D1475212

INTEGRAL MINDFULNESS:

CLUELESS TO DIALED IN –
HOW INTEGRAL MINDFUL
LIVING MAKES EVERYTHING
BETTER

KEITH WITT

Integral Publishers
Tucson, Arizona

Integral Publishers
1418 N. Jefferson Ave.
Tucson, AZ 85712

ISBN: 978-0-9896827-6-3

Cover design by Jeannie Carlisle

Acknowledgments

Thank you, Russ Volckmann, for inviting me to do this project and guiding me through the process. Thank you Ken Wilber for creating a theory of everything and for our indescribably delicious conversations in your loft. Thank you Jeff Salzman for your friendship and wisdom. Thank you Becky, my lovely wife for forty-one years (and counting) of love, guidance, and the life we've cocreated. Thank you Patricia Albere and all my teachers, counselors, and friends who have helped me develop through my strengths and flaws. Thank you to my clients and students who have trusted me to share your lives and work together to create more love, growth, and success in this world.

Our birth is but a sleep and a forgetting:
The Soul that rises with us, our life's Star,
 Hath had elsewhere its setting,
 And cometh from afar:
 Not in entire forgetfulness,
 And not in utter nakedness,
But trailing clouds of glory do we come
 From God, who is our home:

– from Ode: Intimations of Immortality from Recollections
             of Early Childhood by William Wordsworth

"He who is not contented with what he has would not
be contented with what he would like to have."

~Socrates

TABLE OF CONTENTS

FOREWORD

Jeff Salzman

This is the book I wish someone had given me in my 20s. It would have saved me a lot of trouble.

Like young seekers in all times and places, I was looking for the right things to believe in and the right ways to live. I was mad at my religion of origin, Christianity, but how about Buddhism? Of course I needed therapy, but should it be Freudian, gestalt, NLP, wilderness? How about meditation? Martial arts? Which teachers (and what about their flaws)? Does any of this even matter? What is enlightenment anyway? What the heck is even normal?

Oh, the struggles Dr. Keith Witt could have saved me.

But no, I was left to kiss frogs, which I did with a dilettante's abandon. Funny thing is they all, in one way or the other, turned into a Prince. I gained something precious and unique from every retreat I attended (clothed and naked), every therapy session, every self-help book, and every evening talk with every swami, *arhat* and *tulku* who ever traipsed through the people's republic of Boulder.

Handsome princes all, but I never knew which ones to believe, because they all contradicted each other. Is it God or Emptiness? Should I build my personal power or dismantle my ego? Are other people my mirror or my guides? Is everything a projection of my mind or is my mind a projection of my brain?

Help! They didn't just disagree; they negated each other and often vilified each other in their claims to be the one true path.

Help came eventually when I stumbled upon *integral theory* and the writings of Ken Wilber, which provided a larger framework that included – and illuminated – the whole field of transformation.

The integral thesis is simple: every spiritual and psychological tradition holds a piece of the Truth – a piece that no other tradition offers. Each is a work of art, the art of human development, and some are masterworks.

When we see transformation through this lens we become friendlier to all practices and lineages, and understand how they all fit together into a richer whole. Integral theory thereby renders the gifts of any single tradition both more accessible and more profound.

The fundamental integral insight provides more complete answers to the ultimate questions of being human: "Who are we? What are we doing here? How shall we live?" This wider, more inclusive perspective helps us to bring more loving intelligence to all the important areas of our lives: intimacy, family, work, sex, health and spirituality. In *Integral Mindfulness*, Dr. Keith Witt provides a handbook for integral living. He is most qualified to do so. As a psychotherapist in private practice, he has been helping people heal and grow for over 40 years. If we consider 10,000 hours of practice to be the rough requirement for attaining mastery in any discipline, Keith is a master five times over, having conducted more than 50,000 therapy sessions in his career. When it comes to the human condition he has seen and heard it all.

Keith is also a virtuoso of integral thinking, and his work, teachings and many books have been illuminated by the power of the integral vision. He has personally studied and practiced in many traditions. He is an expert in the flourishing science of the brain and mind. Centered in Santa Barbara, California, he has been at the forefront of the latest psychotherapeutic thinking,

Whether Keith is addressing a troubled marriage, difficult co-workers or spiritual longing, he brings an *integrated essence (a new "simplicity beyond complexity")* of the best practices of psychotherapy, brain training and spiritual insight. As you will soon see, Keith is a master simplifier, metaphor maker, installer of sticky ideas.

I met Keith 10 years ago, as the community of integral practitioners was beginning to form worldwide. Since then he has become a leading thinker and teacher of integral, mindful living, perhaps best known for his *Therapist in the Wild* video series, where he "tells truth, spreads love, and takes fearless stands on the great issues of the day – sex, relationships, men, women, sex, pleasure, bullshit, sex, hypocrisy and sex." In *Clueless to Dailed-In* you'll get all this and more!Thank you, Brother Keith, for your basic friendliness to life and its struggles. Thank you for this book that shows us how to see, experience and express ourselves in ways that both reveal more of who we are and help us contribute our best to each other and our world.

INTRODUCTION

Dialed-in is Integral mindful awareness. Mindful awareness is being aware with acceptance and caring intent, on purpose, with compassionate judgment, in the present moment. *Integral* mindful awareness is mindful awareness guided by the elegant, priceless perspectives of Integral understanding, which can help us know who we are, what's *really* happening around us, and what our purpose is *right now.*

Dialed-in makes everything better. We're healthier, more joyful, less irritating and way less crazy. Relationships are more fun and less pain. Children thrive. Sex keeps getting yummier. Spirituality intensifies. The world constantly unfolds into interconnecting patterns that make sense and guide thought and action.

The good news is that we can learn how to be aware with acceptance and caring intent, on purpose, with compassionate judgment, in the present moment, *and we can keep improving at it as long as we live.*

The even better news is that Integral mindful awareness – mindfulness informed by foundation perspectives like what type of person we are, or what state of consciousness we're in – accelerates and stabilizes the entire growth process. It deepens understanding and equanimity. Integral mindful awareness makes us wiser and more caring.

It dials us in.

Integral mindful awareness – being dialed-in – is irresistible after you get it. Unfortunately, our brains resist changing habits of thinking and doing, because habits are encoded to protect and guide us. Even bad habits were originally programmed to help somehow. Habits of thought and behavior direct much of our waking hours – mostly good habits, but inevitably some bad ones. As we wake up to who we are, we observe more good/bad habits, enhance the good, and transform bad into better. That's dialed-in!

Humans like excitement and novelty (you don't want to go to the same movie endlessly), but we also resist change. *Cultures* resist change. *Family systems* resist change. *We all* resist change. Change requires risk, commitment and courage to think and act differently.

Change accelerates with insights and practices. Dialed-in generates insights and practices that eventually become effortless happiness-boosters of daily life.

Explore Integral mindful awareness, and you'll find it explaining the universe in ways you keep agreeing with again and again. The Integral system alone is psychoactive – once learned past a certain point, Integral transforms you forever.

This is not another book about meditation or Buddhist mindfulness. We'll be talking about these things, practicing some of the techniques, and using some of the language, but this book is about *living*. Do you brush your teeth with Integral mindful awareness? When your husband criticizes your dress and you feel like crying and screaming at him, are you guided by Integral mindful awareness? When you're surfing big waves, and your leg begins to cramp a little, but you've only been out a half-hour and a big set is on the way, do you listen to your body and paddle in, or risk injury going for one more ecstatic ride?

Meditation is a beginning. It establishes and strengthens the neural architecture and attention habits that foster empathy and self-awareness. Mindful *living* extends mindfulness into daily life. Integral Mindful awareness – dialed-in – highlights what's healthier/unhealthier, moral/immoral, right-for-our-type-of-person/wrong-for-our-type-of-person, more-an-expression-of-spirit/less-an-expression-of-spirit at any given moment.

For me it started with meditation

I first meditated in 1965, at the end of a line of students in a Shotokan Karate class. We began each practice kneeling on hard linoleum, our instructor facing us, in an elementary school assembly hall that the school had been kind enough to donate to the Covina Parks and Recreations karate class. Everyone had on a white karate outfit (called a "gi") with belts that signified seniority. Our sensei (teacher) Jim Segawa had the coveted black belt, fashionably old and tattered to show how long he had been a senior instructor. I was the most junior student in the class, wearing a new white belt, and frightened of the tests and pain to come (my type of person is prone to fear, but I had no knowledge of typologies then). Nobody in 1965 Los Angeles knew anything about karate, but my intuition had guided my fifteen-year-old self to this class, and I knew it was right to be kneeling in this line at this moment.

First we all bowed, signifying respect for our teacher and Shotokan's lineage, and then Mr. Segawa led us in a simple mindfulness meditation. "Breathe deeply, close your eyes, and relax your body. Focus on clearing your mind and dedicating yourself to the practice ahead." As I did this, my fear diminished, my body relaxed, and I felt a curious floating sensation – spacey, but pleasurable.

At fifteen I was struggling with adolescent emotional storms, family dramas, and life terrors that involved the Draft, Viet Nam, shameful failure or alluring success in sports and dating, and a dominant American culture with little inherent appeal to my young consciousness. I did know I wanted to become a psychologist, have a girlfriend, and not be frightened, angry, and unhappy so much of the time.

The meditation before Karate class soothed and focused me and I continued it, even when practicing alone. Little did I know that my first taste of mindful self-awareness opened up a crack into the other world, and the light that spilled through would continue to draw me like a moth to a flame – eventually leading me to Ken Wilber's Integral system, a theory of everything.

I've continued to study and teach contemplative practices, and know from personal experience and a vast body of research how mindful awareness accelerates growth, enhances health, guides decision-making, and generally makes life better for everyone. Mindfully aware Keith does better therapy, is a more loving and attentive husband and father, is a more thoughtful friend, and can handle life stresses better than mindless or clueless Keith.

Not as simple as it sounds

So, it's simple right? Meditate every day and all problems will be solved, life will be sweet, and the universe will smile.

I don't think so. I noticed early on that I could still be a jerk, a fool, or just clueless, no matter how much I meditated, did yoga, practiced martial arts, or studied spiritual teachers. Waking up to mindful awareness actually was regularly *embarrassing,* even *shameful.* Did I *really* just talk about myself for five minutes and not ask my wife, Becky, one question about her day? Was that my *fourth donut?* I feel a little sick – what was I thinking? How could I buy a 1966 Mustang just because my friend John thinks it's cool, without bothering to get a mechanic to check if the engine is cracked? (It was cracked, and led to a number of painful and expensive adventures in used car repair and what to do before cell phones when you're shipwrecked at 2:00 AM in the middle of nowhere).

We all get into habits of *not* paying attention to mistakes or character flaws. I'm sure you know people who never apologize, continually blame others, deny mistakes, or take out their bad moods on friends and family. Haven't you yourself acted badly sometimes? It's hard to admit being ugly, mean, or at fault.

Development

A signature characteristic of healthy adult development is becoming progressively aware of bad habits, acknowledging them, and growing them into good habits. Think about it, don't you feel more mature when you catch a bad habit – say it's not listening to your seven-year-old – and change it into something good like listening respectfully?

To make matters worse, we *really* don't want to see ourselves as stupid, inept, mean, or at fault, so our nervous systems develop defenses from infancy onward to *avoid awareness* of embarrassing thoughts and actions. Common examples of defenses include denial (I didn't do it!), projection (*You* did it!), or scapegoating (yell at the kid, kick the dog, blame Canada). If you don't notice personal flaws and mistakes, it's less embarrassing in the short run – our neurobiology actually predisposes us to ignore character flaws and mistakes, while still driving us to succeed and self-transcend.

What's inspiring is that we can learn that, in the long run, self-awareness of flaws speeds up development. Evolution reaches for deeper consciousness and more compassion, and we are the apex of the evolutionary pyramid on Earth. Humans can *consciously* enact the genetic mandate to evolve into greater complexity, and that's what drives creativity, innovation, literature, art, spirituality, and generous love. Mindless to mindful is waking up, which helps keep us growing up.

So mindful awareness requires effort, our defenses resist self-awareness, and cruising through the world in habit-mode is essentially *mindless*.

MINDLESS, MINDFUL, CLUELESS, AND DIALED-IN

Mindless is autopilot

Princeton researchers estimate that 40% of our waking day is driven by habits – autopilot. In other words, *mindless*. Driving, eating, talking, even making love, playing, and working, often don't require much awareness – we just act and usually everything works out.

But, everything doesn't always work out particularly well. Not being mindfully aware can get us into trouble. Mindless Keith can do fine in most situations, but risks falling into bad habits and bad vibes when stressed, irritated, or threatened. Even worse, how do I know right action from wrong action, healthy behavior from unhealthy behavior, caring relating from selfish relating if I can't see what I'm doing? Sometimes it's not as clear as "Don't cheat on your wife," or "Don't run the stop sign." We'll be exploring how to foster good habits in Chapter 10.

Clueless is bad for everyone

Repeatedly indulging bad habits without the benefits of self-awareness or moral/behavioral/relational standards – especially when combined with ignoring feedback from experience and other people – is not just mindless; it's *clueless*.

Mindless behavior is not necessarily a bad thing since we can't be rediscovering the wheel with each decision we make ("How do I tie my shoes again?" "It's sunny, should I wear a raincoat?"). Also, mindless bad behavior is often easily fixed with simple attention. Many times, if we just ask ourselves, "What's the best thought/action/decision I could have right now?" we shift easily from mindless to mindful.

Clueless is much worse – clueless is when I ask myself, "What's best for me right now?" the answer is, "I have no idea," or, worse, "I don't care!"

Clueless behavior is what causes 90% of the problems in the world and 90% of the problems in your life. Clueless resists awareness with acceptance and caring intent. Clueless is the opposite of dialed-in.

Examples of clueless?

> • Any addiction – alcohol, drugs, emotional or physical violence, compulsive overeating, – is clueless.

> • Surrendering to the idea that you're just naturally rotten. A successful, cutthroat real estate developer once walked into my office, sat down, sneered at me and his wife, and proudly declared, "I'm Steve. I'm an asshole." (He was right of course – he definitely was an asshole – but, clueless.)

> • Hearing more than one person tell you something critical ("You say hurtful things," "You're selfish," "You need to speak up when you have something to offer," "You bully people when you get mad,") and blowing them off instead of resolving to change and then doing the work. Refusing a loving influence is clueless.

We move through the world either clueless, mindless, mindful, or dialed-in. The better we get at mindful and dialed in, and adjusting from clueless and mindless towards mindful and dialed in, the better it is for us and everyone.

Life is challenging

A lot gets in the way of dialed-in, because we have:

> • Hardwired habits of avoidance, distraction, and destructive impulses.

> • Defensive states that show up when we feel threatened.

> • People who interfere and hinder instead of support and care.

• Social constructs and taboos that hurt us, confuse us, or feel unjust or uncaring.

• Distractions from desires, fears, and mistakes that pull us into the future or the past, usually with distorted stories.

We can keep adjusting to dialed-in if we practice – *and once you learn how, it's mostly just too much fun to stop.*

KEN WILBER'S INTEGRAL SYSTEM IS LITERALLY A THEORY OF EVERYTHING

Over a lifetime of work and over twenty books, Ken Wilber has generated a set of perspectives that are the best understanding of life, love, and development I've ever encountered. He maintains:

Beautiful, good, and true: We're always evaluating the world from what's attractive/unattractive (the "beautiful"), right/wrong according to what we feel is our shared morality with right minded others (the "good"), and what science and direct observation tell us is real and not real (the "true").

Me-first, we-first, and love-first worldviews: We grow through stages of being selfish and less caring of others (me-first), to learning to care and share with others and wanting to follow social rules (we- first), to being caring of everyone and everything (love- first).

Developmental lines and levels: We have different capacities, multiple intelligences (developmental lines) for everything from sex, to parenting, to skiing, to making moral decisions, to writing, to relating, and we *mature through levels* of development on every line.

States: We move in and out of different states of consciousness all the time – like happy, angry, suspicious, dreaming, or caring – states which constantly dictate thought, impulse, and action.

Types: We each dance with various forms of being and doing; we are alchemists of type and have many ways of forming and reforming our unique type of person. For example, we are each more masculine or feminine, introverted or extroverted. Understanding our own and other's type dynamics deepens consciousness and increases compassion.

This integral system is priceless in the "compassionate judgment," and "on purpose" parts of, "Being aware with acceptance and caring intent, on purpose, with compassionate judgment, in the present moment."

For instance, consider purpose. There are a lot of dimensions that influence being mindful and one of them is, what's the best thing to do right now? What is my purpose *at this moment?*

Okay, I'm observing myself right now writing to you. My purpose is to inform and entertain. What's the best way of doing that? Integral helps me figure this out.

I observe myself hanging out with my friends and my family. My purpose is to be a positive influence and enjoy life. Integral helps me determine that. Just asking myself what's most beautiful, good, and true at this moment is priceless guidance, and these are just three facets of the Integral jewel.

I encourage you to observe yourself with compassion throughout the day (mindful awareness) resolving to accept the more or less beautiful, good, and true in yourself and others with a certain amount of humor and equanimity. Tell yourself to reach for beautiful thoughts, actions, and judgments. Be curious about what states you experience, and try to adjust to virtuous states of attention and compassion. Be curious about what type of person you are and keep trying to be in harmony with your heart, not who you imagine someone else wants you to be. Periodically, consider that you move through the day on different levels on different developmental lines, which all continually rise and fall with your states of consciousness. As you practice all of this you become progressively more *dialed-in.*

This book is about:

Dialed-in sex. On purpose with caring and intent, accepting yourself and your partner.

Dialed-in intimacy. How do I optimize *this* relationship at *this* moment?

Dialed-in parenting. The short version? Be aware of yourself each moment as a better or worse parent and keep receiving caring influence to improve.

Dialed-in habits. We train our habits and our habits train us – let's get ahead of the curve.

Dialed-in self-care. Are you conscious and discerning in how you eat, sleep, relate, work, play, exercise, and rest? What's healthiest, yummiest, and best for everyone?

Dialed-in spirituality. What feels sacred to you? Can you let yourself yearn for, stay connected with, and surrender to your sacred values and practices? Do you keep expanding a sense of being in harmony with Spirit?

Dialed-in equals more alive – amplified electric joy, love, fulfillment, and satisfaction.

PRACTICE CONSTANTLY

Most people who teach mindful awareness suggest 10 or 20 minutes, once or twice a day – totally beneficial. I'm going to show you ways of doing that. Daily meditation strengthens your mind/body system and actually enlarges parts of your brain (like the anterior cingulate cortex in your frontal lobe) that are associated with self-awareness, focused attention, and empathy.

But, where the rubber hits the road is how dialed-in you are in everyday life. Just telling yourself to be aware with acceptance and caring intent, on purpose, with compassionate judgment, in the present moment four or five times a day can wake you up in unexpected ways. How mindful are you when you're at the store? At work? In an argument with your husband or wife? Parenting your kid? If little Jimmy just put a hole in the piano, how compassionately do you deal with him? How mindful are you when you're angry, sad, lustful, joyful, or impulsive?

When sensing threats, brains instantly focus on defense and become less mindful. When we're angry, sad, frightened, or ashamed, brains nonconsciously tend to generate defensive states that inhibit empathy and self-observation. But we can adjust to more mindful when we're threatened or in pain. When we do, we get more dialed-in, and good things happen.

So:

Clueless: Bad habits resisting change – not a good idea, lots of problems.

Mindless: On autopilot – it can go better or worse.

Mindful: Observing myself with acceptance and caring intent – pretty darn good.
Dialed-in: Mindfulness turbocharged with Integral understanding – the best.

This book is all about being dialed-in.

Each chapter will explore what it's like to be clueless, mindless, mindful, or dialed-in in important life arenas like parenting, working, loving, sexing, exercising, communicating, eating, having fun, and sleeping. Everything human beings do or think can be more/less clueless, mindless, mindful or dialed-in, and, as you read this book, you'll discover clueless can turn into unthinkable disasters, mindless can be embarrassing or dangerous, and mindful and dialed-in rock.

This book is packed with stories about cool teachers, villains, artists, crazies, warriors, leaders, losers, and healers. All the clinical examples I use – client stories – have been altered to protect the privacy of my clients, but they're all based in sessions with real people. If you feel inspired by any facts, opinions, or people – by "inspired" I mean any intense reaction like joy, agreement, love, rage, shame, grief, interest, disgust, or laughter – you might want to stop and do a search on what's caught your attention. Track down your deeper truth. If we want more knowledge about any particular area in the twenty-first century, we open our personal window-into-infinity (otherwise known as an iphone/computer/ipad), ask our questions, and discern our truths.

Welcome aboard! Let's proceed to Chapter One: What is Mindful Awareness and why is it so good for you?

CHAPTER 1: WHAT IS MINDFUL AWARENESS AND WHY IS IT SO GOOD FOR YOU?

In our clueless, to mindless, to mindful, to dialed-in continuum, "mindful," is the tipping point between living on autopilot and waking up.

Mindful awareness– is, **"Being aware with acceptance and caring intent, on purpose, with compassionate judgment, in the present moment."** This mostly involves nonreactive self-observation.

Integral mindful awareness begins with *mindful awareness,* nonreactive self-observation. To enjoy dialed-in, we need mindful awareness.

This chapter is all about mindful awareness (mindfulness) – what it is and how to do it.

WHAT IS MINDFUL AWARENESS?

Daniel P. Brown, famous Buddhist scholar and teacher, discussing mindfulness training with Integral Life Practice teacher Terry Patten, once said, "Mindfulness has more to do with the continuity of nonreactive awareness."

Non-reactive awareness is self-observation with equanimity – a central component of all contemplative approaches.

Imagine you're making love with your partner and he accidentally elbows you in the jaw. You simultaneously feel a flash of pain and anger, and notice yourself beginning to construct a story of him as a clumsy oaf – or even worse, some kind of *loser.* If you observe all this, on purpose, with compassionate judgment, the anger fades as you notice your defensive

1

tendency to create a hostile story from a painful event. He apologizes profusely for hurting you in the midst of bliss, you observe his distress, and gracefully accept his apology, relaxing with him back into fun lovemaking (which of course involves him also being dialed-in enough to let go of his embarrassment and distress at your anger). This is dialed-in sex, and we'll explore it in detail in Chapter 6.

Anyone can benefit from applying contemplative practices to daily life. Mindful awareness is easy to learn, fits in well with all wisdom traditions, and can be engaged in any time.

At the end of this chapter, I'll show you some of my favorite forms of mindful awareness, attunement to self, others, and nature.

But first, how is mindful awareness different from other forms of awareness?

Awareness does not have to be conscious

Awareness doesn't have to be *conscious*. Our nervous systems monitor millions of inputs, choose seven plus or minus two, and put them together into stories that typically change every few seconds. Each story has unique constellations of memories, emotions, attitudes, and impulses, and we're mostly not *consciously* aware of them.

Your brain constantly checks out the environment and responds reflexively – more likely mindless than *mindful*. Mindful awareness is, "I am *consciously* observing myself moving through the world thinking what I think, feeling what I feel, judging how I judge, doing what I do, and telling myself the stories I tell."

WHAT'S SO GREAT ABOUT MINDFUL AWARENESS?

Why is mindful awareness such a good idea? Well, first of all, mindful awareness is a basic contemplative practice, a meditation, and, as science writer Dr. Larry Dossey maintains, "The body *loves* meditation." Michael Murphy, one of the founders of the Esalen Institute and author of *The Future of the Body*, has a data base on the Esalen website with *three thousand studies* supporting body/mind/relationship/growth benefits of meditations, yoga, and contemplative practices of all kinds. Health benefits associated with regular mindfulness practices include:

• Lowered blood pressure.

• Increased heart rate variability (perhaps, the single most significant indicator of general good health).

• Enhanced intuition.

• Self-soothing abilities, especially in calming distressed or painful affects like anger, fear, grief, sadness, anxiety, depression, and physical pain.

• Kinder, more loving relationships.

• Wider self-knowledge and self-observation, in both relaxed and stressed states.

• Increased equanimity.

• Better decision making.

• More sense of unity with everything and everyone.

I'm convinced – mindfulness practice is a super-good idea.

Mindless awareness has some problems

Why is *mindless* awareness hazardous? Well, first of all, because mindless awareness can lead you to miss out on life and make mistakes. Even worse, mindless awareness allows you to practice bad habits without even knowing there's a problem – choice is not an option if I don't know I have a choice.

What does mindless awareness look like? Here are three examples:

#1: It's your anniversary and your husband takes you to the best restaurant in town. Oh boy! Sounds like fun! You get dressed up, drive over, are seated by a smiling host, and proceed to order and eat a $150 meal. "It's our anniversary!" so you ask the waiter to prepare the house special dessert, Chocolate Bread Pudding, which he serves while you happily reminisce about your wedding reception. The first two bites are delicious beyond belief.

"Wow! I've never tasted chocolate like this! It reminds me of our wedding cake. Remember, your sister said it was so good she..." Suddenly, you're two-thirds of the way through dessert and realize you've been so caught up in the conversation you don't remember anything after the first two bites. That's mindless eating.

#2: Have you ever been driving down the street, your mind wandering, and didn't notice the car whizzing in from the left? You swerve to narrowly avoid an accident – leaving you scared and shaky. That's mindless driving.

#3: Have you ever been talking to your husband and he asks you, "What are you going to do today?" and you're in a hurry and don't have time to talk, so you roughly respond in not-your-best tone, "I don't know what I'm going to do today. I don't have time to talk!" He gets a hurt look on his face, but you don't particularly notice because you're rushed. That's mindless relating.

Mindless behavior causes a lot of problems.

Mindful awareness is much better

Mindful awareness is consciously observing yourself with some level of acceptance and positive intent.

Jon Kabat-Zinn, father of Mindfulness Based Stress Reduction, and author of *Full Catastrophe Living,* has a definition of mindful awareness that I like: Being aware, on purpose, without judgment, in the present moment.

I think that's a pretty good definition, but I think a more useful definition for dialed-in mindful awareness is:

Being aware with acceptance and caring intent, on purpose, with compassionate judgment, in the present moment.

Let's unpack this a little bit.

Aware, acceptance, caring intent, in the present moment

Being aware is observing yourself right now. Try it. Observe yourself right now. Are you sitting or lying down? What are you feeling in your body – both sensations and emotions? What are you thinking? Notice how when you follow a thought, sensation, or feeling, it changes within a few seconds. Observe those changes with acceptance – in that you accept that, right now, this is my thought, sensation, or feeling. Notice how the present moment keeps changing and morphing along with your experience. Try to stay with *right now,* and not get seduced into thinking about the past, future, or someplace/someone/something else. Feel how *right now* is more alive than past/future/fantasy. Your breath is rising and falling right now. The air is moving across your skin right now. Buddhists call this "lively awareness" and being fully present in the moment is central to being dialed-in.

Now take it a step further and cultivate caring intent, as in, "I want to feel and act on my experience in ways that help me and/or others." Generous caring is associated with health, happiness, and superior relationships. (When is it *not* a good idea to feel caring?)

We change states constantly, sometimes happy and constructive, sometimes unhappy and destructive. As we're aware of shifting into destructive, unhappy, depressed or anxious states, we do best if we first accept them with caring intent. Sometimes *just acceptance with caring intent* shifts us into states of equanimity, generosity, and clarity.

Current awareness with acceptance and caring intent is healing and promotes growth, but we can do better. We can harness our human tendencies to constantly judge others and ourselves and use them to become more compassionate.

"Compassionate judgment" is not "no judgment"

"Compassionate judgment," is crucial, because mostly when we observe ourselves, others, and the world, our nervous systems make all kinds of judgments and, quite often, those judgments are not compassionate – particularly the critical ones (positive judgments can be distracting, but, let's face it, very few of us protest when we find ourselves, or someone else finds us, attractive, virtuous, or accurate in our opinions).

Critical judgments especially show up in intimate relationships. Deepening intimacy eventually increases both experiences of profound family connection and tendencies to burden our spouse and kids with our nastiest, yuckiest defensive states. We explore how to identify and deal with defensive states in Chapter 4, and how dialed-in marriage amplifies intimate connections in Chapter 8.

How do judgments show up? I look at you a little weirdly (maybe I'm thinking of the nightmare I had last night about being chased by vampires), and you catch the weirdness, think I'm mad *at you,* and get instantly irritated *at me* with a story of Keith unfairly blaming you for something you didn't do. *My* nervous system registers your irritation, feels disapproved of, generates a shame reaction and a negative story about me being bad, and I'm suddenly in the grip of a self-critical judgment. Even worse, my nervous system then quickly regulates my shame to more anger at you, creates a story about *you* being unfair to me, and I project bad vibes at you, leading you to...

You can see how such judgment circuits – hardwired into our brains – can *non-consciously* create escalating cascades of conflicts.

You walk down the street in a bright pink tank top, meet your friend Irving, and Irving happens to find bright pink tank tops unattractive. Irving is kind of a wise ass, and says sarcastically, "What a *nice, bright* shirt!" leaving you mad and embarrassed (and maybe doubting both your attractiveness and sartorial wisdom – more judgments).

I turn on the news and hear somebody say global warming doesn't exist. I have critical judgment not just about his opinion (it seems *not true* to me), but about him (what an idiot!).

I turn into my driveway, lose concentration as I check out Susie next door climbing out of her car, and run over my trashcan. Susie breaks into laughter, my car is dented, my trashcan is ruined, and I'm totally humiliated, judging myself to be a worm.

Trying to not judge is like trying to not breathe – impossible. Human beings judge. That's all there is to it. Let's get over the whole let's-always-be-nonjudgmental thing and accept that we judge all the time, and what we *can* do is work to judge more compassionately.

Compassionate judgment is experiencing what's more/less attractive, more/less good, more/less true and so on with deep understanding that includes care for everyone, *which is a really big deal.* Compassionate judgment is key to dialed-in, and it develops with practice.

My purpose this moment is writing the clearest sentence I can about purpose. What's your purpose right now? Is it finishing this Chapter? Is it finding your car keys and picking your daughter up from soccer practice? Is it learning how to practice mindful awareness so you can have a dialed-in life?

One of my favorite books – a sacred text of mine really – is *A Book of Five Rings*, by Miyamoto Musashi, the preeminent samurai warrior of 17th century Japan, who just before his death at 60 retired to a cave and wrote about the philosophy and techniques that had made him the greatest sword fencer in the world. I particularly love the end of the last section, *The Book of the Void*: "In the Void is virtue and no evil. Wisdom has existence, principle has existence, the Way has existence, Spirit is nothingness."

"Principle has existence." "The Way has existence." Knowing my principles and my Way illuminate my purpose. At any given moment, we can be guided by understanding what's best for us, based on values organized around our "Way," – our life purpose. Mindful awareness *without* purpose can be directionless and chaotic. We do best when we know what we're about, and are focused on doing it right. Being aware with acceptance and caring intent, on purpose, with compassionate judgment, in the present moment, involves mindfully knowing my purpose in the present moment – *right now*.

Purpose changes through development, but always *feels* the same – charged with meaning and desire to deepen and create in a specific way. When I started surfing, my purpose for two years was to learn how to ride a short board – much more challenging than a long board. Mastering a short board doesn't excite me now, but I get the same *feeling* of meaning and desire when I teach that I did when I was surfing well – teaching currently has that sense of purpose.

How do we best know our purpose? That's where dialed-in Integral understanding can really help. Integral is all about multiple perspectives, and the more perspectives we have about ourselves and others, held with acceptance and caring intent, the clearer it becomes what constitutes the best action/thought/perspective *right now*.

Knowing our purpose when talking with our kids leads to dialed-in parenting, the focus of Chapter 9. Understanding our purpose in sex, love affairs, and marriage leads to dialed-in sex, love affairs, and marriage – Chapters 6, 7, and 8. Being anchored in our purpose at work, protects us from becoming a mindless or clueless boss or employee, areas we'll expand on in Chapter 11.

WHO AM I?

Who is the "I" being mindful? *Who* is being aware with acceptance and caring intent, on purpose in the present moment?

An important step in knowing "me" is recognizing how everything is relationships.

Everything is relationships

Nothing and no one exists alone and separate. Everything is relationships. From subatomic particles all the way to the whole universe, it's everything relating with everything else. Did you ever notice how all stories and experiences involve relationships – either *interior* connections with inner aspects and/or *exterior* connections with others and the world? We each are an amalgam of millions of relationships. Our brain is 100 billion neurons, each with ten to twenty thousand connections to (relationships with) other neurons. We are born relating to others and the world, and continue to do so until death – maybe even after. Not only do we relate with people and objects *outside* of us, *inside* we have multitudes, all influencing one another. Inside we have angry selves, joyful selves, fearful, defensive, generous, immature, or mature selves...you get the idea.

We exist within an infinity of relationships, a universe of relationships. We have relationships with each other. We have relationships with nature. We have relationships with dogs and cats and houseplants. We have relationships with the past and the future.

Research indicates that, as we develop language, which takes off at 18 months when an area of our brain called the hippocampus matures enough, we encounter infinite relationships. Suddenly, at two or three years old, I can talk to you, imagine talking with you, talk to myself, imagine talking to myself, dream about other worlds when I'm asleep, and communicate those dreams to others. Human imagination and capacity for metaphor (that cloud looks like an angel waiting to give us rain, or those cars on the freeway are like ants endlessly migrating) yield infinite perspectives.

It's around two to three that a sense of self, "I am a thinking being," arises – what developmentalists call "A theory of mind." I believe that this is no coincidence. Brains are complex systems that naturally self-organize to greater complexity and coherence. I think that, when a critical mass of interior relationships in the past/present/future are constellated in little kids' brains, a coherent *"me"* is formed that becomes a lifelong enduring sense of self.

"I" am the witness

When we talk about self-observation in mindful awareness, who's observing what? Organizing everything is an *I. Me. Self.* I am the consciousness who answers when my wife Becky says, "Hi, Keith!" Some psychologists call this the ego, or executive ego. Some spiritual practitioners call this the self with a small "s" to distinguish it from a Self with a large "S" who identifies more with all that is arising and less with a smaller personal self.

A milestone of spiritual practices of all kinds – prayer, meditation, yoga, and attunements – is identifying more with a big "S" Self associated with all creation as one consciousness, and less with a little "s" self-associated with our own little ego. We'll delve more deeply into Dialed-in Spirituality in Chapter 12, and see how dialed-in integral mindfulness helps us grow our little "s" self into a big "S" Self.

Who is reading this sentence? *You* are – the you that feels constant and seems to observe and direct all your other selves and states. *I* am talking to *you. I* is the part of me who feels like the same "me" from birth to death. I feel myself to be a *me* observing and directing all the other Keiths inside me right now. When I focus on this, I sometimes envision my conscious self to be on top of a shaky structure of all my experiences, drives, desires, habits, selves, and aspects, directing the whole wobbly system as it lurches one way or another. That's me. That's my "self," who can perceive interior multitudes, drives, and habits (in *here*, in *me*) and observe and direct how to think and what to do, which continually influences how I feel moment to moment.

All these inner components form a bazillion inner relationships with my "self" and each other. I have relationships with all the kids I've been.

9

Keith as infant, toddler, little boy, teenager... – they're all in here. I have relationships with all my potential selves in the future. I have a relationship with myself relating with you right now. I have relationships with myself relating with each of my family members – which change when we're in different states. I have relationships with myself when I'm angry Keith, sad Keith, happy Keith, or dense Keith.

And even though I feel like the same person all the time, I actually shift around quite a lot depending on what state I'm in (tired, confident, anxious, irritated, etc.). I'm a pretty friendly guy right now. If I get mad or scared, I'm more likely to be kind of a jerk.

You change too, essentially becoming somewhat of a different person, depending on all kinds of variables – even though you always *feel* like the same *you*. If you're shifting mindlessly, you might not notice the transition from friendly to threatening. It's often easy to observe such shifts in other people, generally more difficult to observe in ourselves.

It's unsettling to not feel coherent, as if you aren't living your principles all the time, and all of you doesn't fit together into a whole person you respect and trust – which is why people often unconsciously avoid observing themselves acting badly.

Integral mindful living – being dialed in – leads to greater coherence, a greater sense of being consistent, caring, and organized as a self. In attachment theory we call this a coherent, autonomous autobiographical narrative – in which all our stories about our self and our life, past/present/future, fit together into a larger story that makes sense and has us directing ourselves towards a positive present and hopeful future.

Let's quickly recap:

> • We're defining mindful awareness as, "Being aware with acceptance and caring intent, on purpose, with compassionate judgment, in the present moment."

> • We're defining dialed-in as mindful awareness plus Integral understanding.

> • We judge ourselves and others all the time, but can learn to mindfully judge with acceptance and caring intent.

> • Everything is relationships.

• As we engage in life, a part of us – a self (I) – can observe us engaging in life, *and get way better at non-reactive self-observation.*

• This extraordinary self-observation is a unique human *gift* (expands our awareness *light years* beyond other creatures) and *curse* (we can critically judge others and ourselves in the past/present/future and *in our imagination*).

• Compassionate self-observation is crucial to mindful awareness.

Compassionate mindful self-observation can be developed. All you've got to do is practice, and one of the simplest, most elegant set of practices I've ever encountered involves attuning to myself, others, and the world. These attunement exercises form the foundation of both mindful awareness and dialed-in.

ATTUNEMENT: A PRACTICAL STEP-BY-STEP SYSTEM OF MINDFUL AWARENESS.

As I've detailed previously in my book, *The Attuned Family,* attunement to self and others is one of the easiest and most practical mindfulness practices around. We can attune to ourselves, others, and the world by using our "self" to direct us to be aware with acceptance and caring intent.

Let's do it right now!

ATTUNING TO SELF

We start with the breath

All meditation and mindfulness practices start and end with the breath. Sit, relax, and send your attention to your breath. You breathe in; you breathe out. Feel yourself drawing air deep into your belly, pausing, and then allowing it to flow out – an endless cycle we began at birth and will continue to our last breath.

Many traditions suggest you breath in and out through the nose, with the tip of your tongue curled backwards touching the roof of your mouth, and that you slow your breathing during mindfulness practices. The slower you breathe out, the more you self-soothe. It activates your 10th cranial nerve, the parasympathetic Vagus, which actually increases your heart rate variability (how in tune with the present moment your heart rate is) and calms you down. An exhale of 10 to 14 seconds generally calms you down super-efficiently, so it's often a good idea to start an attunement with three or four deep breaths and slow exhales.

Focus on breathing can be a mindfulness practice in itself. At the end of breathing in, just before you breathe out, be aware of your body. At the end of breathing out, just before you breathe in, be aware of your body. This is a central feature of many meditations. If you do just this on a regular basis, your brain will actually change shape. For example, the anterior cingulate cortex (in our frontal lobes) gets activated when we direct our attention, and regularly activated brain areas grow over time, increasing both white and gray matter. Do mindful breathing, and you stimulate the growth of more neurons, neural networks, and myelination in the anterior cingulate cortex, the frontal cortex, and other brain areas having to do with attention, self-observation, self-soothing, morality, intuition, and decision-making.

Sensation

Breathe in and breathe out. As you breathe in and out, be aware of the sensations in your body with acceptance and caring intent. Are you hot? Are you cold? Do your feet hurt? Are you tense or relaxed? Whatever the sensation, experience it with acceptance and caring intent.

Feelings

Now, as you breathe in and out, aware of sensations in your body with acceptance and caring intent, be aware of what emotions you might be feeling right now. Are you feeling happy? Sad? Are you feeling angry? Depressed? Anxious? Are you feeling joyful? Turned on? Ashamed? Guilty? Embarrassed? Are you feeling a little self-conscious? Self-satisfied? Notice how feelings come and go, rise and fall, and just observe your feelings with acceptance and caring intent.

Thoughts

As you breathe in and out, aware of sensations and emotions, be aware of your thoughts. Thoughts come and go. Sometimes we focus on them, sometimes we don't. Right now, just be aware of thoughts coming and going with acceptance and caring intent. If you start following or elaborating on a thought – you know, "We're going out tonight with Ray and Jillian. I wonder if they've spoken with their son who just got married, who..." – try and catch the thought as early as possible, accept it with caring intent, but allow it to pass without pursuit or elaboration.

Judgments

As you're aware of breath, sensation, emotion and thought, direct your attention to your judgments with acceptance and caring intent. What judgments do you have right now about yourself? About me? About this book? About other people? Try not to elaborate, explore, or pursue the judgments you discover, instead just be aware of them with acceptance and caring intent.

Try to observe your judgments with interest. "Oh, I look fat in this shirt." Fine. Be aware of that distress, that shame, with acceptance and caring intent. "Oh, I really like my new hat." Be aware of liking your new hat and feeling like you look good in your new hat with acceptance and caring intent.

"I think the lady next door is nasty and selfish." OK, be aware of your critical judgment with acceptance and caring intent. "I think Jeff at work is really sweet." Be aware of that judgment of him being sweet with acceptance and caring intent.

As you can see, judgments can be negative or positive. If I think you're a nice, attractive, or charming person, or *I'm* a nice, attractive, or charming person, those are judgments – positive judgments. If I feel embarrassed or ashamed of forgetting my dental appointment, or irritated at you for forgetting to meet me at 10:00, I'm caught up in negative judgments of me or you. Whatever judgments you have, positive or negative, observe them with acceptance and caring intent.

Desires

And now, breathing in and out, aware of sensation, emotion, thought, and judgment, be aware of what you desire, what you want right now, with acceptance and caring intent. Do you want to stand up? Do you want to sit down? Do you want to eat something? Drink something? Do you crave the company of a particular person? Do you want to avoid a particular person? Just be aware of your desires with acceptance and caring intent.

Awareness of breath, body, emotion, thought, judgment, and desire with acceptance and caring intent is attuning to yourself. It is mindful awareness of *you*.

Sitting attunement

You can sit and do this for five or ten minutes once or twice a day; and as time passes, your brain will expand as your abilities to calm yourself, be self-reflective, make good decisions, and be empathic become enhanced.

Living attunement

You can also attune to yourself working in the garden, riding on a bus, exercising, or going to sleep. You can do it all day long. The more you do it, the better.

Attuning to others

To attune to others, look at someone, or if they're not around, send him or her your attention with acceptance and caring intent. What is he or she sensing, feeling, thinking, judging, or wanting? Now you're attuning to them. Couples who do this tend to be happier, and the practice makes you more generous and empathic in general.

Next time you're with someone, imagine with acceptance and caring intent what he or she is sensing, feeling, thinking, judging, and wanting. As you do this, you attune to them.

Try it right now with somebody you love who's not around. Think about where he or she is and what they're doing. Are they sitting? Standing? Walking? Driving? Hanging out with a friend? With acceptance and caring intent, imagine them sensing, feeling, thinking, judging, and wanting at this moment. How does this feel? I always get a warm glow attuning to people I love who are not currently with me.

Mothers naturally attune to infants, and most happily married couples do a lot of mutual attunement. Friends tend to attune to one another quite a lot, and this is one of the reasons that if you want to be a happy person, it's a good idea to live next door to a friend. People who live next door to a friend tend to be about 35% happier than people who don't.

Happiness

Interestingly, living next to a friend has a statistically more robust effect on happiness than living with a spouse (which ups your happiness an average of 7%). This makes a lot of sense, because, as we all know, marriages can vary wildly on fun, pain, or mutual care, but we almost always enjoy being with a friend.

Attuning to nature

We don't have to limit our attunements to ourselves and other people, we can also attune to nature. If you're not outside, there's probably a window near you. Look out into nature. Be aware of what's happening out there with acceptance and caring intent. It doesn't matter if it's comfortable or uncomfortable. It doesn't matter if it's sunny or dark, cloudy or rainy, muggy or invigorating. Just be aware of nature. Direct your attention towards nature and be aware of nature with acceptance and caring intent. Cultivate a sense of oneness with a blade of grass, or a whole ecosystem. This is attunement to nature.

These practices are forms of what Ken Wilber calls "Nature Mysticism," and ground us in understanding spirit in the third person, as shining through every object, person, and living being. Nature mysticism is a central aspect of dialed-in spirituality which we'll be discussing in Chapter 12.

We can practice attunement all the time

I love attuning. I find attunements simple, potent, and easy to do. I encourage you to practice attuning to yourself, others, and nature as you move through your day, hanging out with friends or family, at work, or moving through the world.

You also benefit from sitting daily for ten or twenty minutes attuning to yourself, others, and nature – mindfulness practices. Find some combination of attunement practices that works for you, because the important thing is to find what *you* like and do it a lot. The more you practice, the more habitual attunement becomes (what a good habit!), and the easier it will be to add Integral awareness to transform mindful into dialed-in.

Amplifying good habits and improving bad habits is a central feature of dialed-in living, as we'll see in Chapter 10: Dialed-in Habits.

Most meditation is good for you

Unlike some meditation teachers, I love pretty much all contemplative practices. Do you enjoy transcendental meditation, focusing daily on a personal mantra? That's a wonderful, well-researched mindfulness practice. Are you drawn to Buddhist zazen meditation, where you sit and wrestle with an unsolvable problem (called a koan) – like the sound of one hand clapping – and your mind develops as it looks for solutions where no merely rational answers exist? Do you prefer Mahamudra Buddhism concentration and emptiness practices, where you learn to keep your attention focused on one object for long periods of time, and also become able to deconstruct thought, judgment, and emotion through progressively deep inquiry? Do you like Christian centering prayer, as taught by Fr. Thomas Keating, where you connect with spirit and cultivate virtues of love, equanimity, or generosity of heart? These all involve some form of mindful awareness and guide us generally towards attunement with ourselves, others, and nature.

Whatever your practice, if you do it regularly you become progressively better at *being aware with acceptance and caring intent, on purpose, with compassionate judgment, in the present moment.*

Mindful awareness is an awesome foundation that enables you to use Integral understanding to become *dialed-in.*

16

CHAPTER TWO: WHAT'S SO GREAT ABOUT INTEGRAL MINDFULNESS?

I first came to Integral indirectly in the late 1990's. Becky had given me some tapes by David Deida about the masculine and feminine, and I inhaled his system as the best understanding of relational/sexual dynamics I'd ever encountered. My clients were mostly excited and relieved to explore how we all have both masculine and feminine aspects, but in the sexual occasion relate from a mostly more masculine or feminine essence. Since many of us have standards that don't take into account what type of person we are, understanding our masculine/feminine aspects/essence can not only be illuminating, but a relief if we've grown up trying to function against our basic natures.

For example, Mary and Thomas come into a marriage counseling session pissed off and self-righteous. Thomas can't wait to begin, "She agreed to visit my parents over Thanksgiving. We worked it out! We agreed! Now she wants to change the deal! It's just not right!!"

Mary clouds up, "You don't understand! My sister just got diagnosed with breast cancer and Mom's freaking out. They told me they really need us there!"

I turn to Thomas, "You're a more masculine person. A deal is sacred to masculine people and they don't change it unless both parties agree. Mary's a more feminine person. When love seems to require a shift, when it *feels important* to change, it's moral for feminine people to change their minds. This drives masculine people crazy, because, to them, "Don't you get it? A deal is sacred!"

Mary relaxes, "Yes! That's exactly right!" Thomas looks a little puzzled, but way less pissed off. He's intuitively knows the rules change with masculine and feminine, and I'm helping bring that intuitive knowledge into his conscious awareness – helping him be more dialed-in.

In the Integral system of quadrant, levels, lines, states, and types, I've since come to view masculine and feminine as metatypes which organize other typologies such as growth mindset/fixed mindset, introvert/extrovert, harm avoidant/novelty seeking, or thinking/feeling. We will explore masculine/feminine and other types in **Chapter 3.**

Applying how we all have masculine and feminine aspects and a deeper masculine or feminine essence changed me and my psychotherapy. It was like waking up to dimensions I'd always seen, but never so deeply understood. As I attuned to myself and others, the material expanded my world. I've always been an enthusiastic student of typologies and systems of psychotherapy, and I vividly experienced how masculine/feminine understanding radically improved each system, allowing me to happily rediscover it through a wider lens.

Then, on a fateful summer day, Becky brought home a tape of two actors reading Ken Wilber's *A Theory of Everything,* and it blew my mind. As Ken described the experience to me years later, if you're a seeker, encountering the Integral system can be like dropping a catalyst into a supersaturated solution.

Observing each moment from the objective, scientific perspective (the true), the subjective phenomenological perspective (the beautiful), and the inter-subjective what-feels-right/true-to-us perspective (the good) captured my imagination as much as the masculine/feminine material had.

Experiencing each person as having a unique worldview composed of multiple intelligences at different levels of maturity deepened my conceptions of evolution, history, family dynamics, psychotherapy, and development.

Really looking at the states of consciousness we all move in and out of daily, from subtle shifts that can happen below awareness in milliseconds, to the universal rhythms of waking, sleeping, and dreaming was another consciousness expander, and clarified countless complexities of human functioning and relating.

In short, the Integral system was like successive tsunamis that transformed and illuminated the universe, and turbocharged mindful awareness in ways unimaginable to me before I encountered the material.

Integral understanding doesn't particularly *replace* ideas you already have, or even dismiss any of them – all perspectives have some inherent truth, and many, like "Love heals," or, "The truth will set you free," reflect enduring, timeless wisdom. Instead, Integral reorganizes beliefs, knowledge, and experience into frameworks that expand your vision of everything almost more than you can bear. Integral, once you learn it and apply it to your life, is a psychoactive system. It changes you.

The acronym Integral writers and practitioners use for Integral understanding is AQAL, which is short for "all quadrants, levels, lines, states, and types."

I started feverishly studying, writing and teaching, beginning with a lecture I gave at Santa Barbara Cottage Hospital's Grand Rounds in 2003 on Integral Sex Therapy. I wrote *Waking Up* on Integrally Informed psychotherapy, *Sessions,* showing how Integrally informed therapists from different traditions naturally complement each other, and two other books, *The Attuned Family,* and, *The Gift of Shame,* on how developmental neurobiology, therapy, spirituality, and sexuality all fit together elegantly in an Integral embrace.

Integral mindfulness emerged out of this work, and especially out of the thousands of therapy sessions I've conducted using this material and observing my clients' shifts from clueless, to mindless, to mindful, to dialed-in.

COMPASSIONATE JUDGMENT AND PURPOSE ARE AWESOMELY ILLUMINATED BY INTEGRAL

In our *"Aware with acceptance and caring intent, on purpose, with compassionate judgment, in the present moment,"* definition of mindful awareness, Integral understanding especially informs the *"Compassionate judgment,"* and *"On purpose,"* parts. This is because the more we understand about ourselves and the world, the more connected everything becomes, the more related we feel to everything and everyone, the less selfish we become, and the clearer we are at any given moment what we are about.

Let's explore judgment and purpose a little more deeply.

Judgment is neurologically mandated and inevitable

As we briefly covered in Chapter One, we can no more be non-judgmental than we can be non-emotional. Brains monitor the environment constantly for safety/dangerousness, what seems consistent/inconsistent with how we believe the world is constructed, and attraction/repulsion depending on what current drives are activated and what stimuli we're experiencing. These all translate into judgments about what seems safe or unsafe, attractive or unattractive, moral/socially-connected or immoral/socially-disconnected, and observably-true/observably-false. As we'll soon see, these criteria are the automatic evaluations that arise out of Integral's four Quadrants.

Safe or unsafe

We are genetically wired to *survive* and *thrive*, which means our brain's first level of evaluation is safe/unsafe, attraction/repulsion, or, as I prefer, yum/yuck. Yum/yuck reactions are what neuroscientists call categorical emotions, the constant evaluations our brain makes to help us stay alive and thrive.

Survive means, "Am I safe?"

"Safe," is not just safe physically, like, "Is it safe to cross the street?" or, "Is it safe to eat this strange fruit?" Safe also means:

- "Is it *socially* safe right now?" Am I safe from social disapproval or attack?
- "Am I safe from my own critical judgments?" When we violate our interior standards (lie, cheat, self-indulge destructively, or hurt others) our internalized moral system generates painful shame emotions.
- "Am I safe from my own imagined threats?" We imagine threats from all sorts of places – like fears of speaking in public, expressing our needs or resentments, eating taboo foods, or any phobic (irrational fear driven) behaviors.

Thrive means the drives, needs, and desires I associate with a good life are mostly being satisfied.

WHAT ARE "DRIVES?"

Drives are genetic mandates that propel us through life, like hunger, thirst, lust, needs for contact and recognition, instincts to self-transcend, or desires to create. Drives harmonize our inner needs and the countless stimuli life keeps bombarding us with. For instance, hunger and thirst get activated by both internal deficits and external cues (you haven't eaten in a while and get hungry – internal cue – or you pass a barbeque, smell ribs and burgers, and want some – external cue). Another example is lust, which tends to get activated in men by the sight of the feminine form (even abstract hourglass forms can cue lust circuits in a man's brain – guys are super primed to want sex), but also by blood serum levels of free testosterone. Free testosterone also makes women feel friskier, but women's brains respond more to a trustable, powerful, interested male presence than a visual representation of an idealized masculine form.

We each are influenced by an amazing number of genetically based drives and we'll be encountering lots of them in the chapters ahead. Mindful awareness of a drive that's been activated helps me both understand the moment and guide me to right action. For example:

> • I just ate a big dinner, still want the barbeque when I smell it. But I mindfully recognize my hunger is a reaction to an external stimulus and I'm actually full, which helps me more easily pass on by and not overindulge.
> • Sexy Jen from the pool flirts with me one afternoon and indicates that she has no plans for lunch, cuing a wave of lust through my body and instant rationalizations why it would be fine to "Just go have lunch." I realize the incredible dangers inherent in pursuing Jen further and politely decline.
> • You are frightened of public speaking, and your professional association asks you to give a keynote speech at your next convention – a wonderful opportunity. Your sense of personal danger is activated and you want to say, "No! I can't do it because... (some lame excuse)." You realize it's just your survival instinct warped into fear of public speaking and you say, "Yes! I'd be honored to give the keynote!"

So, genetically based forces generate drives to survive and thrive, which develop into habits of evaluation, which generate judgments, preferences, and discernments, which can be more or less healthy, which guide actions, *all of which we can self-observe with acceptance and caring intent, with compassionate judgment, in the present moment.*

Dialed-in, Integral mindful awareness, involves self-observation organized through AQAL – all quadrants, levels, lines, states, and types.

THE BEAUTIFUL, GOOD, AND TRUE STANDARDS AND INTEGRAL'S FOUR QUADRANTS

Human consciousness evaluates the world from multiple perspectives simultaneously. For instance, in the above example with Jen, my subjective attraction to Jen arose simultaneously with my moral objection to cheating on my wife, which is grounded in my scientifically validated understanding that there are a hundred reasons to not have a secret affair. What subjectively is a yum or a yuck for me personally might or might not harmonize with what I believe is a social (moral) yum or yuck, which might or might not be consistent with what scientific research has demonstrated is healthy or unhealthy.

These three perspectives – what I individually experience phenomenologically, what I feel *we* believe is true and moral, and what objective observation and science tells us is accurate – are three perspectives that are irreducible to one another. They are literally three dimensions of human experience that are qualitatively different. Plato, Immanuel Kant, and others call these the beautiful (personal, phenomenological), good (shared understanding of right/wrong, moral/immoral), and true (objectively observable, scientifically verifiable). The beautiful, good, and true are validity standards that can cross-validate each other by observing and evaluating any moment, object, or event in three qualitatively different dimensions.

Integral's four quadrants are four ways of observing the world utilizing these three validity standards. Each quadrant primarily utilizes one of the beautiful, good, or true validity standards.

What are the four quadrants?

Look at the chart on the next page. It is a map of how to observe/experience/evaluate any moment, object or person from four perspectives at once.

The four quadrants are a cornucopia of data and perspectives that you could spend a lifetime studying and applying to any aspect of creation. If you want to delve deeper into them, check out any of Ken Wilber's books, my previous books, or some of the myriad Integral books that have been written in the last ten years. In this book, we're going to focus primarily on practically understanding the three validity standards that characterize the four quadrants, and how to utilize them for dialed-in mindful living.

Briefly, the four quadrants and the beautiful, good, and true involve:

- **The True: The Upper Right Quadrant** looks at everything and everyone as individual objects. I can observe this moment as a series of verifiable, externally observable events – as would be reflected by video recordings, microscopic observations of my cells, or any other means that could be replicated. In science, different people can look through a microscope and all see the same cell. *Most* of us (because not *everyone* believes in science) will agree, "Okay. I believe there is a cell there." You can look at me and go, "Keith has gray hair and blue eyes," and assume everybody can see that. The validity standard of the Upper Right Quadrant is what's scientifically demonstrable – **the true.**

- **The True: The Lower Right Quadrant** looks at groups from the outside, like an audience at a concert, a family system, or school of fish. The validity standard, once again, is what's scientifically demonstrable. We can look at groups and objectively measure how they form, communicate, and progress. I can look at a room and say, "60% of that room is women and 40% men," and everybody looking at that room will come to the same

UPPER LEFT, I INTERIOR/INDIVIDUAL	UPPER RIGHT, IT EXTERIOR/INDIVIDUAL
Intentional	Behavioral

Validity Standards:
    Felt Truthfulness
    Internally experienced
    Subjective
	Validity Standards:
	    Truth
	    Externally Observable
	    Objective

Self & Consciousness	Brain & Organism
BEAUTIFUL	**TRUE**
LOWER LEFT, WE INTERIOR/COLLECTIVE	LOWER RIGHT, ITS EXTERIOR/COLLECTIVE
Cultural	Social

Validity Standards::
    Mutual Understanding
    Internally experienced
    Intersubjective
	Validity Standards:
	    Functional Fit
	    Externally Observable
	    Interobjective

Culture & Worldview	Soc. System & Environment
GOOD	**TRUE**

Table 1: The Four Quadrants, based on the work of Ken Wilber

conclusion. I can record a conversation, evaluate the tape, and say confidently that 10% of the sentences were questions, and 57% statements of opinion – **the true.**

• **The Beautiful: The Upper Left Quadrant** looks at how you individually feel subjectively. Do you feel happy, sad, loving, or interested right now? These are unqualifiable scientifically – they are phenomenological. We can measure brainwaves and neural functioning (Upper Right Quadrant), but that will never catch *exactly* what you mean by, "I feel happy right now." The validity standard for the Upper Left Quadrant is *how something subjectively feels to me* – **the beautiful.**

• **The Good: The Lower Left Quadrant** looks at how *we* feel together at this moment. Social agreement heavily involves a sense of shared understanding, and especially shared morality. If I feel like a moral person and believe you to be a moral person, I'll tend to assume we agree on beliefs like, "Tell the truth," "It's better to be generous than stingy," or "Do unto others as you would have others do unto you." The validity standard for the Lower Left Quadrant involves a sense of what intersubjectively *feels right or wrong to us* – **the good.**

I'm not going to spend much time talking specifically about the four quadrants, though together they provide amazingly full, clear pictures of objects, experiences, ideas, developmental/historical sequences, and people. Dialed-in awareness accesses the four quadrants simply by focusing on what feels beautiful, good, or true in each moment.

Here are some examples of using the beautiful, good, and true to guide us in our clueless to dialed-in Integral mindfulness system, and how they track in the four Quadrants. Notice that no validity standard exists separate from the others, although we tend to emphasize one or the other in different circumstances.

The true

• A mindless relationship with the true might be getting sick every time you eat Thai food (Upper Right Quadrant

25

– anyone can see you get sick), but you keep going back for more – craving that coconut soup and spicy shrimp around 6:00 pm and talking yourself into it again and again ("craving" being your subjective attraction – the Upper Left Quadrant). You are ignoring verifiable Upper Right Quadrant data that Thai Food plus you equals sick (the true). You are also selectively attending to your Upper Left Quadrant data of liking the taste and texture of Thai food (beautiful), while ignoring the pain and suffering you feel afterwards (not beautiful – ugly really). A clueless example of the true would be if your doctor told you you're getting an ulcer because of all the spicy food you eat (he has group data about spicy food and your kind of symptoms – Lower Right Quadrant true), and you keep going to the Thai restaurant anyway. You are ignoring the Lower Right Quadrant data that people who keep consuming substances that make them sick have progressively more severe health consequences (observable statistical data, the true). You are further ignoring the Lower Left Quadrant data that you and your doctor both agree that Thai food makes you sick, and you both have a moral standard that it's wrong (not good) to engage in behavior that makes you sick.

• A mindful example of the true would be noticing the first time you got sick (observable Upper Right Quadrant true) trying once more to be sure (doing an Upper Right Quadrant experiment of what's true, because you like Thai food – Upper Left Quadrant beautiful), and then getting sick and deciding to avoid spicy food.

• A dialed-in example of the true would be exploring what it is about your body, your life, and your cravings that results in Thai food making you sick, and then receiving influence from wise others and your own beautiful, good, and true standards to adjust to becoming stronger and more resilient physically and psychologically.

The beautiful

• A mindless example of the beautiful might be sitting on your porch each evening enjoying the sunset, but then having to work late one week, simply forgetting how relaxed and happy you get watching the sunset, and suddenly realizing with a sense of profound loss two months later you've missed sixty sunsets.

• A mindful example of the beautiful would be remembering how you're nourished by sunsets, and getting out to watch the sunset at your first opportunity when your heavy work week is over.

• A dialed-in example of the beautiful might be feeling your intense yearning to be one with nature, realizing there's not enough nature in your life for you to feel balanced, and planning a trip to the Yosemite Valley.

The good

• A mindless example of the good might be walking on the beach with your friend Mary, hearing her story about how her teenage son Bret just flunked three of his classes and got busted for pot at school, and then going on about how your daughter Beth made the dean's list – not noticing the hurt expression on Mary's face part way into your story. You have disconnected from the Lower Left Quadrant's *we* space where we have inter-subjective attunements and look for shared understanding that feels good and right *inter*-subjectively – between *us*.

• A mindful example would be that this same conversation could be observed by monitoring your words, voice tones, brainwaves, biochemical markers and neural networks as you talk with Mary (the Upper Right Quadrant true), or monitoring the synchrony of her markers and yours as you speak (the Lower Right Quadrant true). You can see how, no matter how accurate such scientific measures are, they can't capture the personal feeling of distress Mary

27

feels at your insensitivity (her Upper Left Quadrant not beautiful standard), or the sense you've broken some social rule (the Lower Left Quadrant, intersubjective not-good).

• A dialed-in example of the good might be hearing Mary's story, knowing how she gets self-doubting when Bret does badly, and reminding her how much you love her, while telling her about this great therapist whom your daughter Beth thought was cool.

You'll find that the more you practice being dialed-in, the more you'll notice judgments arising from your subjective experience (Upper Left Quadrant – the beautiful), your objective, externally verifiable experience (Upper and Lower Right Quadrants – the true), or a sense of shared social understanding with like-minded moral others (the Lower Left Quadrant – the good).

Acceptance and caring intent will guide these judgments to be more compassionate, and compassionate judgment helps us minimize damage, and maximize growth, health, and love.

THE BEAUTIFUL, GOOD, AND TRUE CROSS-VALIDATE EACH OTHER

As we learn to notice and be influenced by *all* these sources, the more compassionate we become, because the beautiful, good, and true continually cross-validate each other. For instance, you might go with your husband to a deserted beach, and he takes off all his clothes and runs naked into the water. Your training is to not be naked in public, so it initially doesn't feel **good** to take off your suit. But it also feels attractive, pleasurable (**beautiful**), to run naked into the water. Your husband approves of you running naked into the water (indeed, he *wants* you to join him!), so in the *we* culture of you and your husband, it begins to feel moral (**good**) in this circumstance to run around naked. You look all around the beach and there are no other people to see, judge, or be offended. There is no objective reason (**true**) to not run naked into the water. So you receive influence, throw off your clothes, and joyfully join your husband skinny dipping. You have mindfully accessed all three standards to refine your

"Don't run around naked in public," value to include that occasional time when it's actually *preferable* to run around naked in public.

Clueless corporation colonizing a dialed-in corporation

A practical morality play illustrating the hazards of cluelessly ignoring the beautiful, good, and true is the saga of Charles Hurwitz and the Maxxam Corporation.

In the 1880's, the Pacific Lumber Company (Palco) was established in Scotai, Humboldt County, in Northern California as a logging enterprise. Palco enthusiastically began converting the largest and oldest living things on the planet (old growth redwoods) into milled lumber, which was honorable and lawful activity at the time. Integrated into the social fabric of the northwest, Palco grew with American culture. By the 1980's, the company was run about as well as a lumber company could be run, by farming the forests systematically and maintaining the riparian ecosystems of mountains, rivers, canyons, and wetlands. The workers had excellent pension and healthcare programs, and the operations were becoming progressively cleaner and more sustainable environmentally.

The company made profits, took care of workers, and treated the Pacific Northwest forests as renewable resources to be cherished – they kept their business beautiful, good, and true – a sterling example of healthy, dialed-in capitalism.

In 1985, Charles Hurwitz of Maxxam Corporation acquired Palco in a hostile corporate takeover using junk bonds and enough shady dealings to instigate New York Stock Exchange and congressional investigations, both of which uncovered evidence of wrongdoing. He then proceeded to enthusiastically rape the company's assets. He clear-cut forests, silted the streams, injured the wetlands, raided the pension fund, and finally – to add insult to injury – went bankrupt to the detriment of the junk bond holders who were his original partners in crime.

During this debacle, Hurwitz marketed an old stand redwood grove near the area's main highway to the government at astronomic profit (threatening to clear-cut huge tracts of old growth trees if they didn't accede to his demands; a classic "greenmail" maneuver), and then hired a public relations firm to sell to the public a false story that environmental zealots protecting old growth were ruining the lumber business, thus creating social conflict in the local towns. In his first meeting with the workers of Palco, Hurwitz told them, "There is the story of the golden rule: he who has the gold rules."

Charles Hurwitz manifested vast wealth for himself while inflicting incalculable emotional and material damage on thousands of people and priceless ecosystems.

What are the personal consequences of engaging in such reckless, greedy exploitation? Like many rapacious industrialists and ambitious financiers over the years, Mr. Hurwitz might not care a bit about the forests, rivers, workers, or investors. Like his infamous business partner Michael Milkin, Hurwitz has been sued, investigated, and vilified, but robber barons appear to be relatively indifferent to such attentions – the good and the beautiful standards are compromised in greedy, unhealthy egocentricism. Ironically, the less distress someone feels at causing such damage, the sicker in mind and spirit he or she is likely to be. A consequence of such ugly, immoral behavior can be spiritual disease – and probably social and emotional conflict and pain – that tends to persist until either death or deepening on the moral line of development. If Mr. Hurwitz developed morally – became less clueless and more dialed-in on the good and the beautiful – part of his process (very much like an addict in recovery) would certainly involve feeling horror and shame as he awoke to the harm he's caused to so many. Given the number of lawsuits that continue to be filed by irate victims, there's no evidence that such up-leveling has happened for Chuck.

Receiving caring influence speeds up developments

If we receive caring influence from our own experiences and inputs from other people and the world, and keep refining our values, behaviors, and opinions towards what's more beautiful, good, and true, we grow faster, are happier, have better relationships, and are generally more value-added people – you know, someone who seems to help everyone else feel a little fuller, happier, or wiser when he or she is around. The ability to receive caring influence is one of the most powerful predictors of health, growth, and happiness.

This is why dialed-in is best served by self-observing feelings, thoughts, behaviors, and judgments with *caring intent*. Also, discriminating from all quadrants (always taking the beautiful, good, and true into account) provides incredible cross validation when reaching for optimal decisions, as we saw earlier in our skinny dipping example.

Worldviews and Developmental Lines and Levels – Me First, We First, and Love First

Most of the time, we operate more or less out of one of three different worldviews – egocentric me-first, relationship-centric we-first, or world/spirit-centric love-first. Humans tend to grow from more egocentric me-first, to more family/tribe/group acceptance-centric we-first, to more brotherhood-of-man, serve-the-planet, world-centric love-first. There are healthier/unhealthier, more mature/less mature forms of each stage, which become progressively obvious as we grow more dialed-in. Charles Hurwitz in our above Maxxam example is a sterling exemplar of unhealthy me-first. In terms of developmental emphasis, we're born into egocentric me-first, grow through childhood into communication/relationships-centric we-first, and then develop as adults towards more world-centric, what-serves-the-highest-good love-first.

Progressive worldviews add new perspectives

You can see how each successive stage adds a perspective.

- Me-first doesn't care much about the welfare of the group, but as growth happens, additionally finds that he's come to care deeply about shared understanding, group welfare, and clear communication – we-first.

- We-first rules for communication – like everyone gets a turn to speak, and people should be treated equally – become less rigid and more fluid as love-first perspectives reveal that shared understanding is not always possible, but creating more love is.

When I was discussing how growing a stage adds both a new perspective and a new level of care with my friend, Jeff Salzman, he told me this great story:

It's like the tale of the three bricklayers. A man was walking by a field at the edge of town, and saw three men laying bricks. 'What are you doing?' asked the man. The

31

first bricklayer replied, 'I'm laying bricks.' The second bricklayer answered, 'We're constructing a wall.' The third looked at the man and smiled radiantly, 'We're building a cathedral.'

Attunement and "Me-First, We-First, and Love-First

Me-First attunes to me

Egocentric is attuned to ourselves, but not especially to others – I primarily want what's best for me. If I'm just attuning to myself and not much to other people, I'm in an egocentric worldview. It matters most to me what's going on with *me* and what *I* want.

Me-first worldviews are normal with children. Children can be altruistic, care about others, communicate cooperatively and follow rules, but they usually spend more moments being egocentric than grownups do.

Egocentric grownups can suffer being irritating and unpopular. Others can find them selfish, and want them more we-first and love-first. We sense they don't much care about us.

On the other hand, healthy me-first moments are those times – eating an ice-cream cone, skiing down a mountain, walking out into the sunshine, suffering a major injury – when making it all about me right now is *exactly* the right thing to do.

We-First attunes to me and you

As we mature, we increasingly are drawn to fairness and clean communication. We care about family and community cultures. This leads us to attune more regularly to others in addition to ourselves.

We-first wants best for *us*, and *we'll* figure it out by *communicating fairly*. A hazard of the we-first worldview is getting lost in blah, blah, the endless committee meeting, but people in healthy community grow more efficient and wiser, gradually expanding circles of care and concern.

Relationship/communication-centric originally attunes more naturally to family, tribe, religion, or nation, than to the world as a whole. As we-first develops, "we" expands towards "all of us," preparing us for the leap into love-first.

32

Love-First attunes to me, you, and all of us

World-centric is attuned to ourselves, others, and world – I want what serves the highest good for me, you, and all of us. In the love-first worldview, rules and customs are less important than care, justice, and connections with spirit.

We spend moments in each stage daily, but normal development leads us to grow from spending more moments in egocentric me-first, to more time in relationship/communication centric we-first, to more time in world centric, what's-best-for-all love-first.

We're usually more me-first egocentric when younger, and grow to more we-first relationship/communication centric entering adolescence and adulthood. As age and wisdom influence our worldviews, love-first increasingly guides us.

Integral mindful awareness – dialed-in –*observes* me-first, we-first, and love-first moments with affectionate understanding. Dialed-in helps us let love-first choose the right perspective for the occasion.

For instance:

> • Your favorite artist – Bruce Springsteen! – is performing at the County Bowl and you've got tickets! You show up, sit down, and Bruce and the E Street Band start rocking. Your job is to be fully me-first – I'm-having-a-blast.

> • Your husband tells you on Thursday that he's taking a ski trip with his buddies to Sun Valley this coming Saturday, which happens to be your Dad's 80th birthday and the whole family is coming in from all over the country. You are so mad you can barely think, but you tell him, "We have to talk about this." You need to be fully surrendered to we-first processing-till-we-both-feel-better to resolve this incipient family disaster.

> • Your twenty-four-year-old daughter tells you she's going to Mexico for two weeks with her (in your opinion) loser boyfriend. You think of all kinds of warnings, threats, and opinions about the trip, her boyfriend, and their relationship in general, but you shut up and tell her to have a wonderful time. Your love-first understanding is

33

that it would create pointless conflict to disapprove (she knows how you feel about him), that she has to find out for herself that this guy is not good for her, and that love is best served by encouraging her to enjoy the vacation.

Maturity on developmental Lines and Levels

If you've ever heard Howard Gardner's term, "multiple intelligences," or Daniel Goleman's, "emotional intelligence," you already have an understanding of developmental lines and levels.

We all are more or less mature in a bunch of different ways. We are more or less mature in how we think, in our ethical standards, and in how we relate with lovers or friends, all reflecting various levels of maturity on lines of development.

Humans are born with capacities to do pretty much anything, in families that take better or worse care of us. As we age, it becomes increasingly up to us how we want to grow. Almost any capacity – to dance, sing, solve problems, be self-aware, or be sexual – is a line of development where we start primitive and then grow through stages. Nobody goes instantaneously from not knowing how to dance to prima ballerina, you have to grow through stages on the ballet line of development. Nobody goes from 2x2=4 to e=mc^2 without progressing through a math intelligence series of stages. Nobody goes from finger painting straight to the Mona Lisa. Even Leonardo de Vinci – talented as he was – had to grow through stages to paint his masterpieces.

Mindful awareness of how advanced we are on relevant lines of development, combined with an Integral understanding of what's more or less mature/healthy on that line, accelerates growth and powerfully informs our purpose in each moment. If I want to learn to paint, I can observe how well I paint now, seek out influences like teachers and other artists to help me make progress, and then patiently work at growing on my painting line of development.

This attitude – pick an area I want to grow, receive influence, and then relax into effort and progress over time – is called a "growth mindset," and has been exhaustively researched by a woman named Carol Dweck, author of *Mindset*. We can actually learn to be a more growth mindset type of person, and we'll talk more about that in the next chapter. Dweck found that growth mindset people are comfortable with effort and progress, enjoy challenges, tend to surround themselves with talented others, are superior bosses and employees, are happier and healthier, and are more likely to have satisfying relationships. Dweck contrasts *growth* mindsets with *fixed* mindsets where people are afraid to make mistakes, experience talented associates as threats, and are way more focused on looking and feeling successful that actually growing on any line of development.

Dialed-in awareness of whether we're in a fixed mindset or growth mindset moment naturally shifts us towards growth mindsets. Knowing what line of development we're currently dealing with, and at what level of development we currently hover, helps us accept where we are and keep maturing onward.

Growth mindsets and developmental lines show up everywhere. A couple of examples are:

> • Talk with any gifted, popular professor at a liberal arts college, and she'll say that one of her goals is to foster critical thinking – helping students practice increasingly sophisticated ways of conceptualizing themselves and the world. She is committed to her students maturing on their cognitive – thinking – line of development, by discovering how they process information now, offering influence, and encouraging them in making effort and progress to understand and effectively integrate multiple points of view.

> • Walk into any dance, martial arts, or singing class and watch the students. You'll see them obviously at different levels of development – we can usually tell just by watching and listening who is more or less advanced. During the class, you'll observe them receiving influence from instructors, and reaching to advance to higher levels on whatever abilities that class requires.

In future chapters, we'll further examine important lines of development like psychosexual development, marriage, parenting, and spirituality.

States of consciousness

Let's attune to ourselves right now. Focus on breath going in and out a few times and be aware of what you sense, feel, think, judge, and want right now with acceptance and caring intent.

Got it?

You have just entered an attuned state of consciousness. As I've previously mentioned we shift states *all the time.*

Big, universal states are waking, sleeping, dreaming, and deep dreamless sleep. Within those we can shift into thousands of different states depending on how our brain is perceiving the world.

Neuroscience

Brains perceiving and reacting instantaneously is called *"neuroception" by neuroscientist Steven Porges, author of* The Polyvagal Theory. *He noticed that brains decide when we're safe and help us be socially engaged, decide when we're threatened and jack us into fight/flight arousal, and decide when death is imminent and collapse us into feigned death. The idea that the brain enacts this whole processing/reacting system independent of consciousness – faster than conscious awareness – was so radical that Steve had to create a new word – neuroception – for it.*

Brains don't just react to safety and danger, they also monitor the environment constantly for drive objects like food, water, attractive sexual partners, or opportunities for recognition, power, or comfort. From hundreds of thousands of perceptions, brains continually choose seven plus-or-minus-two of them, and every few seconds create states with characteristic stories, feelings, memories, and impulses.

As we explored in Chapter 1, we each *feel* like the same "me" all the time, but we actually are constantly changing states where, if we're not dialed-in, we can non-consciously become someone who looks and feels a lot different than our optimal self.

I turn my car left onto a street and a car roars by, honking, and the guy driving is giving me the finger out of his window. I instantly enter a state of anger/fear, generate a story of this bozo driving too fast and unjustly getting mad at me for minding my own business, and "Who does he think he is?!!" My hand automatically reaches for the horn and right before I press it this whole state/story/situation actually becomes conscious. I am driving mindfully, so, even though the state was created – instantiated is the word neuroscientists use – almost instantaneously in fifty milliseconds, I become conscious of it in five hundred milliseconds, a half of a second, and now have the ability to *choose* how to think and what to do.

If I'm clueless, I'm honking, screaming, and lost in a story of how this guy deserves to die. I'm enthusiastically elaborating about what a useless, screwed up *asshole* he is, and *"How dare he?!"*

If I'm mindless, I honk, flip him off, and tell the story later about how this jerk honked at me *for nothing.*

If I'm mindful, I catch myself before I honk back, shake my head at how people can act so crazy sometimes, tell myself, "It's over, so don't make it worse by obsessing about it," and drive home.

If I'm dialed-in, I don't honk or make hostile gestures. I breathe deeply, feel the rising rage state/story and stop it in its tracks. I search back over the last three seconds for what I might have done to cue this apparently crazy behavior. I remember that I made somewhat of a wide turn that could have appeared dangerous from his angle, alarming him enough to go into a fear/rage reaction – and this guy probably has impulse control problems to begin with given how fast he was driving and how quickly he surrendered to *his* rage. I'm calming down as I do this and resolve to be more vigilant on this corner in the future. I drive on, still a little activated, but not particularly upset.

As illustrated in the above story, two of the most important categories of states are states of healthy response to the present moment, and defensive states.

Healthy response to the present moment

When our brains determine we're safe, they help us relax and support us being confident and social. We're more likely to attune to others (have empathy), and ourselves (self-awareness). If we're fully present *now,* not distracted by the past, future, or fantasy, we're likely to be in a state of healthy response to the present moment, where good things happen. We can do this mindlessly just by having the habit of healthy response, or mindfully being self-aware of ourselves in a state of healthy response to the present moment, and reaching for it when we lose it.

Defensive states

When our brains read threat, they tend to instantly create a defensive state (in thirty to fifty milliseconds), where we have amplified or numbed emotions, distorted perspectives, destructive impulses, and diminished capacities for empathy and self-reflection.

If we're clueless, we'll likely surrender mindlessly again and again to destructive impulses. In the previous example, I could have whipped my car around and chased the guy who honked at me down the hill.

If we're mindless, we'll start off surrendering to defensive states, take some steps down the destructive path, but only go so far before we start to feel crazy, and then become more mindful.

If we're mindful, we notice the defensive state beginning and start attuning to ourselves and others immediately, reaching for empathy, compassion, and right action.

If we're dialed-in, we catch the defensive state, adjust to a state of healthy response, and scan from the beautiful, good, and true. We notice how far we've regressed on which developmental line, whether we're in a me-first, we-first, or love-first moment, and how this experience fits into what type of person (like masculine/feminine, aggressive/non-assertive, focused/easily-distracted) we and others might be, and how that's effecting the situation. All this awareness soothes us, organizes us, and prepares us to understand and embody our best purpose right now – essentially moving us into love-first consciousness.

We'll explore much more about states in general, and defensive states and states of healthy response in particular, in Chapter 4.

What's So Great About Dialed-In Integral Mindfulness?

As you can see, starting from a foundation of mindful self-observation, attunement to self, others, and the world, we can build an Integral consciousness that notices our constant flow of states, is aware of us advancing and regressing on crucial developmental lines, recognizes whether we're in a me-first, we-first, or love-first moment, and sees everyone, including *me* and *you,* as unique types of persons. This Integral consciousness is constantly informed by what feels more or less beautiful, good, and true, thus guiding us to be on purpose in whatever activity we're engaged in.

We have learned what Integral mindful awareness is, we have practiced attunement exercises that expand our brains and give us enhanced capacities for compassionate self-observation. We have learned the components of the Integral system and how they contribute to dialed-in.

Now let's go more deeply into understanding our personal similarities and differences in Chapter 3: You Are a Unique Type of Person.

Chapter 3: You Are a Unique Type of Person

Let's do an attunement exercise right now. Take several deep breaths, with slow exhales. Relax and feel your body with acceptance and caring intent. Now let yourself expand accepting/caring awareness of feelings, thoughts, judgments, and desires.

If you've been practicing this for even a few days, you're probably noticing trends and patterns. How we feel, think, and judge are reflections of states of consciousness that come and go constantly and will be discussed in the next chapter. Our typical *patterns* of feeling, thinking, and judging reflect what *types* of person we are. For example:

- You probably typically feel some emotions more often or intensely than other emotions. Are you more frequently afraid or anxious rather than secure or confident? More angry? Lustful? Happy? Nostalgic? Mellow? Satisfied?

- Most of us naturally gravitate to certain thoughts, or kinds of thoughts. For instance, do your thoughts typically drift to your kids, sweetheart, friends, or self? Do you think more about problems or pleasures? Fun you've had, or mistakes you've made? The past or the future? Work issues, home issues, school issues, health issues?

- Do you judge yourself more harshly than you judge others? Others more than you? Do you find yourself chronically not living up to your own standards, or find important people failing your standards? Do you generally find the world satisfying or unsatisfying, beautiful or ugly? Are you moved to tell others your judgments, or horrified at the idea that others might discover your true opinions?

• Do you usually crave pleasures like food, drink, sex, rest, excitement, hobbies, and vacations? Do you more often hunger for opportunities to contribute, like being invited to write, speak, teach, or weigh in on issues? Do you more frequently crave time alone, or contact with others?

No one answers all these questions exactly the same. We are all different types of people!

Habits of attention, desire, emotion, thought, relationship, and judgment constellate together in *you* – they are your type tendencies. As we mature, some deepen, like masculine and feminine, and some can actually change, like shifting from selfish to more caring and generous, or more fixed mindset (avoiding challenge and risk), to growth mindset (embracing effort, progress, and lifelong development).

WHAT TYPES ARE YOU?

If you're a more masculine person, you probably seek out edge of death experiences like sports, gambling, or action movies, and value living your principles. You're ashamed if you compromise core values. Masculine people tend to be goal-oriented, and attracted to solving problems as efficiently as possible.

If you're a more feminine person, you likely hunger for communal contact with family, friends, or community, and desire groups to feel cohesive and cared for. Feminine people tend to be more process oriented and aware of relational dynamics.

If you're a more introverted person, social events probably fatigue you and leave you craving time alone to recharge, while if you're more extroverted, social events are more likely to fill you up and energize you.

If you're more novelty seeking, going to a new restaurant, vacationing in a different country, or meeting a bunch of new people might attract you, while if you're a more harm-avoidant person, such adventures might feel threatening.

Masculine/feminine, introvert/extrovert, novelty seeking/harm avoidant are only three of countless dimensions of how people grow into different types.

Even more, there are healthy and unhealthy versions of almost every type. For instance, in the nine-type Enneagram system, I'm a six, the loyalist/devil's advocate, which is a fear type. I'm a counter phobic version of the fear Type Six, and spent decades of my life seeking out risk, meeting and transcending it, and briefly feeling relief, until the next day when I needed to prove my courage all over again. I believed if I took enough risks, slayed enough dragons, demonstrated calm resolve in enough situations that fear would disappear – but fear never vanished, because I'm a fear type. The best an Enneatype Six does with fear is to develop enough courage so fear never decides, and that wisdom and love mostly have the last word even in the face of fear. Then fear can transform into clarity of awareness of potential risks in the present and future.

Recently, Becky and I were walking on the beach, talking about enneatypes, and she realized she was a Nine, the peacemaker-anger type, who had unconsciously adjusted her anger to fear in a family that essentially forbade anger. This was in response to my insight that I, a Six fear type, adjusted my fear to anger in a family where fear was considered contemptible. The beauty of this dialed-in conversation was that we were not arguing from our different type structures (and God knows we've fought in past years about her fear and my anger), but instead accepted our differences, alert to new insights and life directions, *recognizing we are different types of people.* When people mindfully observe types, this is the kind of growth that becomes possible.

I've heard hundreds of stories from my clients who, not realizing it consciously, suffered from being conflicted about their types and confused about what to do:

- "I'm always alert to whether others are happy with me or not."

- "I can't help constantly looking for what might go wrong."

- "I love to fantasize about how great everything will be when I get married, finish my degree, succeed in my business...."

- "Whatever I accomplish is never enough. I'm driven to start planning the next book, painting, project, or race."

- "I'm ashamed of how frightened I get (or angry, jealous, sexually attracted, critical, accommodating...)."

- "I'm afraid of public speaking. What's wrong with me?"

Habitual impulses and perspectives (driven by what types of person we are) can be constructive or destructive. When we're dialed-in, we can observe our perspectives and impulses with acceptance and caring intent, be aware of our type influences, and choose wisely.

There is no part of us that can't be a resource if properly integrated into our self – usually with some version of understanding and acceptance – even if it looks negative at first glance, like tendencies to fear, jealousy, greed, or rage. Since we generally don't lose or excise central aspects of who we are, we need to integrate dark, destructive, embarrassing, or scary tendencies as resources of energy and insight, rather than try to eliminate them. I can't tell you how much agony I've witnessed from people who hate parts of themselves – usually associated with some aspect of their type – and essentially want to execute these parts. Can't do it. We can grow through some of our repetitive patterns, but many we need to make peace with and integrate into larger, more dialed-in habits and patterns.

For example, some types, like my Enneatype Sixness, involve enduring features which are deeply structured into our personality, probably even at the genetic level. But any aspect of type can be more or less mature and enlightened. I'll always be a fear type who instinctively evaluates risk – that won't change – so growth for me is accepting fear when it arises, utilizing fear's exquisite alertness and attention to detail, and focusing on doing right.

On the other hand, there are lots of traits we can alter with effort and awareness, and often naturally do so as we develop. For example, if you're a more selfish, me-first, type of person, you can learn to be a more generous, caring, we-first and love-first type of person. If you are more of a fixed mindset person, resistant to challenge and horrified at mistakes, you can become more of a growth mindset type person who values effort and progress and regards mistakes as natural consequences of a full life.

Countless typology systems exist like the above mentioned Enneagram (a system I especially love), or varying degrees of the "big five" personality factors (conscientiousness, agreeableness, neuroticism, openness, and extroversion). In this chapter, we're going to focus on masculine/feminine, and fixed mindset/growth mindset, mostly because these dimensions are important, easy to understand, and inform other typology systems – I'm convinced masculine/feminine especially are metatypes that influence all other types.

Understanding just these two typologies can open us up to seeing how *everyone* is a different type of person, and how we can use our understanding of types to be more happily connected and successful.

Myelination

By cultivating states of generosity, caring concern, focused attention, or worldcentric identification, we activate neural networks that become more robust with each iteration. Such brain circuits gradually become more coherent with the rest of our nervous system and the neurons themselves become more heavily myelinated. Cells in our brain called oligodendrocites are drawn to activated networks and start wrapping them in layers of fatty material called myelin. The more myelin wrapping, the faster the circuit and the more robust and hardwired the thought, emotion, impulse, or behavior. This is how states can become traits with practice, and why it's such a good idea to practice attunement all the time.

Knowing that we're different types helps relationships

It's illuminating to observe how different types react differently to the world. Becky loves the desert, while I find it oppressive – a potentially upsetting difference in our "beautiful" standard unless we realize we're different types in this area.

You might love telling personal stories about your home life, while your husband writhes in embarrassment. His "good" standard is offended by what seems to be over-sharing, while your "good" standard feels you're being intimate with friends.

Just *recognizing* different types, or simply *being curious* about what types people are, makes it easier to attune with acceptance and caring intent. We're genetically programmed to be attracted to those like ourselves, which is fine – for instance, married couples from similar backgrounds in ethnicity, education, and socio-economic levels have higher rates of marital happiness. But our "good" moral standards tend to assume others think, feel, and react as we do. This is called "attribution theory" in psychology (more popularly, "the curse of knowledge") when we assume others know what we know. This can lead to confusion, misunderstanding, and moral condemnation if not taken into account.

Helen Palmer tells a story of how Union representatives were amazed at how conflict deescalated when they could observe each other as being different types in the nine type Enneagram system, driven by different passions and reactions.

When we attune to ourselves and others, acceptance and caring intent combined with an understanding of types helps us. We make the shifts from, "I expect everyone to be like me," – worried, ashamed, or irritated when they're *not* – to "We all share the human experience of being a unique type of person, and we all think, feel, and react differently to some extent."

Dialed-in observation of types changes everything.

That said, there are healthy and unhealthy versions of each type, as reflected in my Enneatype Six story. In every arena of life, knowing healthy from unhealthy gives us purpose better than perhaps anything. Healthy/unhealthy naturally harmonizes with the beautiful, good, and true.

Masculine and feminine types

"If you point your finger at me one more time, I'm going to slap you upside the head!"

This was delivered with no humor and utter conviction by a welder sitting across from me with his wife in a therapy session the 1980's. We were on the fourth floor of the Anacapa building in downtown Santa

Barbara, on a hot summer evening, with the smoke from a wildfire rising across the northeastern sky. Everybody was pretty crabby.

I immediately started deescalating the tension with some version of, "I'm sorry, man. You're right, I shouldn't point like that. Also, what's going on with you and your wife right now?"

The guy immediately relaxed back into the session, but his wife needed some minutes to calm down. Feminine people can freak out when masculine violence arises, and she felt the danger in the room as her husband got in my face.

Sensing the smoother vibe, I encouraged him to join me in reassuring her that violence was not imminent, and we got back to the business of helping them love each other better. The three of us were doing fairly well by the end of the session.

Even in those days I was pretty relaxed with masculine rage and challenge. By 1980, I'd been practicing martial arts for fifteen years, and was quite familiar with angry, violent men. I knew that if a guy had it together to give you a chance ("If you point your finger at me one more time...") he'd usually cool down quickly if you respected him one man to another. This welder and I actually had a stronger relationship after that episode.

Years later when I heard David Deida assert "The masculine grows best in the presence of loving challenge, while the feminine grows best in the presence of loving praise," it brought back a flood of such memories: Women weeping with release feeling themselves understood, validated, and praised for their desires to love better and shine in the world. Men first tensing and then relaxing as I challenged them to reach beyond their egos to grow, feel whole, and own their masculine power. When you are whole, vulnerabilities become strengths and resources rather than shameful burdens.

There is a fine line in all of us, a threshold, an event horizon, where passion leads us to lose self-awareness and surrender to hostile defensive mandates – which differ with type. You can tell you've crossed this threshold when no input from the outside can change your mind or alter your pissed off self- righteousness. We easily see how a tantruming three-year-old, or a glassy eyed five-year-old has crossed the line. We have a little more difficulty with rigid, angry, or shut down adults who are deaf and blind to new facts or perspectives. We find it *especially* hard to be aware of ourselves entering such defensive states.

Such loss of control is especially hard on men, since America pathologizes and infantilizes men who lose control and surrender to violent emotion and action. On the other hand, helping men discover these event horizons, and challenging them to keep hold of themselves in clutch situations and do right rather than harm is one of the privileges of being a psychotherapist—and a necessary part of the work. Men are stronger and wiser when they can catch violent states and reach for compassion and vulnerability. Mindful understanding and vulnerability enhance a man's warrior nature by transmuting violent emotions, thoughts, and impulses into resources to be contained and channeled into doing right.

Appropriately channeling violence also makes men more attractive. Most women yearn to feel a man's power and willingness to put it on the line, while still feeling safe from his testosterone-fueled evolutionary capacities for violence. Every man's genome has been shaped by millions of years of male ancestors who successfully held position on dominance hierarchies, met threats from nature and other men, and protected families and tribes from danger and attack.

So, if you're a guy, *never* surrender to violence. Learn to value those around you who have the courage to challenge you as you approach the line between self-control and acting out. That's *real* masculine power, to be so dialed-in that you never lose the responsibility to make each moment better and safer for everyone.

It Began with David Deida

As I mentioned in Chapter 2, in the late 90's Becky gave me some cassette tapes (remember cassette tapes?) of David Deida working with people during one of his workshops. I was instantly fascinated. He had a no-nonsense approach to masculine and feminine that I hadn't encountered before. Briefly:

> • The masculine is anchored in that part of us – deepest awareness – that never changes. The masculine resonates with pure consciousness, presence, meaning at the edge of death, and is drawn to the feminine form and energy.
> • The feminine is all that changes. The feminine resonates with love through the body, free flowing emotion,

delight in being seen as light, community, and is drawn to trustable masculine presence.

• The masculine grows best in the presence of loving challenge, the feminine in response to loving praise.

• We all have both masculine and feminine aspects, but fundamentally most of us – especially in the sexual occasion – are more masculine (the leader in the dance of eroticism), or more feminine (the follower in the dance).

• Masculine and feminine people in proximity tend to generate sparks of erotic polarity, which can turn into attractions and love affairs.

• Relationship styles and worldviews progress from me-first self-centeredness, to we-first let's be equal and talk about everything, to love-first let's open in love to be our best selves, the clearest expressions of spirit on earth.

Deida's system fit together beautifully, and I read his books, studied his tapes, went to his lectures and workshops, absorbed his work, cross validated it with other people's material, and applied it to psychotherapy. I started finding other masculine/feminine theorist/practitioners like Regena Thomashauer, anthropologists like Helen Fisher, and developmentalists/neuroscientists like Ed Tronick and Alan Shore whose work expanded my understanding further. Clients, students, and audiences at lectures love this material – largely I think because our modern and post-modern society has minimized the huge differences between masculine and feminine in reaction to the oppression of women in most of recorded human history, and yet *we all know* it's *really* different being a guy (usually more masculine) or a woman (usually more feminine) in almost every situation.

One of the first things we become aware of as we develop a conscious self in our second year (12 to 24 months) is whether we're a boy or a girl and what that means. A lot of psychologists in the last century thought that such learning was just social conditioning – implying that you could raise a boy like a girl or a girl like a boy and they'd just naturally take on the roles you taught them. *No way.* This doesn't just violate beautiful and good standards, empirical research (true) overwhelmingly supports the reality that, in many ways, men and women grow, think, respond, desire, and relate differently.

It's true that culture radically influences how we experience and embody who we are, and some men have a more feminine sexual essence and some women a more masculine sexual essence. But there are also major genetic differences between men and women that start at conception and keep differentiating the male and female physiology, social networks, sexuality, morality, and general experience throughout life.

For instance, when little girls play a game, if someone starts having a bad time, the game often stops. When little boys play, if someone starts having a bad time, the boys will often argue like lawyers until they've come to an understanding of what's fair.

Little boys use more demanding and intimidating language when playing and suggesting activities. "You be the crook, and I'll be the cop. No! Not like that! Do it like this!" Little girls use more cooperative and inclusive language, like, "Let's play house and I can be the Mommy."

Grown up men want to solve problems and move on. I can't tell you how many times I've seen a look of exasperation on a guy's face when his wife brings up a sex/time/in-laws/money/kids/chores issue and he says, "Not that again! We've *already talked about it*. I thought we were done with that one!"

Grown up women are more likely to want to process. In small groups trying to solve problems, women have been observed postponing decisions so they can keep relating. This *hardly ever* happens with groups of men.

When I train therapists, my emphasis is on helping them discover and enhance their natural healing style – always influenced to some extent by their unique balance of masculine/feminine aspects/essence. I've found adding the dimensions of masculine, feminine, erotic polarity, and me-first, we-first, and love-first relating makes any helping approach much more powerful.

I was studying Deida's material just before the time I read Ken Wilber's *Integral Psychology*, and realized the beautiful confluence of the two sets of teachings. Interestingly, I later discovered the two men had been friends for decades. My first two books – *Waking Up* and *Sessions* – applied many of their ideas to the understanding and practice of psychotherapy.

John and Karen

How is understanding masculine and feminine types useful? Well, check out the following session with John and Karen. They came in depressed (both of them) with Karen despairing about how unappealing John had become in the last couple of years.

Karen started the session with, "We don't connect any more. John comes home and just sits in front of the T.V. I ask him how his day went, and he always says, 'Fine.' What does *that* mean?"

John sighs deeply, "What do you want me to say? It's just another day."

I decide to step in, "When's the last time you two felt intimate?"

They both look confused, and – like many couples – interpret the question sexually. Karen looks reprovingly at John and says, "We haven't made love in months. John's not interested."

This activates John a little bit. "What do you mean? You don't want to."

Karen, in obvious frustration, replies, "Where do you get these ideas?"

John, somewhat self-righteously, "You always say 'No!'"

Now Karen is outraged, "*Always?* You've only asked *twice* since I can remember, and then in the middle of the night." She looks over to me for validation. "Who wants to wake up at 2:00 AM and have sex?"

I step in before they can accelerate any further. "First of all, Karen, you're a more feminine person. John, you're a more masculine person. The feminine yearns to be known and claimed by the masculine. You want him to be intimate in ways you like at times you want intimacy." She nods as if this is the most obvious thing in the world.

I continue with John. "John, the masculine does best when fully resolved, and is usually the leader in the dance of eroticism. How resolved have you been to find the right time and approach Karen in ways she likes?"

John looks down, "I'm never confident with Karen." She looks a little surprised, and I continue with John, though also indirectly talking to Karen. "The feminine likes a resolved masculine person, and especially one attuned to *her*. It's pleasurable for a woman to be deeply known by a man, and to have him get who she is and how she wants to connect. Your lack of resolve diminishes your erotic polarity with Karen, and makes it harder for her to surrender into her feminine side and be danced by you."

I have both of their attention now. Karen is nodding vigorously, because the feminine grows best in the presence of loving praise, and I'm praising her feminine light. John is looking thoughtful because I'm challenging him to step up to know her and claim her, and the masculine grows best in the presence of loving challenge.

I continue a little bit more to extend this beyond sex, because – especially to women – love, sex, intimacy, and arousal are hugely contextual and intertwined. "This is about intimacy, not just sex. Though, don't get me wrong, sex is *important* (guys like John need to hear this so they don't feel ashamed thinking about sex every day). In the dance of your life, John, you're more often the masculine partner and you, Karen, the feminine partner. The feminine craves a trustable, present partner who knows her and attunes to her needs and rhythms, adjusting to enhance her pleasure. Like bringing her a cup of tea just when she wants it, or asking her about her day and *really* being interested. The masculine craves feminine joy, light, pleasure, and devotion, and Karen, you haven't felt safe or connected enough to be generous in these ways."

Both of them relax hearing this. They glance shyly at each other. Even though I'm speaking generically, this feels strangely intimate to them because it rings true and is being discussed openly. Most of us have taboos about these kinds of conversations that we'll explore more deeply in Chapter 6.

John finally speaks, "I want to do this, but I don't know how." Karen looks a little guilty. "There's never any time for us."

I smile at them." I can help you get better at this, so you can deepen your erotic charge and feel more delighted as man and woman with each other. But it will take some work."

John looks resolved for the first time in the session. "I'm up for it."

Karen looks at him with admiration. "Thank you John! I can't tell you how much that means to me."

This is the power of knowing your sexual aspects and essence and developing them to create more love. You can better relax into who you truly are in the moment, and consciously harmonize with your partner.

I consider masculine/feminine aspects and essence to be so central to the human experience that they constitute an overriding typology that informs all other types – they are metatypes. For instance, in the introvert/extrovert system, more masculine introverts or extraverts often present differently from more feminine ones, and so on.

Who Am I?

Ask yourself:

- What is my deepest sexual essence?

- In the sexual occasion, am I more the leader, resting in deepest consciousness, wanting to possess and guide the feminine to deeper pleasure?

- Am I more the follower, relaxing into my body and surrendering to being blissfully guided into deeper pleasure expressed through movement, breath, and sound?

- Would I rather be perceived as a trustable presence, or someone who offers devotional love from my heart?

- Am I more lit up by feeling true to my principles, or expressing love through my body into the world?

- Do I find emptiness a relaxing concept, or am I more drawn to fullness?

- Would I rather stand unrecoiling in the face of anything, or feel like I am a clear channel of emotion, seen by others as light and beauty?

- I have both masculine and feminine aspects that show up differently throughout the day. What are they, and how do they show themselves?

Try talking about all this with your partner and friends, and see what the conversations uncover and reveal. Such discussions with people we love tend to create deeper intimacy and personal revelations.

The feminine in relationship with a masculine partner

In each man's desires and complaints, there is yearning to be loved and pleasured in special ways. If you can offer that love and pleasure from your heart, you become a better woman – an embodiment of the courtesan. Your caresses nourish him. Your kisses give him strength. Your laughter lightens his world. As Regena Thomashauer teaches in her School of the Womanly Arts, embodying the power of pleasure is the courtesan's gift.

This inspires a man to serve you, but you have other influences –for instance, your pain can challenge him to be more kind and present. When a guy complains or whines about something, or when he seems clueless about how to love you, feminine love and current emotion can make him want to reach to be a better man. Current emotion is the ongoing flow of "yums" and "yucks" expressed without residue from the past or distressed anticipation of the future – your feminine spirit flowing from your heart unobstructed. Such surrender to the Goddess in the present moment makes you a better woman.

Men can bully, neglect, and act thoughtlessly – not our most attractive selves. Seeing a woman's distress at his collapse can snap a man back to presence.

Men can also be wise and delightful. When your man is being his best self, allow the light and pleasure from your heart to drench him in love. Devotional love rejuvenates the masculine – especially offered to his best self.

Let his best and worst sides inspire you to be a better woman who who inspires him to be a better man.

The masculine in relationship with a feminine partner

Your feminine partner wants to be an open channel of emotion, be seen as light, and be a wellspring of love into the world. She grows with recognition and loving praise. Embedded in her distresses and complaints are yearnings for deeper love and connection.

Many men are distracted by purpose and challenge, which can dominate their lives with work or recreational activities. We all have heard stories of guys putting work over family, or raising their hobbies to the level of sacred mission. One woman I worked with complained bitterly to her husband that when he finally scheduled a free weekend with her and the kids, he used up most of Saturday and Sunday with epic bike rides with his buddies, leaving him tired and crabby each afternoon and evening.

When a masculine person takes the larger view of what best serves everyone, and then organizes around those insights, his feminine partner tends to relax and feel attracted and grateful. The key to dialed-in is not just to understand your type, but to attune to others, *accept* them, and be the healthiest embodiment possible of your type.

I advocate lifelong development, but growth is knowing what is possible and what pits us against our very natures. A more masculine type can cultivate his feminine aspects, become more sensitive to emotion and devotional love, seek fullness, surrender to community and care for everyone, and learn to let others open him farther than he can open himself, but he will always be at his core a more masculine person who values the resolute acceptance of death, yearns to live on purpose, true to his principles, and enjoys opening his partner into deeper pleasure, love, and spirituality. A more feminine type can learn to enjoy emptiness, be a trustable presence, stand unrecoiling at the edge of death, and surrender wholly to deep soul's purpose, but she will always at her core be a more feminine person, yearning to be a wellspring of love, and relaxing when being a clear channel of emotion.

As you attune to yourself and other people, whether sitting quietly in meditation or going through your day, be aware with acceptance and caring intent of your own and other's masculine and feminine aspects and essence. You'll notice yourself in more or less healthy versions of your aspects and essence, and simple awareness will help guide you to the healthier ones.

FIXED MINDSETS AND GROWTH MINDSETS

Earlier, I maintained that there are positive and negative expressions of most type systems. Occasionally, a typology system reflects dimensions where there are few if any positive versions of some of the types, and this is true for fixed mindsets and growth mindsets. It's abundantly clear from multiple studies and our own beautiful and good standards that growth mindsets are better in almost all ways to fixed mindsets. One of the reasons I'm including them in this type chapter is to illustrate that there are some personality characteristics which are superior and can be cultivated to avoid problems and improve life.

So, what are growth and fixed mindsets, and why are growth mindsets so superior?

Growth mindsets are *so* much better than fixed mindsets.

Lots of us make New Year's resolutions, and most of us don't follow through. Why is this? I believe it's often because we have the wrong *attitudes* towards change – we try something, find it's hard or sloppy, and then get irritated, embarrassed, or frustrated and just give the whole thing up. An attitude towards change, growth, or dealing with the world can become habituated into a type of person – for instance, one who follows through on resolutions or one who doesn't.

We typically have attitudes we bring to bear on everything we do. If I drive carefully, I bring an attitude of caution each time I'm behind the wheel. If I drive aggressively, I bring an attitude of "Don't mess with me!" Such attitudes are called, "*mindsets.*"

Carol Dweck, author of *Mindset, The New Psychology of Success* has found that people live from two major mindset positions, creating two metatypes of growth mindset types and fixed mindset types.

> • A growth mindset believes that effort and progress are what matter most. If I'm learning to play the piano, it's less important that I sound great and more important that I'm practicing and improving. If I have a problem with my iPhone, it doesn't mean I'm stupid, it just means I need to invest some effort and progress to solve the problem, and – if I have a growth mindset – effort and progress in finding and solving problems is what I like. Growth mindset people prefer friends and colleagues who are as smart and capable as possible to help stimulate fresh ideas and change, and are delighted to find somebody who is more knowledgeable or expert than they are.

> • A fixed mindset believes that ability and intelligence is innate, and that failure is shameful. I'd rather do an easy project where I don't risk failure than try a harder project that might involve being frustrated or temporarily stumped. If I have to work to learn something, it means

that I am inherently flawed and I want to avoid that shameful feeling by avoiding the hard activity. A problem with my iPhone scares me because it makes me feel inept and inferior. Fixed mindset people like friends and colleagues who don't seem as smart or capable, because then the fixed-mindset person doesn't feel stupid in comparison.

It seems so easy doesn't it? Clearly, growth mindsets are a better way to go, so why aren't they the universal standard for everyone all the time? Mainly because we are a success-oriented culture where we admire easy victory, and often view struggle to grow as a sign of inferiority. For instance:

> • Your eleven-year-old comes home from school proudly waving a report card with an "A" in every class. You compliment her extravagantly and she says, "It's not that hard, really." Later that day you tell your best friend (feeling a secret glow of pride), "June got straight A's again. She's just naturally gifted."

Or

> June comes home with three B's and two A's. You ask her how she feels about it and she says, "I feel good about my B in Algebra. I was a C for the first part of the class, but I studied hard and now I'm getting it better. Math's like a bunch of puzzles that keep getting harder forever. I kind of like puzzles." You tell your friend later (again feeling a secret glow of pride), "June got three B's and two A's, but she feels best about her B in algebra because she worked hard and saw progress."

Most of us can identify with both these attitudes, but research shows that growth mindset attitudes ("Math's like a bunch of puzzles that keep getting harder forever. I kind of like puzzles.") *overwhelmingly* predict future happiness and success more than fixed mindset attitudes. I use eleven-year-old June as an example because Carol Dweck found that fixed and growth mindset kids diverged wildly at around eleven. Fixed mindset kids are often distressed by the extra challenges of middle school, and academic performance tends to slide through high school. Growth mindset kids continue to improve through high school and even farther into college. We'll explore approaches that support growth mindsets in kids in our discussions of dialed-in parenting in Chapter 9.

Both of the above scenarios tend to feel good to parents. We like to believe our kids are talented and naturally successful, *and* we also love it when our kids display mature growth-mindset attitudes to problems. The take home message is that, in many areas, we unconsciously accept fixed mindset standards without considering that a growth mindset is the best path to success and happiness. For instance:

> • A VP tells a fixed mindset CEO, "We have problems with quality control, and we need to gradually improve the culture in production. People get publicly humiliated for making mistakes, and everyone is afraid they'll be axed in the next series of lay-offs." The boss replies, "We have the best factory in the state! How dare you suggest there's a 'problem with the culture?' You're fired!"

> • Same scenario with a growth mindset boss who replies, "Really sounds like you're on to something! What do you imagine the next step should be? Who could best help us make these changes?"

> • A fixed mindset husband tells his wife, "I'm just not in love anymore. It doesn't feel the same as when we first got married. I don't think we're meant for each other and I believe we should separate."

> • Same scenario with a growth mindset husband who announces, "We seem to have drifted apart. Let's get some help and advice about how to feel closer and have more fun. I think our marriage needs it."

Carol Dweck and others have generated numerous studies showing the superiority of growth mindsets in kids, bosses, athletes, and lovers. Again and again, an attitude that effort and progress are the way to go resulted in better development, more joyful relationships, enhanced performance, more profits, and better employee relations over extended periods of time.

When you do your attunement practices, pay attention to how you feel when confronted with a challenge or problem.

Is there a sense of, "OK, I can do this! What's my next step?" You're probably approaching your challenge with a growth mindset.

On the other hand, if you have a sense of, "This is too hard. I might fail. People might not think I'm the best. I shouldn't risk it!" you're probably suffering from a fixed mindset.

I teach growth mindsets to all my students and clients, and encourage people to look with interest into where they have fixed mindsets. Sometimes a guy will have a growth mindset at work (each month he sits down with his staff and everyone talks about how "We can make things a little more successful and fun around here.") and a fixed mindset at home ("This report card is unacceptable. I want to see A's!"). Or a woman will have a growth mindset about her kids ("Let's just focus on having more fun with your homework."), and a fixed mindset about herself (I'm just not that attractive, so why should I try to exercise and eat right – what's the point?"). My goal is to help my clients *notice* when they're coming from a fixed or growth mindset, and to *make effort and progress* towards having less of a fixed mindset and more of a growth mindset in every facet of their life.

Practice

If you are generally a fixed mindset person, don't despair! Remember, "Aware with acceptance," and recognize you have some work ahead to help yourself be more of a growth mindset type of person. Notice when you start to avoid an important challenge because it is too hard, threatening, or might result in humiliating failure, and focus on effort and progress, noticing (even journaling and recording) both your progress on the challenge and your shift towards valuing effort and progress over outcome and instant success.

Try it yourself

First, are you willing to accept that you're not perfect just as you are, and can improve *everything* about your life with effort and progress?

If the answer is "yes," look with interest at how you relate to yourself, others, and the world today. Include mindset awareness in your attunements to thoughts, impulses, and especially judgments.

> • Do you feel good when things go well, but still have a sense that you can make them even better with effort and progress? Do you get frustrated by mistakes or areas you're clumsy or uniformed, but then tell yourself, "OK, I just need to focus on gradual improvement and everything will be fine." These are growth mindsets which will eventually lead you to greater happiness and success.

> • Do you make a mistake and tell yourself, "I'm an idiot!" and then rage for a while at yourself or someone else? Do you have zero patience for others' imperfections? Do you get irritated or embarrassed when someone seems to be more knowledgeable or skillful than you? These are fixed mindsets that will compromise your happiness and success, and you might want to direct yourself to more growth mindset attitudes and behaviors – with the sense that *effort and progress is beautiful and good.*

Noticing fixed and growth mindsets and adjusting towards growth mindsets can up-level and transform your life, your marriage, your work, and your parenting. It will shift you from a fixed mindset type towards a growth mindset type.

But don't take my word for it. Try it for a few weeks and see how the "Effort and progress is beautiful and good," growth standard impacts your world.

You'll be glad you did.

Dialed-in understanding of types

Mindful attunement gives us capacities to self-observe with acceptance and caring intent, which supports compassionate judgments. Being on purpose generally involves wanting to serve the highest good. Knowing that we and others are unique types with different information processing and motivation systems helps understanding and service enormously.

59

If I know you are a more feminine type of person, your disinterest – even repulsion – with my masculine fascination with Ultimate Fighting is much less distressing or insulting. Knowing I'm a more masculine person helps me feel less embarrassed with my impatience with your love of romance novels.

Even more, as a masculine person I know that much of my purpose will involve success/failure, success/failure...death, and that I'll relax being true to my principles and suffer if I'm not.

If you're a feminine person, much of your purpose will involve love's happening/love's not happening, love's happening/love's not happening... death, and that you'll suffer when love's not happening and blossom when it is. This is also true for the feminine aspects of masculine people and the masculine aspects of feminine people.

Much of our life purpose can be illuminated by knowing our masculine/feminine aspects/essence and working *with* them rather than *against* them.

Similarly, growth mindsets are clearly better than fixed mindsets, and so part of all our purpose is to deconstruct our fixed mindset tendencies and develop our growth mindset tendencies.

If your friend Betty has a fixed mindset about her parenting, *and you can see it,* you'll better understand her outrage when she feels criticized as a parent, and not take it as personally if her anger is directed at you. Being dialed-in this way helps you be strategic in offering what might feel to her like negative feedback.

I once decided to become a tap dancer, and quickly learned I had relatively little natural talent for tap dancing. One of my clients, seeing me dance after my first couple of years of training, burst out laughing and told me, "You look like Lurch in the Munsters trying to dance!" I must admit that stung a little, but I told myself, "Effort and progress is more important that feeling clumsy," and I eventually progressed past the Lurch stage.

Other typologies I love

As you might have observed, I find the Enneagram's nine type system to be compelling and useful. If you want to delve deeper, check out Helen Palmer's books and tapes, or any of Don Riso and Russ Hudson's work. You can't change what enneatype you are, but there are less healthy and more healthy manifestations of your enneatype that become illuminated with Integral understanding of states, lines and levels of development, as well as the beautiful, good, and true.

Secure and insecure attachment styles

I also find attachment theory's types of secure and insecure attachment incredibly useful for kids and adults. It's a system that guides you towards creating secure attachments with others and yourself, which makes it another typology system where you can change your type for the better if you do the work. Once again, attachment styles inform purpose in that we all want to have secure attachment styles ourselves as well as support them in our families.

Whatever type systems you like, you'll find certain narratives and archetypes more or less interesting and appealing. Attractions and repulsions are always reflections of inner forces involving our beautiful, good, and true value systems. For instance, I love the archetype/myth/epic hero typologies. The Warrior and the Man of Wisdom archetypes light me up, but might bore you. The Divine Mother or the Sex Goddess might feel yummy and familiar, or yucky and alien. Simply knowing *the existence of* types expands social understanding immeasurably.

Dialed-in types exercises:

Buy a journal (it's always nice to get one that you find beautiful), and write down your dreams. Notice themes and figures that emerge over time. Notice attractions and repulsions. All emotionally charged characters and stories reflect aspects of you – guides to understanding your unique type of person.

Sit in mindful meditation daily, attuning to yourself and others. Try observing your repetitive patterns of attention, feeling, and interest. What aspects of your typical habits of attention and interest are more/less beautiful to you? Good? True? Learning to accept and integrate what is less beautiful, good, or true, and acknowledge and feel gratitude for what is more beautiful, good, and true in you and others leads to more dialed-in living, and finer understanding of your unique type of person.

Chapter 4: "I love you!" "I hate you!" – What State We're in Natters

What were you thinking five minutes ago?

Can't remember?

What were you feeling an hour ago? Still feeling that way, or have your feelings changed?

What do you think you'll be thinking and feeling in twenty minutes, and how accurate have you found such predictions to be?

What was the happiest, stokiest, most fun time you ever had? Do you remember how you felt and what you thought at the time?

When you attune to yourself, do you notice how your sensations, emotions, thoughts, and judgments ebb, flow, shift, and morph? Isn't there a profound difference between experiencing any of these with acceptance and caring intent, or with critical judgments?

States Permeate All Life

States of consciousness are the atmosphere of life, the sound tracks of daily existence, the meaning-making qualitative experiences of happy/ sad, anxious/secure, connected/lonely, interested/bored, and all the other states. States overwhelmingly generate beautiful and good evaluations, and indirectly drive true (even if science tells me there's nothing to fear from the big black tarantula, there *must* be something icky and dangerous there).

Patterns of states determine our types. Our brains pump out habitual states constantly in reaction to experience. To learn your patterns, mindfully follow the rise and fall of your states – just attune to yourself right now and feel them undulating like ocean swells.

One of my favorite studies in the 1970's used high speed cameras to track micro-expressions on people's faces. The researchers knew that changes in states of consciousness were revealed in tiny shifts of facial micro-expressions. Humans have the most expressive faces of all mammals, and facial expressions actually reflect *and influence* states of consciousness. That's right – influence. If you put a pretend frown on, it will activate unhappiness circuits in your brain (especially in the frontal lobes) and you'll start to feel more bummed out. If you smile, even force a smile, happiness circuits in your frontal lobe will light up, elevating your mood.

Getting back to the high speed photography micro-expressions study, people changed expression, indicating a change in emotional state, *every three tenths of a second.*

What?!

Our states change constantly, usually in patterns governed by inputs from the world, our inner experience, and our type of person.

Brains monitor millions of sensory inputs and are constantly picking seven plus or minus two of them to put together into little stories with their own emotions, impulses, and memories – states of consciousness. Most of these stories are non-conscious, or barely conscious if we pay attention to them.

Brains encode tendencies to enter these states via our implicit memory systems. Implicit memories drive states, and so, what are implicit memories?

Implicit memories start in the third trimester and don't *feel* like something is being remembered

Starting in the third trimester, infants' nervous systems begin turning sensory inputs into interior representations of the universe. This is apparently quite blissful in the womb, but birth is a messy, traumatic transition into a psychedelic exploding universe. Imagine the shock of birth, where an infant's nervous system shifts from not having to breathe, eat, see, or deal with the world outside the womb, to everything all at once!

Luckily, babies bond with mothers and fathers and begin interacting with the world, laying down lots of implicit memories that grow as babies grow. For example, Mom sings James Taylor's *Sweet Baby James* at bedtime to five-month-old Timmy. His nervous system encodes an implicit memory of this soothing, comforting moment, and seven years later Timmy hears the song, relaxes, feels securely held, and begins to go to sleep, *with no sense of something being remembered.* This is implicit memory.

Explicit memory, where we *feel something is being remembered,* like what you had for breakfast this morning and what you and your son talked about in the kitchen, shows up around eighteen months of age when the brain area called the hippocampus has matured sufficiently. *Explicit memory* is what people generally refer to as "memory," because there is a sense of something being remembered.

Implicit memories have all the characteristics of explicit memories – emotions, impulses, stories – but there is no sense of something being remembered. Why do I love Hawaiian ballads and hate mayonnaise? These are obviously connected to experiences, memories, and action patterns that are beneath my conscious awareness, don't feel like something is being remembered, but were almost certainly encoded in response to *something.*

SHADOW

Some psychologists and spiritual teachers call impulses, feelings, stories, traits, and states we have trouble consciously perceiving *"shadow."* As we mature, this non-conscious shadow material progressively becomes conscious – we wake up to new perspectives and deeper understandings. A couple of examples of shadow:

> • I studied martial arts for many years, but never clearly realized my aversion to violence until the week after my son Ethan was born. I had taken the afternoon off to watch *Ran,* an Akira Kurasawa Samurai movie, and had to walk out during the first battle scene. I knew I was watching

actors pretending to be dead warriors, but I couldn't help thinking, "They were all baby boys like Ethan once. I can't stand this useless violence." A shadow part of me that had been at least partially hidden, a profound aversion to violence, was now much more visible.

• Your wife makes a disgusted face when you tell her you spent the afternoon playing video games. "Why are you so angry and disgusted!" you say in an accusing voice (not aware of your tone – *your* non-conscious shadow material). Her face tightens up even more, "I'm *not* angry! I just don't like seeing my husband act like a ten-year-old!" She *can't see* her shadow anger.

Dialed-in awareness catches states and patterns of states with interest – it doesn't matter if you remember how you learned them or if they involve implicit and/or explicit memories, shadow or conscious awareness, all states benefit from mindful attention. Expanding awareness of both healthy and unhealthy states is a mark of cognitive development (how compleity of thought), emotional development (how aware and self-regulating you are of what you're feeling at any given moment), relational development (self-observing your and other's interconnecting states with acceptance and caring intent), and spiritual development (an increasingly intimate and stable connection with unity and love).

In this chapter, we'll briefly explore the range of states we experience daily, and focus on two state distinctions that lend themselves well to dialed-in mindful living:

> • **Yum/yuck** – how we're wired to be more attracted or repelled to almost anything.
> • **Defensive states and states of healthy response to the present moment** – how our nervous system tends to be empathic and pro-social when feeling safe, and closed down and ready fight or flee when unsafe.

Bazillions of states

Daily we move through waking, sleeping, dreaming, and deep dreamless sleep states. When awake, we can be aware in the present moment, or drift into the past, future, or someplace else. We can more or less effectively self-observe states, and our abilities and capacities shift and vary in different states.

What we learn in one state might not be available to us in another state. For instance, in sex education classes in middle school and high school, I really doubt any of the kids are sexually aroused when they hear messages about impulsivity, safe sex, and healthy partners. When teens go to parties, perhaps drink or use drugs, and start fooling around, they enter states of sexual arousal where they become more impulsive, less self-aware, and more reckless. The information from the classes might not be available to them in those states, or repulsive to beautiful and good standards like "It's good to love and have fun." If we want to optimize sex education, let's include instruction on how decision making shifts in intoxicated and aroused states. Let's teach them about how to have fun and reduce harm in *those* states.

Simply knowing state concepts helps all education, and guides development in general. Why aren't we teaching attunement practices routinely in grade school, if self-observation with acceptance and caring intent is so beneficial? Well, lots of people are. Ellen Langer, one of the developers of mindful learning, found that students had more fun and better outcomes with teachers who were open to alternatives, alert to distinctions, sensitive to contexts, and explored multiple perspectives in the present moment. These qualities helped co-create enhanced learning states.

A principle of states is that the more we experience them, the more likely we are to experience them again. States activate neural networks that become more robust with use. This is how people develop superpowers, by practicing extraordinary *states* enough that they become deeply embedded *traits*. This is easy to see in professional musicians and athletes. We tend to notice the *skills* they demonstrate on stages or playing fields, but those skills are all supported by specific states of consciousness that these musicians and athletes have turned into what neuroscientists call attractor states (states our brains automatically reach for) while preparing and performing.

If you practice dialed-in Integral mindfulness enough, it will become an *attractor state* – a state that draws you in through fascination, emotional charge, or habit.

Neurobiology

When a neural network is activated and oligodendrocytes start wrapping the circuit in white fatty myelin, that circuit becomes privileged because myelinated neurons are up to one hundred times faster than unmyelinated ones. Deeply wired, heavily myelinated circuits naturally move to the front of the line when brains choose states to generate. Functionally, this is very much like optimizing parts of your website to be chosen by search engines, or creating more bandwidth with more myelination.

Two state understandings that are easy to observe and contribute mightily to dialed-in living are *yum and yuck,* and *defensive states and states of healthy response to the present moment.*

Let's look at them more closely.

Yum/Yuck – amazingly Reliable, always revealing

Jill – thirty-seven, an assistant District Attorney raising her ten-year-old son after a difficult divorce – sits across from me in my office, fretting about an invitation she just got from her friend Shelly.

"She's organizing a reunion of four of us who've stayed close since high school. She wants to meet in Vegas, gamble, see a couple of shows, and get crazy for a few days."

My clients have had the best of times and the worst of times in Las Vegas, so I'm used to both dread and wild excitement associated with such invitations. I can feel Jill's reluctance and it makes me curious. "There's something bugging you about this."

Jill's face tightens a little in frustration and confusion, "I know. I should be happy to do it. The four of us had fun trips in our twenties, but since Jake was born, I haven't enjoyed partying as much. The last couple of times it seems I wait around a lot while Shelly and the others drink, gamble, and flirt with guys."

I lean forward, "At this point the trip doesn't sound much like a 'yum.' It sounds more like a 'yuck.'"

Jill laughs a little. "What do you mean? Shelly's one of my best friends."

I like where we're going with this conversation. Jill has trouble disappointing people she's close to. "I know Shelly's a wonderful friend, and it's confusing to not be drawn to trips you used to enjoy so much. My wife's spiritual teacher says that our initial reaction to things is usually 'yum' or 'yuck.' The kicker is that if it's not an immediate 'yum,' it's usually a 'yuck.' This happens to track nicely with how brains constantly evaluate the moment, scanning for safety and dangerousness, as well as what we want and don't want."

Jill looks confused. "I used to love to party with them in Vegas and Tahoe. I don't know what's different about me."

I feel a wave of admiration for how Jill has grown since her divorce three years ago. "You've changed a lot. One important difference is that you take your intuitive reactions more seriously and are more willing to be speak up. 'Yum' and 'yuck' are useless unless we pay attention and act. In fact, if we don't pay attention we get increasingly numb to intuition. As we listen better to 'yums' and 'yucks.' intuition improves. You've been getting more sensitive to these messages and that's probably why you didn't say 'yes' automatically."

Jill gets that look of *"This is making sense,"* (a "yum" reaction) that is so enjoyable to see in therapy. "You're right. I never even considered saying 'no' to Shelly before." Jill just shifted from mindless to mindful in dealing with Shelly's request.

Bruce Lipton, in *The Biology of Belief,* describes how cells (amoebas, human cells, plant cells – basically *all* living cells) are always either growing or defending, but hardly ever doing both at once. If you observe a single cell, it is either metabolizing nutrients and expanding, or reacting to threats self-protectively.

This "either you're growing or defending" dynamic continues up the evolutionary chain to you and me going about our daily lives – adjusting every decision and action to feeling secure (we're usually growing) or threatened (we're usually defending). Jill's 'yuck' to Las Vegas is her intuition telling her she's repelled by the idea of partying in Vegas, but her habitual compliance pushes her to say "yes" when she wants to say "no." Such conflicts confuse us, and confusion is often the mark of unresolved psycho/spiritual/relational material.

On multiple levels we spend our lives either defending or growing, guided by our immediate responses to circumstances. Our nervous systems react to each new situation with an immediate *appraisal* of attraction/repulsion, yes/no, or *yum/yuck*. "Yum" magnetizes us, while "yuck" pushes us away. These are reflexive states which we can ignore, blindly follow, or mindfully observe and cross validate with our beautiful, good, and true validity standards.

Yum and Yuck are great guides

How do we ever decide what to do? How do we guide our lives through the incredible intricacies of the world – through the hundreds of decisions we make every day? How do we harness the power of our brain/mind/social systems to understand and thrive? "Yum" and "yuck" states cover a lot territory in the decision making process.

Yum/yuck is not a perfect system. We'll often feel "yuck" to something that's actually a good idea (the colonoscopy I keep postponing, paying bills, asking for a raise), or "yum" to something that's harmful (having a drink with that married man, the second piece of chocolate cake, staying up till 2:00 am watching that old movie, the third glass of wine), but we can't adequately process anything without first noticing how we feel. Enter yum/yuck, our instinctive appraisal system.

Becky has been my best teacher in life. As a seeker, she's been introducing me to extraordinary people and systems forever. For example, she turned me on to David Deida and Ken Wilber, both of whose work rocked my world and became catalysts for seminal insights and writings, including this book.

Her teacher, Djwhal Khul, told her our bodies know what's good for us –they resonate with "yum" or "yuck." When we listen to yum/yuck with interest and acceptance, we tend to make good decisions.

This is a lot like muscle testing, which Chiropractors and Educational Kinesiologists use routinely. Hold an arm out, have someone push it down while you resist, and it will move a little. Now make a false statement like, "My name is Mud," while your friend tries to push your arm down and you resist. Nobody's named "Mud," so I know your nervous system reads this statement as a lie, and your friend will easily push your arm down. Now say, "My name is _____ (whatever your name is)," and have your friend push your arm down while you resist, and you're arm will be much harder to move.

Why is this? I – and many others – believe our body/mind systems are integrated instruments of extreme wisdom, connected to all the interlocking fields that self-organize towards harmony from the tiniest atom to the whole universe. Muscle testing, or yum/yuck, gives us a little window into this wisdom, *if we listen to the states.* In other words, it's a prime guide to integrating our states of consciousness to more satisfying congruence – which generates healthy patterns of perception, emotion, action, and understanding.

Let's try it

Breathe deeply and attune to your sensations, feelings, thoughts, and judgments. Practice maintaining this attuned state. As you go about your day, you'll notice shifts of attraction and repulsion – yums and yucks. Remember, if it's not a clear "yum," it's likely a "yuck."

With each "yum" or "yuck," ask yourself, "What's the kindest perspective and the best action right now?"

If you do this for even a couple of days, you'll have surprising insights. For instance, Jill said "No" to Las Vegas, but invited Shelly and her family to spend the weekend in Santa Barbara with her and Jake, and everybody had a great time.

Defensive states and states of healthy response to the present moment

Dialed-in Integral mindfulness is all about states of healthy response to the present moment. If I'm alone, I'm attuned to myself, on purpose, in the present moment. If I'm with you, I'm also attuned to *us* with acceptance and caring intent, predisposing me to relate well and make good decisions. The more we're dialed-in, the more time we spend in healthy response to the present moment, and the less time we spend in defensive states.

Defensive states arise from our brains non-consciously perceiving threat. Since we are social beings, threats are often social. You frown at me, or tell me you don't like my tone, and I feel alarmed. I remember forgetting my son's birthday last week and feel ashamed. Your wife says, "We have to talk!" and you feel a sinking sensation in your gut. Such threats can cue brains to instantly instantiate defensive states that involve:

- Amplified or numbed emotions. I *hate* that you don't like my tone (amplified), or you feel *totally blank* when your wife says, "We have to talk!" (numbed).
- Distorted perspectives. I create a story of you misreading my meaning and tones and being hyper-sensitive to innocent me. You're not a very good friend if you don't like how I talk!
- Destructive impulses. I don't want to hang out with you anymore – I have impulses to abandon you.
- Diminished capacities for empathy and self-reflection. I'm not attuned to the distress you might be feeling frowning, or disliking my tone, and am unaware of my defensive feelings and reactions to your criticism.

These states prepare us for flight or fight. The amped emotion energizes us for action, or the numbed emotion avoids painful meaning. The distorted perspectives justify our destructive impulses to attack or flee (rather than to connect and cooperate which are hallmarks of states of healthy response). Diminished capacities for empathy makes us more able to do emotional or physical violence to another in service of self-protection. Less self-awareness shifts consciousness resources from potentially immobilizing self-observation and towards immediate defensive action.

Defensive states involve lots of implicit memories we've encoded over our life to reflexively protect ourselves when threatened. They are not necessarily destructive if we can mindfully observe them and consciously adjust amped/numbed emotions towards present moment awareness, reevaluate distorted perspectives with compassionate understanding, observe destructive impulses and reach for non-violent cooperative alternatives, and keep directing our awareness towards empathy and self-reflection.

The more jacked up and defensive we become, the less self-aware and wise we are. Most marriage counselors will tell you how couples can make agreements in the safety of the session where they feel relatively relaxed and pro-social, and then find themselves unable to follow through at home when in the grip of aroused defensive states of amplified anger, hurt, shame, or fear. This is important because relationships rise and fall on how well couples deescalate conflict and up-regulate pleasurable contact.

John Gottman found couples with escalating conflict divorced on average by their sixth year of marriage, and couples that didn't up-regulate shared pleasures divorced by their sixteenth year. So, if you and your honey have escalating conflict and don't know how to create a good time, find a good therapist and turn things around.

Similarly, if we spend time in dialed-in states of healthy response to the present moment, those circuits get more deeply programmed, the neural networks become more heavily myelinated, and we become more aware and resilient when threatened.

Defensive states happen to all of us regularly

Have you ever said something that you regretted the moment it came out of your mouth? Have you ever spontaneously done something where, as soon as you started, you realized you were being an idiot?

Our brains scan the world constantly, associating on what's happening, anticipating what's going to happen next, and *instantly* (within a tenth of a second) activating habits of thinking and responding designed to take care of us and others.

Mostly, this is a wonderful thing. For instance, some version of the following story has almost certainly happened with you. I'm driving down the road and suddenly see a ball roll into the street. Before I even can think about it, my foot's slamming on the breaks. My brain knows that kids chase balls, it's time to *stop right now,* and my foot is stomping that brake pedal before I'm consciously aware of what I'm doing.

On the other hand, I see destructive examples of instant, habitual responses every week in therapy. Here's a typical exchange between Mark and Sherry, a couple who are unfailingly kind to their two daughters and routinely hostile to each other. They come into the office, sit down, and I ask, "What kind of efforts did you make to love each other better this week?" Mark begins with, "Well, I tried to argue less and back off when I was angry more…" and Sherry rolls her eyes and sarcastically interrupts, "Really? Is that what you were doing yesterday when you yelled at me in front of the girls?"

Poor Mark was trying to be positive, but now his nervous system is threatened by Sherry's hostility and he flashes back nastily, "You never give me credit for anything, do you? What about you telling me I was abusive in front of Mike and Sue yesterday? Bringing up *divorce* in front of them! You're such a hypocrite!"

Before she can snap back, I interrupt, "Wait! Stop! Can you hear your violent tones? Are you listening to the insulting words you're saying?" They both stop – confusion on their faces. The truth is, they aren't listening to themselves hardly at all. Their defensive habits are talking, bad habit to bad habit. Mature Mark and Sherry – two people who *never* talk like this to their kids or friends – are basically off line. Defensive, hostile Mark and Sherry – who have lots of emotionally violent habits in relationship to each other – are in charge, bunkered down, thinking nasty thoughts, having nasty impulses, and saying mean things.

Our brains react like this in less than *a tenth of a second.* Yes, that's right, brains are wired to feel threat instantaneously and activate whatever habit is associated with that threat. These defensive habits involve amplified and/or numbed hurt/anger/fear/despair, distorted perspectives, destructive impulses, and diminished capacities for empathy and self-reflection.

When I interrupted, Mark and Sherry got confused because neither one is comfortable trashing *me,* and also because they're being directed by an authority (me, their therapist) to be self-reflective. "Can you hear your violent tones? Are you listening to the insulting words you're saying?" As they attempt what I ask, their brains lock. Trying to hear themselves clashes with their defensive habits of not paying attention – not acknowledging – the crazy activity of trying to hurt this person they love. This is one reason couples rarely look into each other's eyes when dissing one another. It's much harder to turn off empathy when you're looking into someone's eyes. You have to be really angry or sadistic to look someone in the eyes while hurting them.

Our emotional, reactive, habitual, defensive selves are programmed into our brains (with an emphasis on the right hemisphere) to react to threat instantly. Our mature, conscious, and more verbal selves are based in the prefrontal cortex behind our eyes (especially in our left hemisphere), and it takes up to a second and a half for conscious attention to catch up to the rest of us in a critical situation. That second and a half is *huge.*

By the time our conscious self shows up in these situations, the defensive state is already on line and taking charge. Our instinct is to come up with reasons to keep being hostile, just like Mark and Sherry are doing in the above example. We tend to support and rationalize our current states of consciousness rather than question if they are distorted or not, particularly when we are in defensive arousal. It's often easier to look for more reasons to be mad or hurt than to question whether we might be over-reacting. If I had let Mark and Sherry keep talking, they would have hammered away in an ugly dance of accelerating marital conflict. Cases would be made, injuries would be remembered, and accusations and insults would fly.

If we can *be aware of defensive states* with dialed-in mindful awareness, we can choose to slow down and not act badly. What if in the above example Mark and Sherry were self-aware of their defensive states *as soon as they became conscious?* It might look something like this:

They come into the office, sit down, and I ask, "What kind of efforts did you make to love each other better this week?" Mark begins with, "Well, I tried to argue less and back off when I was angry more..." and Sherry rolls her eyes and sarcastically interrupts, "Really? Is that what you were doing yesterday when you yelled at me in front of the kids?" Before Mark can snap back, she gets what she just did – she self-reflects on her defensive reaction – and says, "I'm sorry. I did it again. You were trying to be helpful and I cut you off. I get scared about trusting you, and push you back with my sarcasm. You *have* tried to argue less."

This isn't good enough for defensive Mark at first, "You're damn right you did it again! You always..." but then he catches himself, "I'm sorry. Now I'm doing it. You apologized and I didn't hear you. That's great what you just did, noticing how you interrupted, and I know I can be scary. I'm trying to be safer." Sherry looks at him with love and genuine appreciation, "Thank you! You just caught yourself. I love it when you do that."

This is a *dialed-in* argument, and we'll talk a lot more about the significance of dialed-in relating in future chapters.

Therapy is very much about helping people catch that defensive state after it's been accelerating for a second and a half (which is an eternity in brain time), and turn it into better love. We all need to get better at this, and most of us do throughout our lives.

How can we get better faster? How can we act on that second and a half of escalating defensive state to turn away from violence and towards growth and love?

- We can meditate to enhance self-awareness and create robust neuro-architecture.

- We can attune to ourselves and others frequently.

- We can practice self-reflection when we're hurt or threatened.
- We can ask others for help and guidance when in states of emotional duress.

- We can focus empathically on what *others* are feeling when *we're* upset.

But, most of all, we need to recognize when our brain/body has activated a defensive response, and not indulge it. Be suspicious of your amplified or numbed emotions, question your distorted perspectives, refuse your destructive impulses, and reach for compassionate understanding of you and others.

If we can reach for dialed-in Integral mindfulness, our brains harmonize towards love with others and ourselves – states of healthy response to the present moment.

Have fun with states

Life has enough problems that we don't need more of them by using our beautiful and good standards to judge ourselves or others to be ugly and immoral when we enter defensive states, fixed mindsets, or any other potentially destructive states of consciousness.

Remember, thoughts and impulses are not acts. If you catch the desire to tell some to f@*! off and don't do it, that's a victory! If you have an impulse to make a conversation all about you and instead include others, or feel an impulse to not contribute to a group discussion and speak up when you have something useful to say, those are victories!

If you act badly and get lost in a shame, guilt, or chagrin state, get a hold of yourself, follow or refine your values, make amends, and cultivate a state of warm self-appreciation on how great it is that you're growing into a more caring and self-aware person.

Mostly, don't lose your sense of humor – that state of looking with bemused laughter at yourself or others struggling being spiritual beings having a physical experience, buffeted by the winds of lust, anger, fear, desire, memory, anticipation, and all our other human preoccupations. Dante had it right with *The Divine Comedy*. It wasn't *The Divine Tragedy* *where life sucks.*

Moving right along into dialed-in development

How we experience states (and also our types for that matter) is profoundly influenced by what our current worldview is. Worldviews aren't just me-first, we-first, and love-first predispositions, but also how *mature* we tend to be on the different developmental lines – like how we think, relate, and make moral decisions.

We explore such development further in **Chapter 5: How mature am I right now as a person, friend, lover, parent...?**

Dialed-in states exercises: *Each day, pay attention to moments when you feel good or bad:*

> • *In general, good means you're enjoying a state of healthy response to the present moment. Notice how you feel more generous and undistorted in this state, as well as smarter and more attractive. Write down these moments.*

> • *If you feel bad, you're more likely to be in a defensive state. Let yourself sink into it a little. Are your feeling amped or numbed? Are your perspectives distorted towards the negative? Do you want to fight, flee, or collapse? Are you somewhat disconnected from yourself and others? Observe all these with interest (aware with acceptance and caring intent, on purpose, with compassionate judgment, in the present moment). Notice how dialed-in attention changes everything, and write about it.*

> • *Share what you've written with someone you trust.*

Chapter 5: How mature am I right now as a person, friend, lover, parent...?

Let's attune to ourselves right now. Deep breath, aware of sensation, emotion, thought, judgment, and desire with acceptance and caring intent. Hang out in this attuned state for at least two minutes – enough to get dialed-in.

As you do this, how mature do you feel? Do your thoughts, feelings, judgments, or desires feel grown up, or little-kid-like? However grown up or childish they seem, *the part of you observing them is more mature.* Yes, the self who observes with acceptance and caring intent is usually more mature than the self being observed.

One of the most reliable measures of development is how many perspectives of ourselves we can hold at any time. Can I observe myself writing to you right now? Can I observe myself observing myself writing to you right now? You get the idea. There is practically no limit to the potential breadth of self-observation, and each successive perspective tends to be a little more mature – deeper and wiser.

Darwin awards, Guilty pleasures

One of my guilty pleaures is checking out the Darwin Awards, stories of incredibly stupid mistakes people make – truly epic disasters. Clueless, immature, perfect storms of idiocy. Check out this story from their website:

> Garry Hoy was a respected Toronto lawyer and philanthropist, but sadly he is now mostly remembered

for his embarrassing death. While attending a reception for new articling students, Hoy decided to demonstrate the strength of the boardroom's "unbreakable" windows by throwing himself against them. Unfortunately, they proved less indestructible than advertised and the lawyer plunged 24 stories into the courtyard below.

According to witnesses, Hoy would often do this stunt to impress visitors, but would normally bounce harmlessly off the glass. Indeed, tempting fate, he had already performed the trick once during the reception before making his ill-fated second attempt.

This is a grown man showing off like an eight-year-old to his friends, clueless about life and death stakes. Clearly, Garry Hoy was not observing himself repetitively risking his life to impress people, and suffered catastrophic consequences. The *impulse* to show off is fine – haven't you had Walter Mitty-type fantasies? But, the impulse is not the act. If I mindfully observe my impulses and *choose* Integrally informed action, I'm dialed-in – accepting all impulses, choosing the most beautiful, good, and true.

Dialed-in sees the larger picture and relaxes into mature wisdom.

More/Less mature informs the "Lines and Levels" parts of the All-Quadrants-Lines-Levels-States-Types AQAL Model.

So far in our dialed-on journey we've learned:

> • **Mindful awareness** is being aware with acceptance and caring intent, on purpose, with compassionate judgment, in the present moment.

> • **Dialed-in Integral mindful awareness** is mindful awareness guided by the multiple perspectives of Integral understanding.

> • **Attunement to self and others** forms a foundation for dialed-in, and can be practiced all the time.

> • **Beautiful, good, and true** are three irreducible validity standards we use constantly.

• **Each person is a unique type**, but we share type qualities like masculine/feminine with similar others, helping us understand our similarities and differences.

• **States of consciousness rise, fall, and undulate constantly throughout life** – *especially* defensive states, and states of healthy response to the present moment.

Maturity matters!

Now we're going to add a cool new set of perspectives: how maturely or immaturely we think, relate, and otherwise move through the world.

More mature is almost always better

More mature is superior by every measure – providing *purpose* ("on purpose" being a central feature of dialed-in) as we negotiate the day.

Mature beats immature like a royal flush beats a pair of twos.

Don't get me wrong, we can be silly, playful, even selfish and wacky, but still mature. This means if it's time to stop tickling because your sister says "Stop!" with that certain "I'm not kidding!" tone, you *instantly* stop tickling her – you stay attuned even while caught up in play.

Dialed-in knows more or less mature, and dialed-in living makes mature choices – something poor Garry Hoy was unable to do.

What would Buddha do?

What do mature choices feel like? Think Abraham Lincoln, Buddha, Jesus Christ, Mother Theresa, and Lao Tzu.

I'm sure all these folks had their immature, clueless, and mindless moments, but that's not how we envision them. Any decision that meets the "What would Christ/Buddha/Lincoln/Mother Theresa/Lao Tzu do?" test is likely to be mature. Why? We associate these individuals with serving the highest good and making wise decisions – with being more mature.

So, since we're talking about mature/immature, let's start at the beginning by looking at babies.

I love babies

I love babies. To me, babies are everything wonderful. Each precious soul embodies humanity's promise – incredible potentials to grow, live, love, and contribute.

Every once in a while, a mom will bring a newborn into her therapy session, and this usually keeps all the adults in the room on their best behavior.

Therapy Infant

Surprisingly, babies make therapy much smoother for parents, until around age seven to nine months when they start to crawl. Crawling or toddling infants are nightmares in a session, hopelessly distracting, and shouldn't be allowed back (other than play therapy if necessary) for at least seven years. Babies seem to feel the healing work in the session and participate energetically.

The only problem with babies in therapy is that they are like campfires, you can't help staring at them. I keep wanting to catch their eyes, make them smile. Humans are hardwired to look at and care for babies.

The last time this happened, a couple brought their five-month-old son, Byron, into their session and I kept finding myself catching Byron's eye and smiling. We are genetically programmed to help babies grow by:

- Gazing into their eyes, which activates neural circuits to grow in both baby and adult. Your state of mind trains your baby's. So, I strongly advise you to feel God's pleasure and gratitude for your lovely baby as much as possible when gazing into his or her eyes.

- Holding and cuddling them, which helps babies feel secure and stay present.

- Attending and comforting when we hear distressed baby sounds, and playing with and praising happy babies – activating and strengthening social neurocircuitry for future relationships.

Babies have lots in common. Each enters the world at the beginning of the human developmental epic journey. We drift in diffuse life awareness in the womb, are born into this amazing world, and grow to learn our name and gender. Addicted to relationships, immersed in other people, we grow to think, speak, relate, be sexual, regulate emotions, work with others, and create lives with more or less meaning and satisfaction.

That being said, we're not born identical. We vary according to:

- **Genetic legacy.** This is easiest to see with birth defects and inherited diseases like Down's syndrome or Autism, but babies also vary wildly in emotional reactivity, curiosity, introversion, cooperativeness, shyness, novelty seeking, height, coordination and millions of other variables. In this sense, we are already our specific *type* of person at birth.

- **Gender.** Let's face it, life is *way* different for boys and girls. Boys tend to be less cooperative and more demanding and competitive in their play. Girls tend to use more collaborative words like "Let's," and "We." Boys tend to be more interested in expanding rights, while girls in expanding care. According to Lise Eliot in *Pink Brain, Blue Brain,* "They have different interests, activity levels, sensory thresholds, physical strengths, emotional reactions, relational styles, attentions spans, and intellectual aptitudes."

• **Stress programming**. Mom's stress hormones pass through the placenta into the fetus and powerfully influence how a child's nervous system is programmed to respond to stress, how early puberty will come, how securely the child will attach to parents, and how vulnerable the child will be to diabetes and heart disease. This is why prenatal care, education, and support of pregnant mothers is such a no-brainer smart move for any culture.

• **Parents.** Ethnicity, socio-economic levels, how caring, wise, old, young, selfish, generous, crazy, preoccupied, together, divorced, experienced, knowledgeable, ignorant, bigoted, emotionally coaching, emotionally dismissing, secure, insecure... you get the idea. In modern families, cultural imperatives are mostly played out with two people – Mom and Dad, and sometimes just with Mom.

• **Culture.** Cultures we're embedded in profoundly influence our development. For example, it's way different to be born into a jungle tribe in Venezuela than a cosmopolitan college community in Maine. Kids in rural China will have different upbringings than in Southern California, or in a fundamentalist Christian household, or in a progressive secular family.

• **Attention.** We vary in what captures our attention as we develop. A child magnetized by music or dance has different life experiences than one fascinated with physics or chemistry.

Researchers have studied development exhaustively, and we know now that we grow in different capacities, like how we think, make moral decisions, relate, or experience ourselves in the world. You almost certainly have a more nuanced sense of what's right and wrong than you did at nine. If you've taken tango lessons for two years, you're a better tango dancer now than when you started. Some, like Howard Gardner, call these "multiple intelligences." Integral calls these capacities *lines of development,* and we grow through stages, or *levels of development,* on each line, with each level including and transcending previous levels. Development is in one direction, we don't skip developmental levels, and how far we've advanced in levels *generally* reflects how mature we are *most of the time* on that line of development.

"Most of the time" is not "all of the time." Levels of maturity shift constantly, depending on what state we're in. For instance, I've found that when you lose your sense of humor, you've usually regressed at least one or two developmental levels on your interpersonal line of development.

Physical development is a good example of "including and transcending in one direction." Nobody is born grown up. We're born as infants and must grow into being toddlers, little kids, older kids, teens, and adults. We can't skip any of those levels; each one builds on previous ones, and growth is in one direction.

Or take language. Babies are born "speaking" a sophisticated language of recognition and non-verbal communication. Within minutes of birth, they are communicating with eye contact and facial expressions with Mom and other caregivers. These communications are included and transcended as children develop representational thought (they can have symbols for people and things in their minds), and gradually learn to understand and speak language. Words turn into sentences, into larger concepts, into more understanding and expression, into reading and writing, until, eighteen years later, a person might be reading this paragraph and understand the multiple steps she's negotiated from birth to comprehending developmental lines and levels.

Our cognitive line of development – maturity of thought – parallels our development of language. The infant's universe of sensations, emotions, drives, and non-conscious attunements begins to include symbols and representational thought, where our thought of something is an internalized image or a symbolic representation of that something. One of my son Ethan's first words was "tuk" meaning "truck." He'd see a truck and gleefully shout out "tuk!" reflecting his internal representation.

At age six or seven, kids can develop black and white concrete logic. "If I am taller than Frank, and Frank is taller than Sue, then I am taller than Sue." At age twelve or thirteen, we can think more relativistically, in shades of gray; like, "Phil is nice to me at school, but he gets mean when we play soccer together; so I like him, but maybe I shouldn't play soccer with him." This is called Formal Operational thought, because we can manipulate the forms of thought to look for deeper truths.

What are some other lines of development?

- Moral development. A girl grows from being selfish, to caring for those closest to her, to caring for everybody, to caring and wanting equal rights for everybody. A boy grows from being selfish, to wanting rights for those closest to him, to wanting rights for everybody, to wanting care and rights for everybody.

- Psychosexual development, where our genetic urge to reproduce develops into seeking physical pleasure, into wanting to be accepted by our social group, into craving fulfillment, into healing old emotional/relational wounds through sexual love, into expressing our spirituality through eroticism.

- Physical or artistic skills, such as painting, dancing, basketball, public speaking, story-telling, writing, singing, or playing a musical instrument, are all lines of development.

When we're dialed-in, we notice how mature or immature we are, and keep adjusting both consciously and non-consciously towards more maturity. Of course, we need to know what more or less mature looks like, and our first and most important training ground is our family.

We absorb the personalities of our parents

The bottom line in development is that we absorb the personalities of the people around us, *especially when we're babies and little kids*. I absorbed my loving or scary mother *as a little kid perceiving a huge loving or scary mother*. Little kids' brains can't think in relativistic subtle ways like adult brains' can, so many of our most deeply programmed states are irrational, black-and-white, or just visceral reactions.

This is why defensive states so often feel immature (especially in others – they're harder to see in ourselves), and bringing adult discernment to bear creates more maturity. Adult discernment can take us higher on lines of development like the morals line, the interpersonal line, or the cognitive line, for a moment or for many moments. These higher levels can become more permanent when we've acted maturely enough times to hardwire them as traits.

Humans are social beings, addicted to one another, constantly socially referencing each other and then adjusting to fit more comfortably together. Social referencing influences our states to be more or less mature, depending on how attuned we are.

What is social referencing?

- "Did you just frown at me?"

- "Did I say something that upset you?"

- "I love it when you smile approvingly."

Steve and Karen

Let's make this a little more real by checking in with Steve and Karen, a couple struggling with maturity on their relational line of development.

Steve and Karen – both in their late thirties and married for nine years – are sitting facing each other during their sixth session. Steve says, "Karen never wants me to go surfing, but I love surfing. It mellows me out."

Karen looks dismissively down at Steve, "Boys just enjoy playing with their toys."

Steve, outraged, responds, "You sound just like your sister."

Karen, *more* outraged, snaps back, "How dare you compare me to her! You know what she's like!"

Defensive states are immature by their very nature. They are habitual responses we first encoded when we were kids, in order to protect ourselves. Karen does *not* want to consider that she has a contemptuous side, originally absorbed from her often-selfish and demanding sister. This aspect repulses her so much, that she denies and defends when it shows up. As long as she keeps denying and defending, she blocks integrating – healing and digesting – this wounded aspect into her larger self, thus, unconsciously becoming immature when stressed with Steve.

What's going on here?

We grow through stages on many lines

From birth onward, humans are learning machines. If you've ever tried to master another language, you know how hard it is to absorb enough vocabulary and grammar to have even rudimentary communication. Human *toddlers* grow from knowing very few words at 17 months of age, to having *conversations* at 27 months.

Wow!

Babies learn way more than language – as they grow, they absorb the personalities and cultures that surround them. We come into the world with 100 billion neurons (each neuron with eventually ten to twenty thousand connections with other neurons), but only eighteen percent of these 100 billion are hooked up into neural networks at birth. Newborns look into Mom's eyes, and Mom's brain communicates with baby's brain (especially right hemisphere to right hemisphere in the first two years after birth), causing neurons to form neural networks that are rapidly myelinated by baby's super-charged nervous system.

Spoken language, more a function of the routine-oriented left hemisphere, starts coming fully online around two when the left hemisphere starts becoming more dominant – but language is just part of the upwelling of human development.

Starting before birth – through mirror neurons in our brains and our general social tendencies to harmonize in every way with people close to us – we copy and encode family members' tones, attitudes, expressions, and beliefs. These processes are constantly being reinforced in the inter-subjective webs of talk, touch, play, emotion, dominance, and reflection that surround all families.

As we grow up, we can absorb *personality traits* from the people around us – especially those we spend the most time with like mothers, fathers, siblings, nannies, grandparents, and other caregivers. This heavily influences what types of people we become.

This is a huge big deal! *We infuse the personality traits of the people who raise us – both positive and negative.*

Think about what this means:

- Your beloved father, caring and attuned, exists in you.

- Your feared father, screaming and hitting, exists in you.

- Your adoring mother, cuddling and nurturing, exists in you.

- Your angry mother, emasculating and rejecting, exists in you.

Your protective brother who always looked out for you, your jealous brother who competed with you, your loving sister who supported you, *all can exist to some extent in you.*

One of the main tasks of human development is lifelong integration of different aspects into a more coherent self with a positive life story. This is complicated by the fact that none of us particularly wants to see or acknowledge negative parts of our family that live in us *now*.

There's a branch of psychotherapy called Internal Family Systems (developed by Richard Schwartz) based on people containing multiple sub-personalities, family members among them. Other researchers and therapists, from Carl Jung to Fritz Perls to Roberto Assagioli, have advanced similar constructs. Central to all these approaches is the idea that we have a core *authentic self* who needs to take responsibility for our many sub-personalities and integrate them into a mature whole.

The worm in the apple of these elegant approaches is reflected in Karen's, "How dare you!" reaction to Steve's, "You sound just like your sister." We don't want the burden of unattractive family traits in *me*. When we start acting badly, we tend to unconsciously avoid self-awareness – as in denial ("I'm *not* being contemptuous!") or attack ("You're damn right I'm sick of you being an idiot!").

But facing and accepting who we are is exactly how we liberate ourselves from repulsive or scary inner aspects, and turn them into strengths that help us understand and deal with our own and others' selfishness and violence – to help us be more mature on those lines of development.

We need to develop the capacity to see our defensive traits and states, feel them, acknowledge them, and help them *mature and grow.* Sometimes this is hard because we're still angry about neglect, abuse, or poor parenting that we might still be enduring to some extent. Many of us will never hear family members acknowledge how they hurt us, and we can't do it for them (Karen is not going to change her sister's selfish meanness). Such work has to be done by the person herself.

All of us can perceive, accept, and integrate what exists in us to mature on different developmental lines, and we have a responsibility to do the work, or else suffer the consequences of hurting people we love, the way we were hurt ourselves.

Several sessions down the line, Karen tells me, "I know I get nasty like my sister did, and I hate that part of me."

This makes me smile and nod approvingly, "Good work! You can feel how that habit lives in you, and you want to do something about it to not hurt Steve. Your job is to manage your contemptuous self the way your sister couldn't." Seeing Karen's confused look, I continue, "We don't erase reoccurring personality patterns, we integrate them. If you can hear the mean tone and feel the angry attack, you can catch it, apologize to Steve and better understand how you sometimes get dismissive when you're hurt or frustrated. How would it have been if your sister had done that?"

Karen's eyes narrow, "She *never* apologizes."

This makes me laugh. She looks surprised, "What?"

I get more serious, "You see how you're still so angry you don't want to even *imagine* her kinder? I'm not saying you're wrong. People like your sister who refuse to self-examine and change can stay stuck in horrible habits their whole lives, but *that's not you. You* can heal that contemptuous-sister part of you with acceptance, compassion, and assertion with yourself – don't let yourself use dismissive tones with Steve, and look for deeper understanding. You could say, "I'm sorry" when you attack him. Steve can help. He's a good guy when you're not trashing him."

Karen nods thoughtfully. "He does say I have trouble apologizing, and I have to admit things go better when I do."

We can all take such strides if we look for the positive and negative aspects of our family members we've absorbed, and commit to accepting, healing, and integrating all of them – even the hard ones.

A cool way to enhance integration is to simply notice the caring and the hurting, the loving and the rejecting, the self-aware and the clueless. Who from your childhood acted similarly, and how did you feel about them when they did? We tend to resist such awarenesses, especially in the painful realms. If we can hold on to immature and negative traits with acceptance while directing ourselves to caring and assertive thought and action, we usually make progress doing what difficult family members couldn't do when we were small – heal old wounds and turn violence into love.

More importantly, as the conductor of your inner chorus of selves, you'll keep everyone moving towards sweeter harmony.

> **Integration**
>
> *Listen to your voice today for any similarities to the voices you heard growing up. Observe how you think about and relate with your partner, family, and friends – see if you can monitor your thoughts, words, and tones. Write down any discoveries or insights and share them with your intimate partner.*

WE CAN ALWAYS SEE FARTHER THAN WE CAN BE

Becky and I live on a street that runs near the top of a small ridge a couple miles behind the Santa Barbara Mission. Since we moved here, we've walked to the end of the street and back thousands of times – often together – talking about everything imaginable. On a recent morning walk, we were discussing how the future always exists in imagination. Thinking how important this is in psychotherapy, I said, "How we hold the present and future together determines how happy we are, because we can always see farther than we can be."

Becky looked curious. "What do you mean?"

I was looking down at the city framed by the Channel Islands, considering what a big deal it is to always see farther than we can be. "No matter how good I feel right now, I can imagine myself feeling better. No matter what I accomplish, I can imagine more accomplishments. We can never *be* as good, beautiful, successful, or fulfilled as we can *imagine*. People handle this capacity differently, and, luckily, most people are programmed to be optimistic about the future. Are you grateful and fine with the flow of life from this moment into the future, or do you live in the frustration of never creating the perfection you imagine? A more satisfied life or a more frustrated life can be determined *just* by how you hold, 'I can always see farther than I can be.'"

Becky's face lit up, mirroring the pleasure I was feeling at that moment, being grateful and happy with the flow of life into the future – one of the tastiest pleasures of our marriage has been sharing insights like this.

Being human gives us incredible powers. Starting at age two, we wake up to the idea that "I'm a person who exists!" Developmentalists call, "I know I exist." a *theory of mind*. It means we *consciously* exist in the past, present, and future, imagine endless possibilities, and can consider "I," "you," "we," "mine," and "should." We know of no other beings in the universe who do this – nothing on earth even comes close (the great apes can project about twenty to thirty minutes into the future).

Maybe more amazing than "I am a person who exists!" is our endless curiosity. Soon after learning how to talk, two-year-olds start asking "why," and *never stop asking*.

We are also biological beings constantly pressured by our drives. Our genes influence us to pursue security, comfort, social contact and stature, sexual gratification, success, and happiness. One way or another, all humans seek satisfaction of these drives through action, imagination, intimacy and creativity.

Embedded in the human experience is the challenging problem of reconciling our constant tendency to project into the future – seeing ourselves better or worse, more or less happy – with our desires to feel excellent, successful, secure, joyful, and good enough *now*.

We can always *imagine* ourselves *more* excellent, successful, secure, beautiful, fulfilled, recognized, joyful, and mature than we are now. We can always *see* farther than we can *be*. How we resolve the "I can see farther than I can be" dilemma largely determines life happiness and satisfaction.

"Life is good now, but I can imagine things better, and that helps me grow in a positive direction," is one of the hallmarks of a more optimistic, happy person (it also characterizes growth mindsets). "I'm always frustrated that I can't be better than I am now," characterizes more pessimistic, unhappy individuals.

Even people at the top of the world have to deal with this. Magic Johnson (more optimistic and happy) was once being interviewed by NBA legend-turned-broadcaster Rick Berry (more pessimistic and unhappy) right after winning his first NBA championship in 1980. Rick, a previous NBA scoring champion, was notorious as a driven, crabby player – when he played, he wore a gold necklace reading "Me First." In the interview, he seemed uncomfortable with Magic's overwhelming joy in the moment.

Holding up the microphone, Rick struggled with what to say, and then asked (weirdly it seemed to me at the time), "How many more of these [NBA championships] do you want?" Magic – probably feeling Rick's negative energy as much as the awkward question – seemed momentarily disconcerted, but then flashed his huge smile and laughingly responded, "About twenty." It was a mature response to an immature question.

This illustrates how being able to imagine a better future is *not* a problem. Both Rick and Magic were imagining positive futures – more titles for Magic – and such visualizations are often central to accomplishing goals. Even more, our desire to grow and expand is what makes us human.

Humans out-xxplored Neanderthals

Neanderthals were very successful in surviving and thriving in ancient Europe, but seemed to have little of the restless ambition that characterized our Homo sapiens ancestors. Neanderthals tended to stop exploring when they reached bodies of water like the Atlantic and Mediterranean – they apparently weren't driven to find out what was further on. Starting around fifty thousand years ago, humans expanded around the globe, and nothing – bodies of water, mountain ranges, deserts, endless plains, ferocious predators, or frozen ice fields – stopped them. They could always fantasize something cool over the horizon, and were compelled to go check it out. We have a built-in instinct to progress, advance, and grow.

Neuroscience

All this makes sense, given that the neural architecture for imagining the future is pretty much the same as remembering the past. We've all had good experiences and bad experiences as we've grown. If you remember your life as mostly painful failures with a hopeless sense, you tend to be more pessimistic and depressed. If you remember triumphs achieved and problems taken on as growth opportunities, you tend to be more optimistic and happy. People with essentially the same life experiences can feel happy and fulfilled, or unhappy and dissatisfied, just by how they remember their pasts and hold their futures.

Our happiness largely depends on *how we manage* seeing farther than we can be, which depends heavily on how mature we are on our self and values lines. Happy, mature people tend to feel grateful for who they currently are and what they currently have, and instinctively use thoughts of future accomplishments, connections, and pleasures to guide confident anticipation for progress to come.

Practice

How do you manage your "I can see farther than I can be" gift? Try paying attention during the next week to whether you're using your imagination to anticipate victories and joys, or defeats and sorrows, and to how you feel about your present compared with your future. Write down the results of the following suggestions and questions:

- *If you imagine negative, pessimistic future events, try imagining possible (even probable, since things usually work out OK) positive, optimistic outcomes – research shows that optimistic explanatory styles are associated with being happier and healthier.*
- *If you are imagining victories and joys, does it make you feel more satisfied and grateful for how you are right now, or more frustrated and ashamed of where you are right now? The most productive, happiness-generating attitude is feeling grateful and satisfied now while imagining things even better in the future.*
- *If you do imagine things better, but are still left frustrated and bitter about now, try cultivating gratitude for what you have, and for your power to guide your life towards more love, joy, and success.*
- *Share your writing with someone you trust.*

More unhappy people – especially depressed people – use their ideas about unlikely future success and no fun to diminish the current moment – keeping them immature on key lines of development.

The studies have been done and the results are in:

> • We can always see farther than we can be, and we can't help living simultaneously in the past, present and future.
> • We do better being grateful for what we have and who we are.
>
> • We do *much* better imagining growth and happier lives than imagining becoming less connected, joyful, and successful.

Dialed-in tends to feel grateful and satisfied in the present moment, imagining love, joy, and success in the future.

MATURATION ON DEVELOPMENTAL LINES IS A LIFELONG PROCESS

As we've seen, we all exist at different levels of maturity on multiple developmental lines. We can speed up or slow down the maturation process with how attuned we are and how dialed-in we learn how to be.

Growth isn't just learning new ways of thinking, being, and relating (what Ken Wilber calls "knowledge by description"), it's *embodying* new ways of thinking, being, and relating (what Wilber calls "knowledge by acquaintance"). Experiences change us if we allow ourselves to change, to be more mature on different lines.

We're blessed by our abilities to see farther than we can be. I can always see Keith at least a little more mature (farther than I can be) on any line, like healing, integrating defenses, loving, or creating. This guides me – gives me purpose – as I move about my day. It can help me stay dialed-in.

Chapter 6: Dialed-in Sex – American Tantra

Sex is a big deal. We're going to talk in more detail about dialed-in love affairs and marriages in Chapters 7 and 8, but dialed-in sex is important enough to deserve its own chapter.

We all have experienced clueless and mindless sex either personally or vicariously.

- Bill Clinton/Monica Lewinski – clueless.
- Eliot Spitzer/expensive hookers – clueless.
- Most teen pregnancies – mindless.
- Cheating on your husband – clueless.
- Dirty dancing with your wife's best friend at a rowdy party – mindless.
- Having mercy sex with your husband because he's been whining about "Not getting any," for two weeks, and then feeling contemptuous of him afterwards – clueless.
- Flirting with your secretary because your wife doesn't seem to be into you – mindless.

Most of the above involve fun sexual activities followed by painful consequences, and this sex-leads-to-painful-consequences attitude shows up all the time, and mostly people blame sexuality for the suffering. From *Fatal Attraction* to *Boardwalk Empire,* media sex is often portrayed as dangerous or exploitative, and the occasional pro-sexual *Fifty Shades of Gray* seems to be the exception that proves the rule.

Sex is fun, fantastic for developing intimacy, and can be a central player in joyful monogamy; yet most sexual talk, references, stories, and education seem to trash sex.

94

What do I mean? Well, attune yourself right now, becoming aware with acceptance and caring intent of feelings, thoughts, and judgments, and see what happens as you try on the following words and phrases (actually say them out loud):

- Sexual attraction.
- Sexual arousal.
- Flirting, sexual experimentation.
- Oral, anal, genital.
- Tongues, French kisses.
- Doggy style, penis, vagina, porn, masturbation.
- "Fuck me!" "Harder!" "Slower!"
- "Let's do it in the back seat! (on the kitchen table, in the hot tub...)."

I'll bet at least some of these seem slightly too majorly naughty or forbidden.

Now imagine talking to children or teens about any of the above (how do you respond when your ten-year-old daughter asks you, "What does 'doggy style' mean?"). How does *that* feel? Just imagining such conversations feels immoral to many people. God help us in America if we talk with children about sex, so what kids, and especially teens, mostly hear – if they hear anything at all – is, "Just say no!"

What the *#%!?

Remember the beautiful, good, and true validity standards?

> • **Beautiful:** Sexual activity and talk both attracts us and repels us – it hits both the beautiful and ugly notes of the "beautiful" standard. We might like romance novels, or even to a certain extent happily appreciate beautiful women (or men) displayed in dance or film – these meet our "beautiful" standards – but there are lines we can't cross without feeling icky. For instance, frank sexual talk is generally forbidden. *"How are you doing Tim?" "Fine, except I have a herpes outbreak and Jane and I have to use condoms till it goes away. What a drag!"* I don't think so!

Tim's complaint is a not-beautiful statement in most social situations.

• **Good:** Sexual conversations in most forms, and lots of sexual behaviors, don't feel *good* (as in "Good boy, Andy," "Good girl, Amy"). They seem to violate our shared cultural moral standards of: don't talk about, look at, be explicit about, or acknowledge sexual interests or practices. *"Marty, I'd like you to be on top tonight. I like the way your pelvis feels slamming into mine when you come."* A couple *might* have this conversation, but in all likelihood one partner would be embarrassed enough to shut it down pretty quickly.

• **True:** Families that have open discussions about sex at all ages have children who are less sexually inhibited, have less teen pregnancies, and are more likely to be satisfied in their own age appropriate sexual relationships. Seventy percent of religious fundamentalist households have no substantive conversation with children about sex – and this is the demographic that most vehemently asserts that sex education should happen at home. Couples who discuss sexual likes/dislikes/yearnings and behaviors tend to be better educated, more stable, and happier. Most couples I've worked with have sexual material that's forbidden to acknowledge or discuss, and occasionally they freak out when I ask sexual questions. One example: Jean and Harry got married sixteen years ago and have two kids they adore, but both feel they've become "just friends," and miss deeper connections. They've come to me for help. Halfway into the hour I ask Jean, "Do you masturbate?" She blushes and looks down (classic shame reactions), and says, "Yes, about once a week." Harry is astounded, "What!? I never knew you did that!" (Notice how he can't even use the word "masturbate"?)

The "Let's Talk About Sex" party

About twenty years ago my family was part of a home schooling group that included doctors, contractors, business people, teachers, therapists, and a bunch of kids from age two to twelve. We were united by our desires to create a community dedicated to helping our children thrive and be healthy, in as personal and developmentally pro-love, joy, and individual expression ways as possible. We camped together, shared resources, took trips, and generally were fascinated with learning and growth.

Sex came up in a few conversations, so I invited everyone to a "Let's talk about sex" party at my family's house. I can't remember much about what we said, but I do remember everyone coming over and talking about sex. Most of the discussion was between grown-ups, but the kids either participated or wandered in and out of the room as we talked. My favorite take-away from the "Let's talk about sex" party was how *everyone* – kids included – normalized the whole deal. We talked about sex the same way we talked about teaching kids how to read, or how to handle the inevitable inclusion/exclusion issues that arise in such communities.

Twenty years later, almost all those kids are happy young adults who seem to be doing pretty well in their relationships, jobs, and lives. The homeschoolers created a little culture within the larger cultures we were embedded in (Santa Barbara, California, United States) that had extraordinarily open standards of communication – we all helped each other talk about pretty much everything (I also had a "Let's talk about anger" party that year).

Talk about sex

Dialed-in sex is one area where we can use the "true" standard to help us refine our "beautiful" and "good" standards. Let's start talking about all aspects of sex with our spouses and children. This accelerates growth on everybody's sexual and social lines of development, because the more you talk with acceptance and caring intent about anything, the easier it gets to discuss, and the less conflicted you are about what you're discussing.

"Easy to say!" you might be thinking. "Everyone thinks frank talk in families is a good idea, but how do we go from taboo to open? You had a bunch of like-minded families to help you!"

Well, let's explore some approaches to working our way into sexual candor and openness. It begins with deeper understanding.

STAGES OF SEXUAL DEVELOPMENT

Our sexual line of development grows through stages, just like all lines, and as we discussed in Chapter 5, each stage includes and transcends previous ones. What are stages of sexual development?

- **Genetic**: Like all mammals, we are programmed to reproduce. Our genes want to be passed on. Little known evolutionary fact – our emotion circuits developed out of our sexual circuits. That's right, reptiles have sex, but are not particularly cuddly and emotional – feelings and relationships arrived with mammals who have an emotional/relational limbic area that grew from the reproductive circuits in the brain stem. This explains why when we are dialed-in sexually, it really helps us be dialed-in emotionally and relationally.

- **Pleasure**: We crave and enjoy sexual pleasure at all ages. Infants stroke their genitals, kids fool around with other kids, teens kiss and touch leading eventually to oral sex and intercourse. Being turned on lights up multiple pleasure-seeking circuits in our brains.

- **Belonging**: We want to be accepted by our family, friends, and culture, so we have standards of what's okay sexually, feel ashamed if we violate them, and moral if we follow them. When I was a middle-schooler in 1962, it was acceptable to have your girlfriend sit on your lap while you smooched as deeply as you both wanted. I remember my friend Mark Dillard saying at the time, "We kiss and kiss and kiss – you get tired of it after awhile!" (Not having a girlfriend at the time, I was totally envious of Mark Dillard.) It was *not okay* to fondle breasts, penises, or vaginas. It was unspeakable to have intercourse, so nobody even discussed condoms or how to use them. To this day, "Belonging," in most American cultures, requires strategic abstinence and/or silence around sex… *or the appearance of abstinence and/or silence.* Remember President Clinton's Surgeon General, Joycelyn Elders, who was fired because she said masturbation was normal and should be taught in schools? High school students *overwhelmingly* masturbate – easily 90% of boys and somewhat less of girls – but it was literally unspeakable to advocate talking about it in high school health classes. When Joycelyn Elders, in the role of the nation's chief public health official, starting talking about it, she was slammed.

- **Fulfillment**: As teens, we start dating and sexing with our dates, and the developmental trend is towards craving a fulfilling relationship. This expands our connections beyond the sexual, to include deeper relationships and more secure bonding; but, sex is still a prime mover. What characterizes a boyfriend/girlfriend from a friend, is regular sexual connection.

- **Yogic healing**: Most adults are wounded in their sexuality. This is inevitable when we've been taught to feel ashamed if we're not normal, and *none of us* are normal by the cultural standards we were raised by, because those standards are *genetically impossible* to follow one hundred percent. (*Example: I can't tell you how often a woman has complained to me about her guy looking at other women. Men are genetically drawn to the feminine form – so guys are going to look! The task is how to look in ways that don't hurt anyone.*) Couples who face their sexual injuries, and work with a partner to use their love affair to heal and grow, are engaging in sex as a healing yoga.

- **Spirituality**: The most refined level of sexual development, the spiritual level, uses intimacy, arousal, love making, and orgasm as practices to generate unity with Spirit. The templates for such practices have come to us largely from Eastern traditions, but Americans don't seem to respond well to surrender-to-the-Guru schools, and so Western practitioners have combined Eastern practices and principles with education, psychotherapy, and workshop formats. I call this American Tantra, and will explore it in more depth later in this chapter.

Dialed-in sex can be some healthy version of any of these levels, or any combination of them, *while recognizing that there are many healthy versions.* What's morally acceptable expands radically with attuned acceptance. Such expansions turbocharge intimacy and sexuality, and bring more spirituality into sexual occasions of all kinds.

Checking out our beautiful, good, and true standards is a great way to approach sexual growth.

- **Beautiful:** Be openly curious about what sexual images and practices attract or repel you and others – the beautiful standard.

- **Good:** Talk respectfully with your partner and family members about what feels moral or immoral, with lots of interest in where you disagree. Can you allow yourself to influence and be influenced? That's dialed-in.

- **True:** Science, lord of the "true" validity standard, looks with interest at people having better and worse health benefits and more or less erotic charge with different combinations of erotic thinking, speaking, and sexing. In general, more open communication, integrity, and acceptance of all sexual pleasures between consenting adults in healthy relationships, supports growth and happiness.

Social science is unambiguous. Introspection, respectful attention, and open sexual conversations enliven and deepen us – so let's do it! The more you talk, the more beautiful and good the talks naturally become; but make no mistake, effort is almost inevitably involved because we all carry social taboos blocking sexual awareness and growth.

CRUCIAL SEXUAL KNOWLEDGE

Ignorance causes more problems than malice when it comes to sex, and I've found that knowing how we are wired sexually helps us understand and accept ourselves and each other. So here is some basic Sex 101:

Lust, romantic infatuation, and intimate bonding

Lust, Romantic Infatuation, and Intimate bonding are evolutionary drives, expressed through states of consciousness.

Lust happens when a guy sees an attractive feminine form, or a woman feels the desiring attention from a high status, safe guy at the right time. Lust activates charged states of consciousness that magnetize us to lust objects.

Lust is impersonal. If you're a woman and some masculine icon tells you he wants you – you know, Brad Pitt or Bruce Springsteen if you're over 35, or Liam Helmsworth if you're a teen or in your twenties – you'll probably feel a flood of energy course through your body. It might not feel exactly like sexual energy, but it's *really tasty*. If you're a guy and a beautiful woman smiles, flirts, or flat out tells you she wants you, you're likely to feel a surge of sexual desire, and impulses to *pursue her right now*.

Lust tends to be more easily promiscuous and non-exclusive. People generally don't get particularly sexually possessive about someone they simply lust after and have sex with, but with whom they haven't entered a state of romantic infatuation or intimate bonding. This is why a prostitute's customers rarely feel jealous of other customers, why a college student waking next to someone he or she picked up the night before for a casual hook-up is unlikely to feel jealous of whoever else has shared this bed, and why 40% of single women from 19 to 39 have a guy they call occasionally for sex with no hint of monogamy.

Romantic infatuation is *personal*. You connect, are attracted, get to know someone, and dopamine-driven in-love circuits in your brain light up and can stay lit for up to eighteen months or longer. During that time you have heightened awareness of your lover, and desire her/him above all others. You also feel increased sexual urgency (due to elevated levels of dopamine and testosterone in crucial brain circuits), natural forgiveness of your lover's faults, and increasing needs for contact.

Romantic infatuation occurs when your nervous system decides that *this* person is a very *special* lover – someone you specifically hunger for. Now a guy, who previously didn't care much if his lover dated other guys, gets jealous if she just smiles at another man, never mind has sex with him. A woman who's previously enjoyed casual hookups without complications finds herself thinking about her lover all the time, and can't get enough contact, sex, and intimacy with him. Most people in states of romantic infatuation aren't much interested in sex with others, and suffer badly if their lover strays.

Infatuation is wonderful when shared with a like-minded lover, and torment if the other doesn't return our affection. If you're caught in an infatuation that is not reciprocated, get support and help from friends and therapists. If your love is returned, strap in for an extended pleasure joyride, and realize the blissful states you're feeling and the conclusions you're drawing about your lover will shift when you progress into intimate bonding.

Intimate bonding occurs as romantic infatuation fades and you're more "at home" with your lover. Sexual urgency diminishes, defensive patterns (shared defensive states like we discussed in Chapter 4) accelerate, and it requires more conscious effort and depth of understanding to keep your love affair alive and growing.

When you are in the intimate bonding stage of a relationship – which often follows an initial one to three year romantic infatuation joyride – sex and romance become less urgent and easy. The excitement/ sexy neurotransmitters dopamine and testosterone are down, and the bonding/attachment neurotransmitters oxytocin and vasopressin are up, and people feel more securely connected, while less obsessively "in love."

Even though you feel less sexually urgent, intimate bonding is *important* – as in life-partner important. Sex might have cooled, but if you discover your partner has cheated, your nervous system still spasms into jealousy, depression, obsession, and outrage. We intensely value life partners, and neurological mate protection circuits light up if we feel another to be encroaching on our relationship.

From an evolutionary standard, we can feel any combination of these drives *with any combination of partners.* Yes, you can feel lust for one person, be in love with another, and be in intimate bonding with a third!

I probably don't have to tell you that I don't recommend such combos, but I want you to know that you're wired for them, and dialed-in sex *consciously* interweaves them together with your chosen partner throughout a relationship, to create fulfillment and protect us from infidelity. Those cultural jokes that men tell to friends getting married such as, "Enjoy sex now, because it's going stop before you know it!" have basis in fact, and couples in the intimate bonding stage often need to consciously attend to mutual sexual fulfillment to keep eroticism alive. This practice helps inoculate you from cheating, and sustains fun sex.

On the other hand, since most of us crave the heat of desire and infatuation, even in satisfying intimate bonding, we can find ourselves longing for the sweet rushes of lust and romance (longings that can cause us to seek loopholes in our monogamy commitments). We can amplify lust and romance in intimate bonding, but it usually requires two people putting in some effort. For example, since change, risk, and excitement raise dopamine (and correspondingly testosterone) levels, people often get sexual boosts from novel experiences they share with their intimate partner, or from transgressive rushes they might feel from breaking taboos. Dopamine-boosting novel experiences can range from roller coasters, to hotel rooms, to vacations, to having your wife's old college roommate join you in bed (watch out for this last one – it can cause painful complications).

"I see her I want her!"

Men are dominated by the "I see her I want her!" sexual arousal system, while women have at least three different sexual arousal systems Many studies have found men to be attracted to youth and beauty, while women seem more drawn to secure resources and presence, but what gets men and women off sexually?

Sex researcher, Meredith Chivers, put sensors in women's vaginas and on men's penises and showed them lots of different kinds of porn. Hetero, homo, lesbian, bonobos (a kind of smaller, friendlier chimp), masturbation, naked beach shots... pretty much anything she could think of. She measured physical arousal, recorded where people's eyes went to on the video screen, asked what kinds of arousals they felt, and compared how their conscious experience tracked their physical states.

Men's arousal systems were consistently lit up by the feminine form doing almost anything – basically, "I see her I want her." I suspect the "I see her I want her" system is strong in men because sexually indifferent guys couldn't compete with sexual enthusiasts in our evolutionary past. Even gay guys have their version of "I see him I want him." Chivers found that men mostly knew when they were turned on, and this jived with the physical data.

Women had much more complicated responses. They didn't report being turned on by lesbian porn, but many of them showed physical arousal watching lesbian porn. Where men looked at the women in the videos, women often were drawn to the women's bodies and *the men's eyes* in the videos, suggesting that to them, seeing attraction/desire in a man's eyes looking at *me* is exciting.

Chivers' work, combined with other researchers like Marta Meana and Lisa Diamond, suggests that women have at least three different arousal systems:

> • **I am the Sex Goddess**: Feeling beautiful and desirable
> – a delicious embodiment of feminine erotic light – is a
> turn on.

• **Ravish me:** Being taken confidently by a strong, attuned man *at just the right time* sends most women right over the edge. Ravished is not raped. Rape is an act of violence without love or consent – ravished is magic surrender to masculine power.

• **Cozy, cozy:** Intimate warmth/safety/privacy relaxes into friendly amour.

I think men have the "I am the sex object," "Ravish me!" and "Cozy, cozy" arousal systems too, but they are drowned out by the volume of, "I see her I want her!" I also know that some women get off seeing attractive men, just as men get off seeing women, and can enjoy being the dominant "top" during lovemaking. There seems to be incredible variety in human sexual preferences.

Love maps matter

Love maps matter. What gets you off is what gets you off – and that goes double for your lover.

Becky and I have a wonderful routine on weekend mornings. We sleep in, share insights, make love, and then eat breakfast and read the papers. I learned years ago that psycho-spiritual insights are aphrodisiacs for Becky under the right circumstances, and I draw from that well often. I might share a study that shows people feeling better imagining how problems happen and how problems might be solved, or an idea Ken Wilber has about spirituality being both a state of consciousness as well as a line of development.

During these talks, Becky relaxes, gets interested, and then feels frisky. This is lucky for me, since I'm much better with insight than buying flowers or planning nights on the town (as Clint Eastwood said in one of his *Dirty Harry* movies, "A man's got to know his limitations.")

The point here is to pay attention to what gets you or your partner in a sexy mood. What titillates us is based on our sexual drives, but experienced through a filter of how we're wired, or as John Gottman calls it, our *love map.*

Much of your love map is wired in by the time you're ten or twelve. Straight or gay, top or bottom, breasts or legs, tall or short, short shorts or lingerie, wham/bam or cozy/cozy, nice guys or bad boys – mostly in place by early adolescence, waiting to be discovered as you mature.

A real problem occurs when what we find beautiful – what gets us hot – isn't what we find good. For instance, to one successful businessman I worked with, secret affairs felt incredibly sexy and erotically charged, but cheating still felt wrong. This reflects the difficulties inherent in accessing the charge of transgressive sex (naughty or forbidden behavior we find exciting), while still staying acceptable/moral to our "good" validity standards.

Mostly people ignore such discrepancies or pretend they don't exist. Bad idea! A train wreck waiting to happen!

Therapy

Fifty plus thousand therapy sessions over forty-one years have convinced me that secret affairs and lack of sexual communication are epidemic cultural problems that are totally interrelated.

A much better strategy than denial, self-indulgence, or dissociation is to find a good therapist and discuss *beautiful/good* arousal discrepancies in detail, with lots of interest in what the *true* has to say about happy intimacy. Most of us can find ways of integrating what gets us hot with what makes great relationships. We'll talk much more about this in Chapters 7 and 8.

Let's open up conversations everywhere

Dialed-in sexuality opens up conversations and experimentation everywhere, at every age, and it's never too late to start. I have a column on my website called, "Ask Dr. Keith." Check out this exchange I had with Jennifer a few months ago.

What about when we don't feel like BABES anymore?

Jennifer J. wrote to us on our Ask Dr. Keith page: "I'd love to see an episode on sexuality in older people ... women who don't feel like babes anymore, men who need more stimulation or Viagra to have erections, fading libidos, etc."

I responded, encouraging older people to have dialed-in sex:

Thanks Jennifer! This is a big deal issue. These problems are shared by millions.

What to do?

Accept that you are a sexual being! If you've got a partner, accept that *you are both sexual beings!* We are informed by our sexual essence from birth to death.

Have sex and/or masturbate regularly – keep your sexual circuits and organs happy and alive.

Talk with your partner about sex. What do you and your partner like, want, fear, or feel ashamed of? Talk with the intent of radical acceptance. If you two can't sustain these accepting talks, find a therapist to help.

Expand your understanding of sex. All forms of sexual/ sensual pleasure are on the table, including masturbation, fondling with and without orgasms, sexual talk, images, videos, books, toys and fantasies. Anyone for *Fifty Shades of Grey*?

Talk to your MD or OB/GYN in detail about your sexual feelings and functioning. I *love* Viagra, Cialis, Levitra, and hormone replacement therapy – they are central players in the rejuvenation wave of the future that we're all riding to some extent. If your doctor is uncomfortable with these conversations, find another doctor.

If you are the more feminine partner in lovemaking, keep reaching for full surrender to your inner Sex Goddess. Open into deeper pleasure with movement, breath, and sound.

If you are the more masculine partner, anchor in your love, power and principles. Focus on being nourished by her pleasure as you open her to deeper bliss. Relax and lead the dance; bathe her in your admiring delight.

Whether you are more the leader or the follower, feel your erotic spirit emanating from your body, dancing with your partner's erotic spirit – this spirit is largely independent of age, disability, and appearance.

Practice

Practice attuning to yourself and your lover, during sex and also generally during the day. Lovemaking is a time to embrace your divine masculine and feminine essences and polarities. Leave your insecure ego at the door and put on your, "I'm hot, desired, and enjoying a great time with someone I love," persona – which you can *consciously practice regularly*.

Work out, eat right, meditate, resolve problems that arise in relationships (with your partner and with the many parts of yourself), and get enough sleep – they all help with sex as well as improve pretty much everything else.

There are a gazillion other ideas and techniques for enhancing sex as you age. Begin with the ones I've suggested, and never stop exploring and expanding. Remember, when *you* have good sex with yourself or someone you love, it serves *all of us*.

AMERICAN TANTRA

Eastern traditions have a long history of sexual/spiritual philosophies and practices, commonly referred to in the west as "Tantric." Over the last century, many westerners have studied these approaches (often with trips to India), and teachers like Michaels and Johnson (*The Essence of Tantric Sexuality*) have translated Eastern traditions into Western forms.

In general, enhanced sexual intimacy has been an increasingly hot topic as American culture normalizes the importance of sexuality and the need for sexual wisdom and fulfillment in individual and relational health.

Lots of practitioners teach an incredible array of systems amplifying sexual intimacy and pleasure. Alan and Donna Bauer's *Extended Sexual Orgasm*, and Steve and Vera Bodansky's *Extended Massive Orgasm*, get to the nuts and bolts of achieving and amplifying orgasms. Margot Anand (*The Art of Sexual Ecstasy*) has a more theatrical and eastern tinged approach that includes invoking nature spirits, movement, dance, and erotic ceremony. David Deida uses a more rigorous – almost martial arts tinged – approach of blasting through blocks and liberating your masculine/feminine aspects and essence. Esther Perel (author of *Mating in Captivity*) is big on understanding and transcending cultural limitations and demands around intimacy and sexual charge. Cumulatively, I call all these more flexible, less traditional approaches "American Tantra," because Americans are diverse, individualistic, and tend to resist surrendering to any one path.

When I meet practitioners in these areas, I joke with them that by the time a couple is ready to go to one of their intensives, the hardest psycho-therapeutic work has usually already been done. Most American couples can't safely *discuss* sexual wants and yearnings, much less experiment with extended sexual play or tantric ceremony. I'm stoked when a previously sexually silent couple can just have a productive sexual conversation in my office – never mind going to organized erotic workshops. Such talk forms the foundation upon which individualized American Tantra programs can be constructed.

You can see the inhibition of sexual communication weirdly played out in American culture, where people are fascinated with public displays of affection up to kissing and hugging, and completely shut down around talking about anything more sexually explicit. For instance, I subscribe to "People News" from Stephen M. Silverman, and the following are a couple of typical entries:

> • Anne Hathaway and her fiancé Adam Shulman are in Paris this week, and clearly feeling the allure of the old city – as they were spotted kissing at an outdoor cafe, while enjoying glasses of champagne.

> • Bradley Cooper & Zoe Saldana Share Kisses at Sundance. Cast mates and rumored off-screen couple Bradley Cooper and Zoe Saldana weren't coy about their relationship status at Sundance! The co-stars were spotted taking their romance public, smooching at a

cocktail party for their film *The Words* at the Park City, Utah film festival.

Nobody *ever* speculates any further about sexual engagement. If Anne and Adam and Bradley and Zoe are lovers, what kind of sex do they like? Does Zoe like to be swept off her feet and ravished in hotel rooms? Does Adam get off on Anne wearing high heels? Powerful taboos repel us from such talk – taboos so strong that many married couples *never* share their sexual landscapes fully *with each other*, even after decades of marriage.

Jim and Bobby make sexual progress

That's why it was so much fun recently to work with Jim and Bobby, a couple who had just returned from a sensuous tropical vacation and wanted to keep the sexual thrill going. Neither believed they had much trouble talking explicitly about what they liked – and they really were much more open than most couples. On the other hand, subtle resistances still caused them problems in sexual communication, and they had an ongoing problem keeping sex hot at home.

With partners like this – generally self-reflective, communicative, and experienced in personal transformation and erotic development – my job is to help them expand their range of self-awareness, communication and action, and then guide them through the defensive distress that inevitably emerges from such work into more dialed-in sexuality. In the initial session with Jim and Bobby, the expansion part involved exploring their favorite connections and fantasies, and suggesting a few relatively safe practices. The defensive distress part came up in the next session after they tried out the new ideas, had some problems, and activated their defensive states – which always show up eventually when people work with sexual identities, yearnings, judgments, and practices.

In the first session, I started by asking them, "What is your best sexual/emotional connection?"

Bobby answers immediately, "Gratitude and appreciation for each other."

Jim takes a little longer, looking thoughtfully out the window and finally saying, "Her enthusiasm, sexual desire, desire to be playful."

I ask, "What's your favorite sexual scene?"

Bobby: "Dressing up, adorning myself as the sex goddess – being appreciated, found attractive, worshipped."

Jim: "Directing Bobby to do sexy things." He looks embarrassed, "Kind of being the master in the master/slave thing."

Bobby blushes, "I have to say I like that too. But sometimes it's hard to get there."

I ask Bobby, "When you two start fooling around, how many minutes until you are in the mood?"

She laughed a little, "Often right away, but it can take five to ten minutes if I've had a stressful day."

"OK," I said, "This week I'd like you to stake out a two hour interval and have Jim initiate lovemaking." I turn to Jim, who gets impatient when Bobby doesn't immediately get into it when they start making love, and say, "You need to be loving, patient and present for at least ten minutes after you begin. That's your job." He nodded – guys like to have a specific mission.

Bobby breathes deeper as Jim agrees, and I tell her, "Bobby, your job is to relax and let Jim lead you into bliss."

Looking back to Jim, I continue, "The first directions you offer are the most important ones. Each needs to be an easy 'yes,' like, 'Close your eyes and taste this strawberry.' The president of a Los Angeles Hypnosis Association once said that if someone does what you say three times in a row, they are likely to be relaxing into trance and much more available to further direction, so the first things you suggest – or order her to do in the master/slave sense – need to be easy and fun."

They both nod, and two weeks later they come back into my office and sit down, with Jim looking pissed and Bobby scared. *"Time to deal with defenses,"* I think to myself as they settle into armchairs facing each other.

Sipping from my teacup, I ask, "So, what happened?"

Jim: "She got controlling and wouldn't go along."

Bobby: "He got angry and I couldn't relax."

I smile reassuringly. "We talked about how stuff would come up, and here it is. How did you handle the situation?"

Bobby: "We had a fight and then stopped talking to each other." Jim nods his head in agreement.

"Great strategy!" I say with a smile, and they both laugh.

This gets us connected, and we proceed to explore the negative stories they tend to generate about each other, and the hostile habits of blaming and attacking they unconsciously surrender to when feeling sexual criticism, shame, or pressure.

We went on to make fairly good progress with these issues, and I ended the session with my admiration and encouragement. "This conversation, where you two can talk in an accepting and caring way about your hurtful experiences and negative stories, and listen for the kernels of truth in the other's beliefs, is what will guide you towards deeper intimacy and sexual bliss. *This conversation* is a prime example of what I call American Tantra, the ability of equal partners – educated, sophisticated, but still driven by defenses and closed down by inhibitions – to keep expanding the conversation and trying new ideas and practices to create more love and passion. As long as you *keep the conversation alive,* and *keep reaching for more love and passion with each other,* you'll continue to make progress and keep getting more dialed-in."

Bobby and Jim left the session more hopeful and willing to try some more practices, and so far they're still making progress. If they continue, they'll keep discovering amazing capacities for love and passion, but it will be harder than they think. That's really the secret knowledge about American Tantra – it requires courage and willingness to be wrong and to change over time, but two people committed to ongoing practice can generate incredible levels of love and passion.

America is a society of unique individuals, so we each co-create our own growth systems with therapists, teachers, health practitioners, and lovers. We have always been a great melting pot of ideas and approaches to everything imaginable. American Tantra reflects this as it draws from multiple sources and traditions to help people find their way to deepening love and sexual bliss.

SEX HELPS YOU LOSE WEIGHT

A recent study revealed that a third of men have had fantasy sex with *over one thousand women.* Men are genetically wired to crave diversity of sexual partners, and most guys create sexual variety using autoerotic daydreams, often fueled by sexy media images. Men aren't alone on the romantic fantasy highway. Over fifty percent of paperback books sold in this country are romances bought by women, about virile, present, loving men claiming and ravishing smart, radiant women.

Remember the sixties? If you do, you'll recall that men's main sources of erotica were *Penthouse* and *Playboy*. Back before internet porn, "men's magazines" weren't about working out and having outdoor adventures, they were about pictures of (mostly) naked women and sex. I always loved the Penthouse Letters to the Editor section (it was my second favorite part). The letters read like soft-core porn, and each issue would usually have one offering that rang my erotic bell, or – more rarely – offered a new perspective.

One woman wrote that she lost weight by having sex five times a day. Largely clueless about the potential horrors of sexual compulsivity and sex addiction, I thought this strategy fantastic. Besides constant sex sounding just right to my 28-year-old male libido (many twenty-something guys think about sex *every 52 seconds*), I was also intrigued by her claim. Like most Americans, I've always been somewhat obsessed with weight loss, and wondered if frequent sex actually worked for weight control.

Fast forward 36 years (*36 years? – really?*) to current research on diet, lifestyle, metabolism, stress management, sex, and weight. It looks like that woman might have been onto something.

Weight is not just about calories and dieting – not even close. Weight is a function of genetic heritage, lifestyle, stress levels, exercise patterns, what kinds of food we eat, and when we eat them (yes, *when* we eat matters – just eating breakfast means you effectively consume around 150 to 300 fewer calories that day). Eating is also social (digestion is personal). People tend to bond with others around food, and often turn to food when they're lonely. The intersections of social engagement, stress and food are where sex comes in.

We all know that regular exercise and frequent small healthy meals optimize healthy weight, but stress management and social satisfaction weigh in heavily. How we manage stress affects weight gain and loss, and *loving human touch alleviates stress.*

Loving touch reduces the stress hormone cortisol – one of the main culprits in weight gain. Some monkeys groom others up to a sixth of their waking hours, and such friendly touch reduces participants' cortisol levels. Interestingly, in the monkey studies, the *groomers*, givers of sensual attention, had the lowest cortisol. It was especially soothing to soothe others.

Stress *increases* cortisol. When our brains believe we are threatened, our hypothalamus tells our pituitary to tell our adrenals (which are on top of the kidneys) to pump adrenaline (a "let's get jacked up and moving" hormone) and cortisol (a "let's prepare sugar levels, blood pressure, and immune systems for battle" hormone) into our blood to get us ready to fight or flee.

When we have too much or too constant stress – over days, weeks, or years, like extended battle, grinding poverty, political repression, abuse, or neglect – our cortisol levels first get high, then get flat, telling our bodies to turn muscle into fat.

Chronic high cortisol also results in craving carbohydrates and eating more. Even worse, constant high stress elevates levels of an enzyme in cells called HSD, which keeps cortisol high *inside* the cells, *even when cortisol levels drop in the bloodstream.* HSD causes cells to hang on to the fat they've got and store more fat – especially in the belly and hips. This is why dieting rarely works – it's stressful to limit food, stress increases cortisol and HSD, and our bodies end up holding on to, and storing more fat.

Like the grooming monkeys, loving touch reduces cortisol, and helps us deal with stress. Sex is particularly great because making love typically gives our body the equivalent of twenty minutes of aerobic exercise (with exceptions to those who prefer super-quickies), and increases the bonding chemicals oxytocin and vasopressin – associated with that post-coital glow when we're cuddling in warm aftermath. Also, most couples report feeling less stressed *in their general life* for up to twenty-four hours (or even longer) after making love. Feeling securely connected as a lover apparently has huge, long lasting stress reduction benefits. Men who believed there was plenty of affection in their marriages were 300% more likely to report themselves happy and satisfied.

After working with couples for over four decades, I can't think of any other activity that lasts for (typically) fifteen to forty five minutes that has such consistent and wide ranging health effects as love-making.

Maybe it even helps us lose weight.

SEX AND SHAME

Back in the day before I settled down to a monogamous existence, I had a brief, passionate affair with a beautiful woman named Jan. We spent

114

two weeks falling in love, circumstances drove us apart, and I suffered somewhat shocking grief and loss for the next three months as my body/mind system adjusted from in-love to lost-love.

Even though she was seven years younger than me, Jan was much more experienced in the dynamics of love affairs, and one afternoon as we lay in post-coital bliss, bathed in the sunlight streaming in from her bedroom window, she asked me, "Is there anything you *really* like. You know, something that especially turns you on?"

I was surprised at my reaction. First of all, I found it totally endearing that she'd ask this question, clearly eager to step into whatever Sex Goddess role my answers might indicate. Her erotic generosity felt beautiful and very personal. Second, I felt embarrassed, not particularly at the brief array of sexual fantasies that cascaded through my mind, but at the fact that I *didn't trust her enough* to share them. Here I was, naked, vulnerable, in the most intimate physical space imaginable, and I didn't trust my lover enough to share potentially embarrassing desires and fantasies.

In 2007 I published *The Gift of Shame*, which explored the shame family of emotions (shame, guilt, embarrassment, chagrin, mortification, etc.) and how badly they have been misunderstood and mismanaged over the last hundred years. Shame is a gift if we can understand it as a social emotion that enables mammals to instruct their young, and as an interior compass that guides us to identify, follow, and refine our moral standards.

In my chapter on sexual shame, I make the point that sexual taboos, rules, and learning are so highly charged that even a little bit of misattunement or disapproval can release a flood of shame, guilt, or – as in my response to Jan – embarrassment at who we are or how we react.

Like most therapists, I've found that sex comes up all the time in sessions. Almost without exception, where there's sex, there's some kind of shame emotion stirred into the mix.

This is especially true for couples who, unlike me with Jan, have the courage to actually share their deepest, most embarrassing sexual yearnings. If those yearnings aren't accepted and respected, disapproval, resentment, and even repulsion ensue, often with disastrous consequences.

For instance, some women I've worked with are aroused at the idea of sexy dancing in front of desirous men. These days, such excitement can be pursued and supported by programs like burlesque classes, or schools like "The S-Factor" where women learn pole dancing. Unfortunately, often when a woman reveals such fantasies to her husband or lover, she's met with his embarrassment, or stony disapproval, shutting both partners down, and setting the stage for sexual shame and secrets.

Another common example is a man sharing fantasies involving threesomes, vibrators, lingerie, pornography, anal sex, or oral adventures. If his partner finds such activity unappealing or embarrassing, she radiates disapproval – sometimes including disgust, anger, or fear – leaving him ashamed and conflicted.

The point here is not that you need to like what your partner finds sexy, or engage in sexual behavior that is uncomfortable for you. I know of no couple – straight or gay – where both are turned on by exactly the same things – people are *way* too complicated for that.

The bottom line (when you talk about sex, almost everything becomes a double entendre!) is that every long term love affair becomes a compromise between how often *you* want to make love, versus how often *I* want to make love; between *your* favorite romance/sexual overtures/activities and *my* favorite overtures/activities; and between what *you* believe is "normal" or "healthy" sex, versus what *I* believe is "normal" or "healthy." These compromises are inevitable and necessary.

Where everything goes to pieces is when partners lose attunement and indulge critical judgments of each other for what they like or don't like, leaving them ashamed and separate.

I encourage lovers to *accept* whatever desires and fantasies they and their partner have and *make love* in ways that are acceptable to both.

Diana and Bill

For instance, Diana and Bill are in their mid-forties with kids in grade school. Bill, repeating a long-standing refrain, complains bitterly, "You never want to have sex anymore! You always say 'no!'"

Diana, equally pissed off, responds, "I have to tell you, Bill, 'Let's fuck,' is not my idea of a romantic come on!"

Bill, always willing to dig himself deeper into this particular hole (see what I mean about double entendres?), fires back, "I didn't realize you were such a prude when I married you!"

I interrupt before they can fire any more salvos. Both are angry, embarrassed, and ashamed (though, since shame is the 'look away' emotion, neither are particularly aware of it). "Stop it, you two! This is the most unsexy conversation I've heard this week, and I talk about sex all the time! Look at each other, remember you are lovers, and make some progress. Bill, I don't hear you asking what kind of overtures Diana *does* like."

Bill's a good guy, and looks gratefully at me for saving him from more self-inflicted wounds. "OK. I'll bite. What kind of overtures do you like?"

Diana, still smarting from the "prude" comment – which is only one or two steps better than the ever-popular "You're frigid" attack – doesn't feel very generous at this moment, but she's also acutely aware that I'm taking a stand for love and passion, so she heroically gets a handle on her anger and responds from her heart, "I like it when you're friendly when you get home, and help in the kitchen when the girls are doing their homework."

Bill looks genuinely bewildered, as many men do with statements like this. "What does that have to do with sex?" Diana looks to me for help, which I'm more than happy to provide.

"Come on Bill. We've talked about this before. Women's sexuality tends to be contextual, and run off whether she feels known, loved, and supported by her guy. Sure, women have at least three arousal systems – the 'I am the embodiment of sexual beauty,' the 'ravish me,' and the 'cozy, cozy,' systems, but long term lovers like you and Diana need the safety of 'cozy, cozy' to access the others."

Both are nodding at this point, and the rest of the session moves into Bill being more intimate and engaged, and Diana responding more generously to his efforts. With some perseverance they'll be a little more accepting and responsive this coming week, which is how couples usually change in sexual areas. Most of us have been trained by family and culture (often via shame emotions) to be *un*conscious about sexual desires and behaviors, so it's amazingly hard to even remember sexual stuff, much less talk and act differently.

Which brings us to *you*. Where is it hard for *you* to be aware of and accepting of sexual desires and activities in you and your partner? What can *you* do to make your romantic/erotic relationship more fun for you and your partner? Are *you* willing to change what you think and do to create more love and pleasure? Are *you* willing to be more expressive about who you are sexually, and more accepting of who your partner is sexually?

If you resist some of these questions – and most of us do – that's your sexual shame talking. The more you're aware of it and let your wisdom guide you, rather than your shame, the better it is for you, your partner, your family, and all of us.

Practice

Write down your answers to the above questions about your sexuality and relationships, and share them with your partner. Encourage him or her to do the same. As you discuss your answers, pay attention to whether you feel you're creating more intimacy and potential for passion, or less. If it's "less," be a strong advocate for progress and keep the conversations going – with help from therapists, if necessary – until improvements happen.

LUST, TO ROMANTIC INFATUATION, TO INTIMATE BONDING

We've talked about sexual states of arousal, masculine and feminine types in the sexual occasion, and how mature people can open up sexual dialogue and keeping the conversations going.

When we're attuned to ourselves and others, have solid information and good communication habits, intimacy happens, growth happens, and people hook up into love affairs, families, and friendship networks.

In Chapter 7: *Dialed-in Love Affairs,* and Chapter 8: *Dialed-in and Clueless Marriages,* we further apply this material to hooking up, bonding, and creating/maintaining stable, satisfying marriages.

Chapter 7: Dialed-in Love Affairs

Most love affairs are terrifyingly random. You meet someone at a party, sit next to an attractive stranger at a concert, or notice someone giving you the eye across the room, and WHAM! – before you know it you're in bed, hopefully having an outrageously good time of course, but rolling the dice about whether this relationship will ultimately build you up or tear you down. Sexual polarity tends to trump other judgments, *unless we are dialed-in.*

This is one of the reasons why, in my opinion, computer dating is a godsend. Computer daters actually do some vetting of potential partners, independent of "I see her I want her," or "OMG! He's cute and he likes me!" In the U.S, 25% of current marriages are between people who meet online, and that number will keep growing through the 21st century, but online discernments still run the risk of missing key elements in potential lovers.

Much of our relationship craziness simply arises from ignorance – often created by cultural blind spots. We can sometimes see such blind spots more clearly in larger-than-life stories of celebrities, the modern mythic heroes and anti-heroes.

Take, for instance, Lady Gaga.

Lady Gaga and cultural blind spots

People often say America is a celebrity culture, but this seems unfair to me. *All* cultures are celebrity cultures! Humans are fascinated with extraordinary people everywhere. In the U.S., we just have more celebrity *coverage.*

In previous eras, famous figures passed into legend, like Queen Elizabeth, Jesus, Kublai Khan, and Odysseus. Their lives took on mythic resonance that fascinated and instructed people – largely through storytellers, minstrels, and priests, until the printing press and widespread literacy hit the world like a comet a few hundred years ago.

In our modern information age, such stories erupt quickly as people achieve notoriety from accomplishments (the Beatles, the Clintons, Kobe Bryant); huge falls from grace (Barry Bonds, Bernie Madoff); or sheer dedication to celebrity (the Kardashians).

We are especially attracted to celebrities' love lives – who and how they love. I think this reflects our fascination with each other – especially with mythic figures in the big stories around us, illustrated as they are by celebs.

Lady Gaga is one of my favorites. Great music, fearless performer, straight from the heart communicator. What's not to like? I was taken by statements she made in a 2012 interview in *Vanity Fair*. Excerpts include:

- "I have an inability to know what happiness feels like with a man."

- "I think what it really is, is that I date creative people. And I think that what intimidates them is not my purse, it's my mind."

- "It starts out good. Then when I'm in these relationships with people who are also creative, or creative in their own way, what happens is the attraction is initially there and it's all unicorns and rainbows. And then they hate me."

- "It's a hideous place to be in, when someone that you love has convinced you that you will never be good enough for anyone."

- "When I fight with someone I'm in a relationship with, I think: 'What would my fans think if they knew this was happening? How would they feel about my work and about me as a female if they knew I was allowing this to go on?' And then I get out [of the relationship].²"

I have no personal knowledge of Lady Gaga, but I like her music and performances, and she is obviously a brilliant, talented woman. What seems revealed in these quotes (perhaps just what she was feeling that day, but also perhaps deeply held beliefs) are stories she tells herself about love – variations of painful patterns I've heard from clients of all ages. This Lady Gaga version seems to include:

- Relationships start well.

- People (especially creative people) become intimidated by my mind and begin to hate me.

- My lover and I fight, and leaving seems the best option, so I get out.

Her conclusions seem to reflect what I've come to see as enormous blind spots in American culture. Far too often, people have repetitive relational experiences, tell themselves stories that explain the patterns, *and never think they can create different stories.*

We don't do this with physical health problems. If that ache in my back gets worse, I get help – maybe from an MD or chiropractor – to find out what's wrong and what to do. Healers might not always be right, but I assume their training, experience and access to special knowledge can help explain my problems and generally make things better.

Way too often, when it comes to emotions, sex, or relationships, we come up with a negative story, and keep playing out the same drama without considering *that we can probably change the script.*

For instance, a new Lady Gaga story might be, "I can be more able and willing to do what it takes to get back to love. I can choose partners more able to get back to love, and we can help each other improve our abilities to communicate and resolve issues."

Intimacy is like learning to sing and play the piano (something Lady Gaga has obviously dedicated thousands of hours to). Effort and progress can result in natural abilities growing to modest abilities, growing to extraordinary abilities.

This growth mindset attitude – focus on effort and progress is better for development and achievement than focus on success and failure – applied to love could be widely taught at every level to children, teens, and adults. It could also be more widely embraced by celebrities – our mythic role models.

Many high profile people don't have the time or energy for committed intimacy (public lives can be brutally demanding), and often keep the details of personal growth private when they do successfully use therapists or other helpers to resolve relational issues.

How often does any celeb – even Dustin Hoffman or Harry Belafonte, who publicly acknowledge extensive years in therapy – talk *specifically* about personal transformations they've experienced through changing relationship patterns? Except in the context of drug and alcohol rehab, hardly ever.

I think this is a cultural blind spot – not seeing love as a developmental line that we grow on, just like we grow physically, athletically, or musically, and where we often need help to grow in healthy ways. Too often, people assume relationships work a certain way for them and that's it.

Therapy can be enormously helpful in changing destructive patterns. It's really less about treating symptoms (the traditional medical model), and more about helping people elevate abilities to love and understand.

Lady Gaga reaches millions of men and women around the world, and clearly cares about her fans. What if her story changed to, "I used to believe that lovers became intimidated by my mind, started to hate me, and then I had to leave; but, I live differently now. I'm more dialed-in to who might be a superior partner. When I fight, I'm getting back to love quicker and easier."

On the other hand, given her wild talents, maybe this already *is* her new story.

Use your attunement skills to create healthy love affairs

In this chapter, we'll talk about using your attunement skills to train your brain to notice key variables in yourself and potential lovers. Then, we'll talk more about online dating, healthy flirting, and why the closer you are, the weirder it gets!

Dialed-in love affairs are *not* problem-free! All love involves suffering, and that goes double for love affairs. Dialed-in love affairs *are* relationships where, when problems inevitably arise, you have a fighting chance of working through the problems to bring them back into love.

All relationships start with *choosing* someone to go deeper with. Even if someone asks you out, you still have to choose whether to say "yes" or "no." How can we possibly discern healthy and unhealthy candidates? People are so complicated, how do we get deeper than, "He seems nice and attractive," or, "There's something about her I like."

We actually are astonishingly more sensitive and perceptive of other people than most of us believe – but we often lose discernment abilities when we're distracted by states of attraction, lust, anxiety, or pride.

We don't have to blunt our native social genius – we can actually *amplify* our social genius! We can train our nervous systems to scan for positive relationship variables with what I call a "Five Star Practice for creating beautiful relationships."

A FIVE STAR PRACTICE FOR CREATING BEAUTIFUL RELATIONSHIPS

Say you're single and yearning for love. What's the first step? Most of us have asked ourselves some (or all) of the following questions at some time in our lives:

- "What do I do to find someone?"

- "How do I find someone where we're both *into* each other?"

- "How can I tell if a potential lover is good for me?"

- "What's the difference between someone who'll rock my world or ruin my life?"

I've heard these questions for decades, and here's one set of answers – a Five Star Practice for creating beautiful relationships.

The Five Stars are five questions you ask yourself about other people and yourself. That's right – just ask yourself these five questions about everyone you meet, and your chances of having successful relationships skyrockets.

This practice is awesomely simple.

Ask yourself these questions about everyone you meet:

> 1. Is there erotic polarity between this person and me? Is there a sexual spark?
> 2. Does this person stay healthy physically and psychologically?
> 3. If we were in a relationship and had conflict, would this person be *able* and *willing* to do what it takes to get back to love?
> 4. Would this person be a superior parent?
> 5. Does this person live life from a sense of deep, even sacred, purpose? If I do, do they (or would they) sense it and admire it in me?

If the answer to one of these questions is "no," a relationship with this person is much more likely to end in negative drama. If the answers to all five questions are "yes," or "maybe," he or she is more likely to be a fun, honest, constant lover.

The best way to start attracting a Five Star Candidate and becoming a Five Star Candidate is to notice the presence or absence of these qualities in yourself and everybody you meet.

Neuroscience

We learn new routines quickly in the left hemisphere of our frontal cortex (our left frontal lobe), but our habitual responses come from our right frontal cortex (our right frontal lobe), which learns very slowly. That's why it's hard to learn new habits quickly. Our left hemisphere needs to decide on the new routine many times before it becomes a reflexive habit that our right hemisphere will automatically kick in without us having to think and decide.

Try asking these questions about lots of different people for a couple of weeks, whether you're interested in them or not. You'll be amazed at what you discover. If you like these new perspectives, do it a few months more and you'll find that noticing the Five Stars starts to be as automatic as noticing how tall someone is, or what kind of outfit they're wearing.

The Five Stars arose out of a conversation Becky and I were having with our kids Ethan and Zoe when they were teenagers, around twelve years ago. We were all hanging out in the kitchen and talking about relationships – a frequent topic. Ethan, who was just beginning to date, asked, "What do I look for in girls?" Meaning, "What do I look for besides she's hot and I like talking with her?" (not bad criteria themselves, if you think about it).

Challenged to give everybody a useful response, I reached for the simplest, most fundamental qualities I've discovered that characterize superior partners – which turned out to be the Five Stars.

These five dimensions aren't random – they are conclusions based on my decades of clinical practice and massive bodies of neurobiology, psychology, anthropology, and sociology research. Some of my favorite findings include:

> • We absorb huge amounts of information just meeting someone briefly for the first time. One study looked at the differences in interpersonal evaluation between people who had three to five seconds of face-to-face contact with another, and those who knew that other person for five weeks. Both groups had about the same accuracy in evaluating the other.

> • Our brains naturally – unconsciously – scan the environment to look for threat, safety, beauty, social position, and potential need/desire gratification (like food, water, sexual partners, warmth, light – basically all the tasty/secure/comforting/yummy stuff we yearn for).

> • Even better, we can train our brains what to look for. For instance, if you've ever picked fruit or vegetables from a garden, you'll find that very quickly you automatically start discerning the ripe from the unripe, and where on the

tree or vine these prime delicacies are likely to be hanging out. In other words, brains love to play, "Where's Waldo?" with people, objects, or qualities we decide we want to monitor for.

• When we make eye contact with people, mirror neurons in both our brains resonate, revealing our states of consciousness and intentionality – what we're feeling/thinking and what we intend towards each other. This is an imperfect system, since all of us can lie and hide from ourselves or others, but we share quite a lot with someone just looking into their eyes.

Back to Ethan's question, "What do I look for in girls?" I caught everyone's eye and began, "First, look for erotic polarity. There has to be some sexual chemistry to make dating worthwhile. If you have zero erotic spark, what's the use of dating? Often, at best, you'll go out and end up liking them and want to be attracted. People try to talk themselves into it – you know, "She has a pretty face," or, "He's such a nice guy." Trying to talk yourself into sexual attraction is usually a disaster. You need that spark of erotic polarity to give a love affair a chance."

Sexual Spark?

At this point you might be asking, "How do I know if there's a sexual spark?" Just for a moment, reflect back on all the people you can remember feeling sexy with. Now, do the same for a few people you had absolutely no sexual attraction for. There's your answer.

At this point I had everybody's attention. Becky said, "Wait, let me write this down," and grabbed a pen. Inspired by their collective interest, I continued.

"Next, does this person do what it takes to stay healthy physically and psychologically? Are they addicted to anything? Do they neglect their body? Do they let important relationships languish, or routinely dismiss or attack others who offend them? If they encounter a problem with their physical, emotional, or relational well-being, do they seek out and receive help to get better?"

One of the kids said, "How do you know all this stuff just meeting a person?" I responded, "All you need to do is ask yourself the questions. Your nervous system will eventually start noticing erotic polarity and whether someone effectively maintains physical and psychological health. These questions become habits of perception."

"What else?" said practical Becky, scribbling furiously.

Influence

This theme of receiving influence is a central dialed-in characteristic. You'll notice how it fits into growth mindsets, turning defensive states into states of healthy response, and progressing on developmental lines. If I never listen to my tap-dancing teacher and resist following her advice, I'm destined to keep noisily stumbling around until I learn how to receive her influence.

I continued, "A third question to ask yourself is, 'If you were in a relationship with this person and there was conflict, would they be able and willing to do what it takes to get back to love?' This means talking, self-reflecting, asking for help, forgiving, and refusing to stay angry or alienated." Everyone in the family nodded. The four of us had years of experience getting back to love with each other and friends, and we'd also all seen relationships end in conflict. I continued with a question I knew would raise some hackles.

"A fourth question is, 'Would this person be a superior parent?'"

Zoe immediately piped up, "Wait! What? I'm only fourteen! What possible difference does it make if a guy would be a superior parent? I don't want kids with him, I just want to date him!"

I smiled patiently, "I know it sounds weird, but think about it. If you don't believe someone would be a superior parent, you're intuitively sensing something me-first egocentric, or selfish, or self-destructive, or narcissistic, or whatever would be bad for a growing child. Besides the imperfections of birth control (remember, nothing tests at 100% effective, even surgery), these kinds of selfish traits of non-superior-parenting types will show up with lovers, meaning with you."

Seeing them nod, I plunged forward to the last question. "Finally, does this person have deep soul's purpose, or are they seeking it? Is there some sacred service they commit to – like their work, family, art, or a spiritual path? Also, will this person see and value you living from – or seeking – deep soul's purpose? It completely sucks to have something sacred to you that your lover doesn't see or dismisses."

I wanted to emphasize here that there are differences between masculine and feminine types of people, so I went on a little. "Deep soul's purpose is especially important for men. Guys with no purpose, or who refuse to acknowledge the pain of no purpose and seek meaningful passions, tend to collapse in the clutch in intimate relationships. Even worse is a guy who organizes his life just around you. Women tend to be repulsed by this." Both Becky and Zoe nodded at this last part.

People's eyes were starting to glaze a little, so I quickly wrapped up. "The best way to use these questions is to ask them about everyone you see, whether they're a potential partner or not. You want to train your nervous system to just notice automatically these qualities in people, like red hair, or brown eyes. Even more importantly, if you want to attract a Five-Star person, be a Five-Star person. Cultivate all these qualities – like me and your mom!" I put my arm around Becky, looked triumphantly at the kids, and we all laughed.

Becky posted the Five Stars on the fridge, and I started sharing them with my clients. I've had so many requests for them that I keep a stack of handouts in my office, was asked to do a TEDx Five Star talk, and offered a Five Star class with en*theos Academy.

Try practicing being the Five Stars and noticing the Five Stars in other people. If you're in a relationship with someone, ask your partner and yourself the questions and see how you both answer. If it's "no" to any of the five, don't rush out and hire a divorce lawyer – have a conversation. If it gets nasty, practice Star #3 and do what it takes to get back to love. If that doesn't work, you can call a therapist for help.

However you use them, you'll probably be surprised at how quickly your social radar expands, and how you blossom and deepen utilizing the Five Stars.

As you gradually become a Five-Star candidate, you'll tend to attract other Five-Star people. Depth attracts depth, generosity attracts generosity, and love attracts love.

The Five Stars are a magnificent gateway into dialed-in love affairs, but we have to meet people to have opportunities to get to know them better. In this modern age of hectic schedules and social isolation, how do we find potential lovers?

One modern gift to love affairs is computer dating.

Why online dating is so cool

I love online dating. I think online dating services like Chemistry.com, EHarmony, Jdate, plentyoffish, positivepartners, and Match.com are among the most beautiful and good outcomes of the linked-in information age. Computer dating has revolutionized meeting potential lovers and life partners the way Viagra revolutionized treating erectile dysfunction. Yes, it's that wonderful.

For example, fifteen years ago Janine – a college professor – came to me depressed, thirty pounds overweight, and the adult survivor of a crazy stepfather's sexual and emotional abuse. She entered therapy lonely, suicidal, and despairing on ever finding love again. As we worked through her issues, her strengths began to shine more brightly. She was intelligent, disciplined, dedicated to her students, and – in her rare love affairs – enthusiastic and creative sexually. Like many women in their early fifties, she thought that finding a lover, much less a life partner, was about as likely as winning the lottery.

Enter computer dating. Janine, with the encouragement of her friends and me, went online and eventually met Frank. Today, they are in the twelfth year of the best relationship either has ever had. Sure, there were problems, but Janine and Frank were strong in Star #3 – able and willing to get back to love – and the three of us had couples sessions that helped them move through blocks, resentments, and horrible relationship patterns. Janine and Frank courageously progressed, and now live in wedded bliss in a beautiful house in the Santa Barbara foothills.

Jacob was fifty-five when we started therapy. I helped him through a train wreck divorce (he was devastated at the loss of his wife, even though she was an immature, stingy partner who got progressively more abusive the longer they were married), and he swore he'd never go online to find women. Jacob grew up seeing lascivious sex ads in risqué magazines featured in newsstands and sleazy tabloids – you know, "Single white male looking for Asian sex goddess into bondage and water sports" – and thought computer dating was the bottom of the barrel when it came to meeting women. Finally, after recovering from his divorce and fully embracing the reality that he was a good man who deserved a good woman, Jacob went online and today – ten years later – is happily married to Carolyn. He wakes each day next to a woman who loves him and a life that includes a grateful and satisfied life partner.

Back in the sixties and seventies, people found partners primarily at school (fine for the 18 to 25 age group, pretty impossible for the rest of us), at work, or at church. Therapists were taught to encourage lonely single adults of all ages to "be more social," "take classes," and "join groups." This seemed fine to me, except a little duplicitous and hypocritical for those people who specifically yearned for a lover/life partner. I always wondered why people couldn't just say, "I'm single and want a lover who might turn into a life partner." In those days, there were heavy societal taboos against publicly announcing you were lonely, looking for love, or wanting a specific kind of partner. Tellingly, one of the most popular albums of all time – Sergeant Pepper's Lonely Hearts Club Band – featured John Lennon lamenting, "Ah, look at all the lonely people."

Thirty-something people took classes (swing dance classes were particularly popular in Santa Barbara), went to bars, and occasionally attended singles groups, sometimes finding people they resonated with, and sometimes falling into creepy situations. You can't really exchange much relevant information in a noisy bar or a singles' mixer. It seemed especially difficult in relatively small towns like Santa Barbara, which had limited social choices compared to big urban areas.

The personal computer changed everything. I loved it when the dating services started, and knew immediately they would eventually blossom into huge, multimillion-dollar enterprises. Like all human social connection inventions (the written word, the printing press, the letter, the telephone, the cell phone), they were bound to grow and become

130

progressively more refined. It's now culturally acceptable to find partners online. People of all ages – especially boomers and those in their forties and fifties – normalize the online dating process, and can find help everywhere to guide them through.

There is even a new professional niche of "love coach," – a person who helps you with your photo and profile, and works with you throughout the process of meeting potential partners, evaluating their suitability, and dealing with the inevitable distress of having to reject and be rejected. If you can't afford (or find) a love coach, a good friend is wonderful – especially a woman friend (sorry guys, but women seem to be much more relaxed and helpful with this). I've helped shepherd many of my clients through the online dating dance, and – even though it's not easy – it tends to be honest and effective.

Meanwhile, the dating services have gotten progressively more sophisticated. Chemistry.com gave anthropologist Helen Fisher millions of dollars to research male and female arousal/mate selection systems and how to figure out what kind of person you are and whom you might hit it off with. Check out her book, *Why Him? Why Her? Finding Real Love by Understanding Your Personality Type*, for some mind-blowing, cutting-edge knowledge on how we bond. For instance, she found that most of us are more Explorers, Builders, Directors, or Negotiators, and that Explorers like other Explorers, Builders like other Builders, but that Directors and Negotiators do better with each other than with their own types (another cool typology system to add to the AQAL model of quadrants, levels, lines, states, and types).

Helen Fisher's research is just the tip of the iceberg of all the information that science has given us on love, sexuality, and healthy intimacy. If you watch my three TEDx talks, you'll get more details of the potential for educated love in the twenty-first century – love that is made much more possible for people everywhere through computer dating.

DRIVES CAN'T BE SAFELY IGNORED

We are genetically wired to be social and sexual. These are drives, like hunger and thirst. If we deny them we suffer horribly. That's why most prison wardens agree that solitary confinement is cruel and unusual punishment. It drives criminals crazy, and crazier criminals are exactly what prison wardens want less of. We need to embrace our drives to bond with others and to create intimate partnerships where sex is part of the deal. Sure, there are thousands of problems that arise. Most of these problems involve suffering from misunderstanding, immaturity, bad habits, ignorance, and emotional violence. Many issues can be resolved with education and therapy if people have the courage to love and receive influence from caring others, but first you need to get into the game. You need a relationship to work on your relationship.

That's why I love computer dating.

Healthy flirting

What about starting relationships with people we encounter in person as we go about our lives? Once we determine a possible Five Star candidate, then what?

I'm a great believer in healthy flirting.

Flirting often naturally happens when a more masculine person (usually a guy) and a more feminine person (usually a woman) connect.

This is not to say that any of us is purely masculine or feminine. All of us have masculine and feminine qualities. Ask any gender researcher and they'll tell you there are more differences and variations within all women and all men than between men and women. This reflects the incredible diversity and complexity of humans.

That being said, almost everyone is more masculine or more feminine in their deepest essence when it comes to the sexual occasion. You are either more lit up being the leader in the dance, being nourished by feminine erotic light, or the follower in the dance, allowing yourself to be guided to deeper pleasure by masculine depth and presence. When people connect in any way, they create little sparks between each other – polarities – that can be sexual polarities when a more masculine person connects with a more feminine person. These aren't always consciously felt as sexual. "He seemed so nice," or, "I loved her smile," reflect pleasure in this person's aura – pleasure that often has some subtle-to-obvious sexual component that we might or might not be aware of.

What is healthy flirting? When attraction happens, signals are exchanged, and sometimes relationships begin to form instantaneously.

I walk through the park on my way home from swimming and pass an attractive woman walking towards the pool, towel and fins in hand. I smile and wish her a good swim. She smiles back. I'm aware of her friendliness and feminine radiance, and she is relaxed and positive with my Keith presence. Seems like healthy flirting to me.

But, what if I pressed my flirting? Tried to converse more, asked for her name or contact information? Extended the conversation because she is magnetic and I don't want to let go of the erotic charge? She either finds me icky and unsafe, or is flattered and participates, giving me more access and encouragement. Either way, I've pressed the flirting boundary too far. I've taken a normal attraction, fed it, and I'm on the way to a *distracting attraction* (no longer an enjoyable casual exchange, but now more personal and obsessive) where I'm likely to keep thinking about her or even pursue her. This would be fine if we're both available, but in this case a potential nightmare since at least one of us (me!) is married.

If a couple of single people negotiate a flirtation into deeper engagement, oh boy! If you're single, feeding-flirtation skills lead to more lovers and fun. Feeding-flirtation expertise begins with attuning to yourself and that magnetic other, and then generating the right energy for the moment – skills that can be learned and refined with practice.

Healthy flirting spreads good vibes, helps us feel generous and attractive, is welcomed by others, and under the right circumstances can lead to juicy relationships. Unhealthy flirting risks soap opera dramas, turns people off, or takes them dangerously close to distracting attractions, romantic infatuations, and secret affairs.

Since erotic polarities naturally constellate between masculine and feminine people, it behooves us to have solid guidelines. We flirt all the time – whether we're conscious of it or not – so let's flirt well. Let's feel the polarities and feed them just enough to have fun and help others feel known, seen, and attractive, but never so much or in such ways that bad stuff happens.

Try to observe flirtation in all its forms this week. When you flirt, keep reaching for everyone-feels-great sweet spots in the polarities. You'll find you can adjust the intensity and quality of the energies to suit both your instincts and your values, and you'll notice others enjoying and trusting you when you get it right. If you're looking for a partner, feed the flirtations with Five Star Candidates.

The more conscious we are, the more choices we have, and principles like managing erotic polarities to serve the highest good can guide and focus our choices from clueless and mindless to mindful and dialed-in.

Love affair nightmares

What about the fact that, no matter how wonderful a love affair is in the beginning, problems always show up. Are long term happy relationships impossible, are we all hopelessly neurotic, or are there other human forces at work?

Long term happy relationships are difficult but not impossible, and, even though we are all neurotic to some extent, few of us are *hopelessly* neurotic. There *are* other human forces that complicate intimacy, and we usually need to understand and manage them to create dialed-in love affairs.

The closer you are the weirder it gets

Cindy sinks down into the light brown armchair in my office on a sweet Santa Barbara autumn day. The sun shines through the French doors, and a slight morning breeze caresses us with crisp, delicious airs. I swam this morning at sunrise at Los Banos outdoor pool near the harbor, and have that stoked sense of having worked out in nature – a feeling that usually persists throughout the morning. I'm glad to see Cindy, but worried about her obvious distress.

The pleasures of this day are lost on Cindy. She slumps in her chair, devastated and bewildered at what just happened with her lover, Tim.

Cindy's face is drawn in pain as her voice quivers with frustration and – unknown to her at this moment – outrage, "I don't get it! Everything was so wonderful for five months! We didn't fight. We traveled to Bali and had so much fun. I don't think I've ever been in love like this. Then, *after just one argument*, Tim says we have to break up! He really means it! Nothing I can say has any effect. He says, 'We're just not right for each other.' How can he walk away from something so beautiful? It doesn't make sense!"

A familiar combination of sympathetic grief and compassion rise up through my solar plexus and heart. I've been at this point countless times with men and women throughout the years. It's comforting to know that I can help her grow through the crisis, but sad to know that Tim probably won't make it back to love with Cindy. Totally rejecting a lover after one fight usually reflects profound narcissistic wounds that resist insight and change – a deficit in the Third Star, being able and willing to get back to love from conflict. There's a good chance that Tim is a lost cause, but Cindy isn't.

I start the process with the bottom line, "Cindy, one of the main risks of love is that – often – *the closer you are, the weirder it gets.*"

What...?

There are two forces (at least) that complicate love affairs and cause enormous confusion and suffering.

First, falling in love – romantic infatuation – is an altered state where you amplify your partner's strengths and ignore their weaknesses. When you fall in love, a place in your brain stem called the ventral tegmental area sprays dopamine – an excitement/pleasure neuromodulator that's central to all addictions – into your brain like a sprinkler system, keeping you intoxicated with your partner. People in love *notice* that their lover isn't perfect. They can perceive flaws, but they generally aren't particularly worried about them. Being in love feels like a state of grace where bad things that happened in previous relationships just aren't possible with *us*.

When, after days, weeks, or months, romantic infatuation fades, character flaws and bad relational habits aren't medicated away with sexy, romantic, dopamine-driven fog, and lovers find themselves pissed off, scared, or distrustful in ways that are alarmingly reminiscent of previous relationship nightmares.

A second force that complicates love affairs is that, as you get closer to another person, the levels of familiarity and intimacy keep rising until they recapitulate states we experienced with family members growing up. Almost everybody's first romantic infatuation was with Mom – holding, nursing, cooing, caring, and protecting. This *wired our brains* to love and act in specific ways, and – since no mother is perfect and human development always creates some form of crazy defensive habits – when we feel certain levels of closeness with somebody, those old habits can get triggered when we're stressed.

135

As we grow from baby to adult, the best and worst sides of our mothers, fathers, brothers, and sisters come out one way or another, and we develop habitual patterns of dealing with them. When levels of intimacy with a lover *feel* as deep as early family relationships, the habits we learned growing up – and especially defensive habits we learned when we felt attacked, threatened, or misunderstood – automatically kick in.

With poor Cindy and Tim, after five months of bliss, that one fight lit up Tim's most primitive defenses. From what I learned from Cindy, I suspect he was indulged and neglected by shallow parents, which contributed to him always assuming bad feelings were *somebody else's fault*. The distress he felt during their argument was so intolerable that he had to make Cindy wrong and gone. This is the signature narcissistic defense: demean and withdraw. Some of us (most of us) can sometimes blame others and want to take off, but we're still able to hang in and work through problems. Deeply narcissistic people can't do this, and tend to take off like Tim did.

This is why I counsel people to take their time with lovers, and, rather than worry about problems coming, *assume* problems will show up to challenge your mutual problem-solving abilities. You never know if you and your lover are able and willing to get back to love during a conflict until a conflict actually shows up and demands attention. It's a horrible sign if somebody goes crazy and leaves (like Tim did), or relentlessly attacks. It's a fantastic sign when lovers can resolve problems back to love – legitimately warranting more confidence.

Eventually, Cindy got all this, and became wiser in choosing lovers – Tim was just a little too good to be true. The road she had to travel to this new understanding was long and painful, beginning as it did with, "Cindy, one of the main risks of love is that – often – *the closer you are, the weirder it gets.*"

WHAT TYPES ARE WE? WHAT STATES ARE WE IN? WHAT'S MY MOTIVATION?

Let's look at what dialed-in Integral mindful living might look like for these two:

• Tim learns to observe his Narcissism – how he compulsively demeans women and withdraws. He learns to tolerate their penetrations of his bright shell, and opens himself to healing up the frightening black holes below. He commits to meeting his shadow and integrating into evolutionary relating, capable of tolerating pain in service of love, and doing the work to sustain the love of a good woman.

• Cindy recognizes her allure with Narcissists, and chooses mature men able to get back to love.
• Ebbs and flows of beautiful, good, and true currents naturally help them navigate life. They become sensitive to these currents of experience, accept them with caring intent, discuss them, and grow through the process.

• Cindy and Tim see defensive states like the sun rising, and learn to instantly shift into dialed-in.

Attuning to myself and you opens the channels. Integral understanding provides directions to be on purpose, with compassion, in the present moment.

DIALED-IN LOVE AFFAIRS FOR EVERYBODY

Give this chapter to a potential lover, or, better still, *read* this chapter aloud to a potential lover. Try the Five Star methods and discuss each Star with your lover.

If you're already in love, relax, have fun, and when problems show up, do your best to get back to love. Get help if you need it.

That's how we create dialed-in love affairs.

Chapter 8: Dialed-in and Clueless Marriages; Heaven or Hell

By all means marry; if you get a good wife, you'll become happy; if you get a bad one, you'll become a philosopher. – Socrates

At sunrise of my wedding day, I ran up into a canyon behind my house. The canyon is called Seven Falls because a stream cuts down through a series of cliffs, moderately difficult to climb, and during the wet season water cascades over them. That day the canyon was still and beautiful as the sun rose. I was completely alone.

After I climbed the first two rock faces, I took off all my clothes and walked naked up the stream, carefully scaling the sandstone walls until I came to a point where the stream rushed through a huge v-shaped rock interface, directly facing the Channel Islands in the distance. I sat on a rock in the fresh morning sunlight and meditated on the streambed stretching down beneath me, the ocean framed by the canyon walls. I relaxed into unity with nature and, as the meditation deepened, two red dragonflies arrived and hovered, suspended two feet in front of my eyes, and mated.

It seemed like a good sign, and it was. Becky and I had an outrageously fun wedding, followed by twenty-six years (and counting) of a magnificent marriage.

Two days before, we had hiked up the canyon to the pump station, and had a screaming fight. "Well let's call it all off then!" I screamed at her, my voice echoing into the mountains.

Looking back, I wonder about my lack of curiosity about the extreme contrasts between the intense, magical love I felt for Becky on our wedding day, and the aggressive rage I had felt two days before. Back then I did what most couples do, normalize outsized shifts in states of consciousness from "I love you!" to "I hate you!" to "I love you!" in minutes, hours, or days.

Marriage is difficult and irresistible

Most people expect to get married, and most do, but it's a rough ride. Modern marriage challenges us in ways unimaginable a hundred years ago. Men and women have equal power financially, sexually, parentally, and in decision making. Forty-one percent of households have a wife making more money than her husband. Significantly longer lifespans challenge us to stay in love for decades longer than previous generations, and modern secular society accepts divorce as a fact of life. In the U.S. over 25% of children are raised by single parents, and 41% of children are born to single mothers (many couples have kids without getting married).

Even though most people seek marriage (and expect marriage to go well – few marry *expecting* divorce), the common wisdom is that marriage is difficult.

We've all heard the confusing American statistics in one form or another:

- Around 50% of first marriages and 65% of second marriages end in divorce, but almost all marriages begin with confident predictions of lifelong love.

- Statistically, second marriages don't last as long as first marriages, but people describe themselves as happier in second marriages.

- A sixth to a third of married people cheat on their spouse (and this is the conservative figure – some studies show a third to half).

- Fifteen percent of marriages have one partner with a secret bank account.

- Men who cheat spend more money on presents for their lovers than for their wives.

- Two-thirds of women and half of men say they are "very" or "extremely" likely to marry for money.

- Sixty-three percent of 18 to 24-year-olds believe most marriages are not happy, but 77% of them want to marry before having children, and 80% believe marriage makes a relationship stronger.

- Young people in the United States are marrying later than ever before in history; around age 29 for men and 27 for women.

We want marriage; marriage Is difficult and dangerous

Thursday, Keith and Becky are screaming insults at each other, their voices echoing across the canyon of Tunnel Road trail in the foothills behind their house. Saturday, they love each other beyond measure, mythic figures in a dream wedding. Reconciling such extremes into more consistent love is central to dialed-in marriage.

Modern marriage is the most demanding intimate relationship that has ever existed – even dangerous, since over 25% of murders in this country involve love triangles. Historically, marriage was either more casual or economically motivated than today.

- **Casual:** Many hunter-gatherer tribes have about the same rates of divorce as modern couples. In Europe well into the middle ages, a couple could marry by jumping over a broom together until the Catholic church took over the sanctification of marriage – certainly partly as a means of social control.

- **Economically motivated:** Agrarian cultures needed stability and kids to work the farms. Arranged marriages (still popular and accepted in India) were calculated to preserve and expand wealth and social status. The male domination in agrarian cultures made it difficult to impossible for women to choose to leave (significantly, in contemporary college educated couples, women are most likely to initiate divorce).

Historic marriages were shorter (we live almost twice as long now as a hundred years ago), survival based (couples needed each other to survive

140

and needed kids to work the farm and take care of them in old age), and didn't particularly expect lifelong love, friendship, or eroticism.

In today's world of men and women having equal power financially, socially, sexually, and in parenting, people want a best friend, a great lover for life, a superior parent, a reliable business partner, and a good communicator, and *often feel ripped off or outraged when just one of these characteristics is absent!*

Relating in an intimate relationship is a line of development with progressive stages. Dialed-in marriage understands that we need to negotiate these stages together.

A challenge in a happy enduring marriage is that both partners need to grow through progressive stages of intimacy in complementary ways. Take secrets for example. Many marriages begin with couples having me-first habits of keeping secrets. As they grow more intimate, the standard shifts towards we-first transparency, which yields more closeness and familiarity, but can become predictable, entitled (as in *you're obligated to tell me everything about you*), and can smother eroticism and fun. Dialed-in couples who challenge dissatisfaction with shared willingness to grow, can progress to love-first standards where transparency is a privilege that needs to be respected, and secrets might be desirable if they lead to more love and eroticism.

Crazy blind spots can lead us to bliss

Practically, we grow by enjoying each other and using crazy blind spots as opportunities to progress on the marital bliss line of development.

A good place to resolve crazy blind spots is to notice when you turn someone into an object, and commit to do whatever it takes to make them a person again.

We can do violence to objects. Most of us have trouble deliberately hurting a person.

Treating people like objects is always a bad idea

A couple in their forties sit facing one another in my office, stiff, uncomfortable, and believing their marriage is a mess. Eric is a successful accountant and Camille is a part-time bookkeeper and mostly a stay-at-home mom, dedicated to her family. On paper, it looks like they're living the American dream – successful, faithful, not addicted to anything, and living in a nice house in a beautiful city raising two healthy, pleasant kids doing well in good schools.

141

But, of course, if everything were really wonderful in their world, they wouldn't be sitting in my office. I can tell from the minute Eric starts talking – or rather, complaining – that they have some serious problems. The more he shares his laundry list of Camille's faults, staring off into space rather than looking at her or at me, the more Camille – more passive and hungry to please – visibly shrivels, listening with a pained and long-suffering expression.

"Camille doesn't hear me when I talk," Eric drones on cluelessly. "She doesn't understand me at all. She doesn't realize how hard I work to please my clients. She just doesn't get it that when I get home, I need the kids to be quiet and give me some space. She..."

Usually I interrupt these kind of selfish and one-sided attacks, but on this day I'm intrigued by Eric's escalating hostility combined with the rather stunning level of emotional deadness between them, so I let him continue.

Suddenly, Camille leaps up and screams, "FUCK YOU, ERIC!" She then runs out of the room, and starts hammering the wall in my waiting room so viciously, over and over again, that I later have to hire a carpenter to fix the door.

The minute Camille storms out, Eric looks at me in shocked surprise. I smile ruefully, then walk out to Camille, still furiously banging and shaking. When she sees me, she calms down as quickly as she erupted and accompanies me back into the office. Eric regards her with tender concern, while she, on the other hand, sits glaring at him, breathing heavily. Their roles have completely shifted. And the energy in the room has changed, too. All the tired, spaced-out, aggravated vibe has dissipated, replaced with an air of intimate, charged danger.

I wait for about twenty seconds, and then say, "Everyone hates being treated like an object."

"What do you mean?" Eric asks.

What I meant was that most human cruelty and rage involves treating others as objects, not as thinking, feeling, sensitive people, and that's what I went on to describe to Eric and Camille.

Any objectified person on the receiving end of cruelty, rage, or disrespect is going to respond with defensive states. Your body instinctively reacts to perceived threats by unleashing a cascade of hormones like adrenaline and cortisol, activating the fight/flight reaction that is a legacy of our cave-dweller days. If a terrifying saber-toothed tiger on the rampage is chasing you, survival depends on you either fighting back with whatever weapons you've got – good luck with that by the way–or taking flight and hoping for the best. Usually, the more threat you feel, the more stress hormones flood your bloodstream, preparing you to fight or flee. Under such circumstances, it's natural to get upset and lose perspective – and especially lose empathy for any tormentor – and blow your top.

The fight/flight reaction also explains why anger so often leads to violence – violent thoughts, impulses, tones, words, and actions. Such violence isn't necessarily physical, or even directed at others. You can be the recipient of your own violence and anger if you regularly attack yourself with judgments, guilt, and shame. Defensive states don't just have distorted perspectives and violent impulses towards others, they have them towards ourselves, too.

Let's get back to Eric and Camille. Eric's mindless litany of criticisms – which in truth didn't pour out of him because he really felt neglected by his wife, but from his anger and anxiety about his job, his status, his loneliness, and his future – turned Camille into an object. He unconsciously exploited her more passive and gentle nature, and went after her because such attacks gave him some marginal relief. Eventually, Camille reached a critical mass of bottled-up rage. Instead of attacking Eric to his face as he'd done to her – her nervous system knew this was a dangerous invitation for abuse from an aggressive man – she literally attacked an object. The wall couldn't scream back or hurt her, unless she bruised her hands.

As Eric and Camille were calming down, I suddenly remembered something about objectification and anger – a scene from my teen years in the sixties – and I told them the following story.

The rattlesnake and the rat

One of my first lessons in objectification didn't come from people at all. I learned it while writing a high school biology paper about a rattlesnake and a rat.

In 1966 my father was a biology teacher at Northview High School in Covina, California. In those days teachers were allowed to keep caged rattlesnakes in the classroom (something rather unthinkable nowadays – can you imagine the liability nightmare? For good reasons, as my dad's snakes did get loose once!). He kept two Pacific rattlers in a glass terrarium. They would only eat live rodents, so every month or so he put a couple of lab rats in the cage and let nature take her course.

I was enraptured with dinosaurs, predators, and rattlesnakes in particular, so for one of my science papers I asked my dad if I could watch the feeding process and report on it, and he gladly agreed. I had no idea how creepy and significant the experience would turn out to be.

We went into his classroom on a Saturday, and there lay the two rattlesnakes, one about two feet long and the other slightly bigger, coiled motionless around the rocks at the bottom of their terrarium. Totally pure scientist blasé, my dad picked up a small rat and a bigger rat from a rodent cage and dropped them into the terrarium, while I gazed in fascinated horror at the unfolding drama.

The rats completely freaked out, skittering desperately to escape before ending up hopelessly cowering in tiny corners of the cage. Meanwhile, the snakes woke up and began writhing around. Suddenly, one of them coiled and reared up, looking to me about twice as big and ten times scarier – and its rattle started the famous, horrible chattering. (Here's a nice piece of trivia: European horses brought to the New World went nuts when they heard this sound – doubtless a genetic memory.) The snake's mouth gaped open, the venomous fangs prominently displayed so that it became almost a caricature of terrifying reptilian danger. Its head shot forward unbelievably quickly, striking viciously at the smaller rat. *Wham! Wham!* Two lightning-quick bites, and the poor little rat flew around the cage in a panicked blur of motion for a few seconds and abruptly collapsed. The snake leisurely coiled around the corpse, and, starting with the head, slowly swallowed the rat whole before settling back down into its original position in the terrarium.

This experience was stunning enough, but it was not the main lesson I took from the whole episode. The other snake was apparently not hungry, and so the remaining rat spent *the next two days* stuck in the terrarium with two rattlesnakes until my dad finally took it out because he said – and this blew my mind – "The rat might hurt the snakes."

I've always wondered what those forty-eight hours had been like for that rat, trapped in a small cage with two vastly larger predators that could have cared less about it. Objectively, it was fairly safe, since one snake had just satiated itself, and the other clearly wasn't hungry (unlike humans, reptiles never eat unless they really need a meal – snakes don't seem to have much fun, really), but the rat couldn't know it was safe.

I realized that the rat was obviously just an object to these snakes, as it was to my father when he put it in with them. The rat's terror, alarm, and imminent painful death weren't relevant to anybody – not my father, me initially, and, of course, the snakes.

I've thought a lot about that rat in subsequent years, and what went on in its little rat brain for those two days. Especially as this feeding session took place when our country was in tumult, and at the time I was a teenager trying to figure out what my place in the world was going to be. I often felt trapped in a cage of the times myself, and found it offensive that people were being treated like objects everywhere. Civil rights abuses were rampant, and the Vietnam War was raging on the news each night, with daily, mounting American body counts that a lot of people didn't seem to care much about (and seemed to care even less about the Vietnamese being killed by the thousands). Teenagers, just two years older than me, were being drafted by the thousands (cannon fodder objects) and forced to fight overseas – the American equivalent of the child soldiers that horrify us so much today in Africa. That the society I was living in normalized objectification as business-as-usual struck my teenaged sensibility as profoundly wrong – completely violating my "good" validity standards.

I've occasionally recalled that rat while doing therapy, like in the session with Eric and Camille. I see on a daily basis how much hurt comes from people turning loved ones into objects to attack, seduce, manipulate, or use.

Any of us can be that rat trapped in a cage, spending endless hours alone, knowing we are objects of convenience for somebody who wants to use us solely for their own gratification.

And any of us can be that snake, attacking or using another being for our own selfish purposes, without a care about how that being really feels.

Once Eric and Camille got the message about not treating each other like objects, it marked a real breakthrough in their marriage, because they'd finally become conscious of each other's humanity, even when upset. They could be distressed, yet still see the other person as a real human being with fears and hurts. Their love and compassion for each other deepened over the years, and I'm happy to say that the man who could so easily insult his wife, and the woman who attacked my wall, are now entering the fourth decade of a pretty good marriage.

What to do when we find ourselves objectifying another, especially our spouse? One dialed-in technique is emotional dialysis.

Emotional dialysis

James Grotstein is a psychoanalyst/author who lives and works in Los Angeles. He's brilliant, funny, and can make dry psychoanalytic giants like Melanie Klein and Wilfred Bion sound hip and interesting.

I saw him speak once in Los Angeles, where he was the "mop up squad," as he called it, at a neuroscience and psychoanalysis conference. He stood at the podium, the epitome of an elegant elder psychoanalytic statesman – regal, white hair swept back over his forehead, rumpled suit, and endearing, absent-minded-professor brilliance. His job was to integrate the multiple perspectives advanced by the many clinicians and researchers throughout the weekend, and Jim did a credible job. He was especially entranced with Dan Stern's book, *The Present Moment in Psychotherapy and Everyday Life,* and discussed how experienced therapists anchor themselves in *right now.*

At one point, Dr. Grotstein became impassioned as he described Bion's idea that mothers engage in emotional "dialysis" with their babies, helping them process and program emotional experience, through intimate inter-subjective relationships of understanding, holding, nursing, caring, vocalizing, and gazing.

Then, with a sly twinkle in his eye, he pointed out how therapists perform similar inter-subjective dialysis, helping clients process, understand, and integrate thoughts, memories, and emotions into more coherent life stories. "The therapist gives the patient visitation rights with himself," he said to general laughter, but there was a poignant undertone. Most clinicians in the audience knew the feeling of helping another work through emotional toxins to reach the soulful purity of authentic self that we all yearn to identify with as "*me.*"

I love "emotional dialysis." It totally applies to all relationships – even with ourselves. It involves self-observation of whether we're in an unhealthy me-first moment of selfishness, an unhealthy we-first moment of reflexive rigidity, or in love-first response to the present moment.

Check out the following two hypothetical conversations between a gay couple, Tim and Andrew, discussing the upcoming wedding of Andrew's niece, Wanda.

First conversation:

Andrew: "Wanda hates it when you drink too much and get rowdy at parties, so lighten up at the wedding."

Tim: "What do you mean, 'rowdy?' She and I have closed more than one club, dancing and drinking. You get so uptight with your family!"

Andrew: "You never listen! Don't embarrass us again!"

Tim: "Again? What do you mean, 'again?' How dare you call me 'an embarrassment!'"

Andrew: "How dare I? Remember Cabo last year? You know, when they called the cops?"

Second conversation:

Andrew: "Wanda hates it when you drink too much and get rowdy at parties, so lighten up at the wedding."

Tim: "I thought she liked partying with me. God knows we've done it enough over the years."

Andrew: "You're right, and we've had lots of fun! But this wedding is a big deal to her, and I think she wants us to be more mellow at the reception."

Tim: "Did she say anything?"

Andrew: "Not exactly, but she went on about how her fiancé's family are 'conservative.'"

Tim: "I can see your point, but what if she wants us to – you know – liven up the party. The family can be *so* boring!"

Andrew (laughing): "Well, let's stay attuned to her during the night and try to make it great for *her.*"

Tim: "I like that. Help me out if you think I'm pushing it too far."

Andrew: "No problem. Thanks for listening."

Which conversation do *you* prefer? I absolutely prefer the second. Tim and Andrew are dialysizing the initial distress by listening and bringing more acceptance and cooperation to bear with each exchange. They are taking the toxins *out* and leaving the love *in* – essentially engaging in emotional dialysis to purify their exchange. You can feel how the anger subsides and the attunement, understanding, love, and humor blossoms.

Apparently, such exchanges might happen more frequently with gay partners. In a couple of studies, John Gottman found that gay couples were especially good at using humor and a sense of equal power and fairness to slow down conflict and speed up repair in difficult situations.

All good therapists perform emotional dialysis. During marriage counseling sessions, I can feel the toxic and nutritious elements of clients' exchanges, and I deliberately help them strain out the toxins and focus on the nourishment. Often, after we make the transition to more accepting understanding, I'll point out what just happened, and encourage the same at home. Many toxic processes are variants of, "I hate myself," or "I hate *you!*" If you can focus on emotional dialysis as soon as you notice such violent perspectives, good things happen.

Try it next time you feel bummed out about yourself or someone you're talking with. Accept the icky feeling while simultaneously attempting to soften the hostile parts and grow the parts that want more warmth and shared understanding. I suspect you'll discover such emotional dialysis heals and purifies.

Evolutionary relationships

About 50% of marriages end in divorce (which makes marriage the number one predictor of divorce, if you think about it). On the other hand, 50% of marriages become life-partnerships, and I'd say about half of those are mostly mutually satisfying. What characterizes the happy marriages? Well, one big characteristic is that people grow together and support each other's development, or *personal evolution.* They become evolutionary relationships.

A couple of years ago, my friend Patricia Albere asked me to talk with her about evolutionary relationships on the Evolutionary Collective Conversations program she offers periodically. Her passion is understanding and supporting clean, authentic intimacy – profound mutuality. She and I both believe such relationships are the cutting edge of evolution.

Patricia Albere is a transformational educator and contemporary spiritual teacher with a passionate focus on Evolutionary Relationships and Collective Consciousness. For the last forty years, her core commitment has been to teach from the emerging edge of consciousness, awakening others to the profound depths and infinite wisdom possible between two or more people connected to something higher and greater.

It was a fun hour. I think the term "evolutionary relationships" is a redundancy, since I believe evolution has always been relational, from the Big Bang all the way to now, and that all relationships have at least some aspect of reaching for greater coherence and understanding – they are *evolving*. But, I also understand that there are forms of mature mutuality that are extraordinary and require great depth – and these are what Patricia calls "evolutionary relationships" and what she has such love for.

One aspect of evolutionary relationships that I don't think is widely enough discussed is that *our ability to be intimate* grows as we mature – it is a *line of development*. As we discussed in Chapter 5, lines of development are characterized by successive stages that can't be skipped – we must crawl before we walk, and walk before we run. Simple awareness grows to self-awareness, grows to family awareness, and grows to awareness of everything. We're not born speaking in full sentences, or thinking coherent thoughts – we need to gradually learn how to speak and think.

All animals have stages of relating. A chimpanzee starts out totally dependent on his mom, and learns to move around, fend for himself, and play with other chimps. As he becomes more independent in the troop, he reaches sexual maturity and begins mating with sexually available females and competing with other males for dominance. Once he earns alpha male status (if ever), he's ascended as far as you can rise on the chimpanzee social ladder.

Two hundred thousand years ago, when the two critical mutations on the FOXP2 gene gave humans the powers of symbolic communication and grammar, we began growing into new capacities for self-awareness and intimacy. These new capacities created potentials for *new levels* on almost every developmental line.

Since then:

- We extended artistic impulses into incredible masterpieces, as demonstrated by cave paintings 30,000 years ago in France, progressing to the artistic miracles of today.

- We expanded our abilities to hunt with new weapons and cooperative strategies that resulted in the extinction of thousands of other species (not a good thing, but an incredible demonstration of increasing technological/ ecological power).

- Socially, we grew into *tribes,* with traditions (first oral, and then written) including intricate rules and roles, into *nations* with shared identifications, and even further into *spiritual/philosophical communities* joined by values like universal care and rights for all.

New developmental levels are never realized all at once. For the last two hundred thousand years, the human race has been growing into *capacities* created by the FOXP2 and other mutations, and those capacities extend beyond where *any* of us currently are – we don't know the upper limits of any human developmental line, including profound intimacy.

How does this apply to evolutionary relationships? Well, think about it. If there are ascending levels of mutuality, and we are stable at wherever we are *now,* love can guide us to new, higher levels. Those higher levels will have new characteristics, rules, roles, and possibilities – they are like new countries to be explored – but we have to grow to be relatively stable at those new levels to figure out what they're about.

For example:

- It's normal for eight-year-old boys to want to hang out mostly with other boys, and for eight-year-old girls with other girls, and to not be particularly sexually driven.

- If they keep growing, teens start craving contact and intimacy with the opposite sex, and want social/sexual connections that feel age appropriate to whatever cultures they identify with.

- Further on, it's normal for many 18 to 25-year-olds to experiment with sexual relationships. Some are promiscuous. Some are celibate. Some try non-monogamy. Some cheat on their lovers or are cheated on themselves. Around the world, these are all normal variations and experiences for young adults.

- If these young men and women keep maturing, they tend to want more stable relationships that involve the shared values of monogamy and transparency. When someone begins insisting on monogamy and deeper honesty with lovers, they've grown to a new relational level where such shared values are necessary for the kind of intimacy they crave.

• People can develop deeper connections through self-awareness, embracing different perspectives, and conscious eroticism – often demand characteristics of deeper marital mutuality.

Levels stretch beyond these, but we need to grow to get to them. Not surprisingly, at higher levels, *the rules change* towards honesty, transparency, and mutuality.

Intimacy

We encounter new relational interests, demands, and experiences as we develop. It's always a fun exercise to examine what relational needs and values you have right now – try writing them down. For instance, some single people I work with value the autonomy of not being committed to a particular partner. Some people in a relationship value the companionship of being married to a "best friend." What are your values and needs regarding relationships?

A further fun exercise is to discuss what you've written with intimate friends, lovers, or family members and see how the conversations progress. Do you feel more intimate? Less intimate? Do the conversations lead to deeper love? More conflict? All of the above?

Just doing these exercises requires a certain amount of relational maturity, because it's a developmental achievement to be able to stand somewhat outside yourself and your relationships and observe more objectively. Such self-reflection and conversation challenges you to reach for deeper understanding – and deeper understanding is the hallmark of evolutionary relationships and dialed-in marriages.

"That's all very well," you might be thinking, "But how do I apply it practically?"

It's often good to remember your powers as a partner and lover – powers to create more love or bewildering chaos – and there are a million techniques to create more love. One cool one is paying attention to relational passwords.

Relational Passwords

In the movie *2001: A Space Odyssey,* director Stanley Kubrick had HAL the computer be an immature, petulant, super-powerful machine God who waged war on two poor astronauts who were just trying to make it to Mars.

Most of us have had similar computer/human intimate moments ("What? Where are my files?! Evil computer God! What have you done with my files?!").

On the other hand, when a document comes out the way I want, I'm soothed that my computer has listened and – *yes!* – done exactly what I told it to do.

The needs for computer security and privacy have given us *passwords* – secret combinations of letters and symbols accessing special personal realms of knowledge and power.

Well, nervous systems – arguably super-computers – also have passwords that open us up to both blissful and horrific states, memories, and reactions. In intimate relationships, partners naturally generate both negative and positive passwords they instinctively go to in moments of distress or pleasure.

Negative Passwords

"You're just like your mother!" in an argument tends to be on the horrific end of the continuum (though, in defense of loving mothers everywhere – I have heard this phrase used as the most profound form of compliment). Usually the password, "You're just like your mother!" evokes outraged states in a spouse – often leading to indignant fiery defenses and nasty counterattacks.

Doesn't it seem a little strange that a husband or wife – having used such a loser password repeatedly with agonizing/destructive effect – would fling it *again* in an angry moment? If insanity is repeating the same behavior while expecting different results, isn't it insane to look at your

152

angry wife for the fiftieth time and say the magic, "You're just like your mother!" password?

Yes, it is insane – reflexively lashing out is mindless in the short run, and clueless in the long run because you refuse to notice the bad habit and resolve to learn better responses. But there is a neurological method to this madness. This husband's brain has been conditioned to believe, "You're just like your mother!" actually protects him and serves his wife by trying to wake her up to change for the better. He has not yet done the necessary work to condition his nervous system to automatically deliver superior responses, so he reflexively – habitually – goes to the old clueless standby.

We can change such habits by consciously deciding enough times to say something potentially more likely to get us back to love. This is one of the best methods for replacing the old, "You're just like your mother!" clueless, passwords with smart dialed-in passwords.

Positive passwords

There are positive passwords we can hear or say with magical effects. They can help us shift from disturbed, regressed clueless states into more caring, mature dialed-in states. For instance:

- "I'm sorry you're distressed. How can I help?" delivered with love, feels pretty wonderful.

- "You're right. I do need to change this bad habit. I will make progress," can reassure your partner that you receive positive influence.

Each time we mindfully refuse a negative and choose a positive password, we take a step forward in social power and capacity to love.

Brenda and Doug

Brenda and Doug, a couple in their late twenties, finally got the power of passwords in the middle of a heated argument, almost two years into their therapy.

Brenda would never validate or acknowledge Doug's points. His angry, dismissive demeanor and shut down emotional body were like fingernails screeching on a blackboard to her, and the last thing she wanted to do was be generous, caring, or inclusive.

Doug would never let himself see Brenda's yearning for love and communion beneath her superior, alarmed, or dismissive attitudes, so he kept grinding her in conflict rather than learning ways to reach her heart.

In this breakthrough session I said, "Look Brenda. You want Doug's warmth and masculine presence. A positive password validates the worth of his ideas and acknowledges the efforts he's making."

I turned my head, "Doug. If you want to be heard by Brenda, your password is to see her as her adorable self, yearning for love. Always speak to that adorable Brenda. Remember, you get who you talk to. Talk to the bitch, you get the bitch. Talk to your adorable Brenda, you get adorable Brenda."

They both sat in stunned silence for a bit. Such insights can be both exciting and confusing.

Later in the session, Doug became dismissive and critical, caught himself, and smiled, saying, "I know you're adorable and want to love me better right now." Brenda laughed, warmed up, and responded with her own positive password, "You make good points about how critical I can be, and I will get more appreciative and praise you more." Doug lit up hearing this.

Brenda turned to me and said, "This has to be a chapter in one of your books, Keith. This password thing is so true."

She's right. Our nervous systems are programmed to respond in certain ways, and we can use this to support harmony/love/evolution.

Password Exercise:

> • *Make a list of pronouncements you typically make to your upset partner that never work, and usually make things worse.*

> • *Now make a list of specific statements that have helped or might help.*

> • *Do the same two exercises for negative and positive statements your partner makes to you. You know, upset pronouncements that never make things better, and then a list of specific statements that actually help when you hear them.*

• *Share all this with your partner, and see if you can have a conversation of positive passwords. If you can, I guarantee you'll get closer and sweeter.*

If the exercise doesn't work, but you still want to make progress, call a therapist and ask for a little help. Sometimes – like with Brenda and Doug – having a supportive third party point out positive and negative passwords makes them more visible and changeable.

Either way, noticing the power in relational passwords expands your choices in how to love better – and such choices help you move from clueless to dialed-in.

Dialed-in marriages

Dialed-In Marriages are always adjusting to love, transparency, and authenticity

You might be noticing the progression from dialed-in love affairs to dialed-in marriages involves ongoing self-observation, growth, and the giving and receiving of influence. If you practice attuning to yourself and others daily, you'll accelerate your growth.

The interpersonal and psychosexual lines of development are particularly important in marriages, and modern marriage requires conscious commitment to health and growth on both.

Attunement – being aware with acceptance and caring intent, on purpose, with compassionate judgments – positions us to make superior decisions. Understanding healthy and unhealthy states, driven by whatever types we are, along with sound principles of superior relating, gives us the opportunity to know the differences between clueless, mindless, and dialed-in, and cultivate the *responsibility* to always be reaching for dialed-in.

Since this is so easy when we feel great about our husband or wife, I've focused a lot on adjusting from conflict into attuned bliss – a big deal, since couples researcher, John Gottman, found that escalating conflict predicted probable divorce by the sixth year of marriage. That being said, he also found that couples who couldn't have good times together eventually divorced after an average of seventeen years – apparently it's just as important to generate good times as to de-escalate bad times. This is one reason I've written so much about sex. Arranging for your love affair to keep feeling alive with your spouse is a pretty effective way of keeping the good times rolling.

But relationships are not just *me*. They are *you and me*. No matter how much emotional dialysis you do, or how superior your relational passwords are, or how transparent and authentic you become, your partner needs to reply in kind, or your marriage deteriorates.

"What about when my spouse can't be touched, no matter what I do?" Often when I hear some variation of this question, I talk about the castle, the gate, and the threshold.

The castle, gate, and threshold

In fairy tales, the castle can be a fortress of strength or a prison of solitude, depending upon who is in charge. Castle as fortress-of-strength shows up frequently in Tolkien's *Lord of the Rings*, protecting Frodo, Aragorn, and the good guys – Minas Tirith and Rivendale are my favorites. Castle as prison-of-solitude usually involves a princess locked up and needing rescue – think Rapunzel or Sleeping Beauty. I suspect most psychotherapists find the castle metaphor arising periodically in their sessions – it certainly shows up regularly with my clients. The following exchange with Sharon and Dennis, a couple in their forties married for seven years, illustrates how useful understanding the Castle, the Gate, and the Threshold can be.

Our fifteenth session has just begun, and Sharon stares out my French doors into the tiny garden beyond, completely avoiding Dennis. I catch her eyes, "You look locked up in a Castle."

Sharon relaxes a little, "Yes, exactly, and I don't know how to get out."

Dennis' eyes widen, "I didn't think you wanted to get out." There is a moment of surprising warmth.

At this point, we are all beginning to focus on the most alive parts of the Castle – the Gate and the Threshold. The Gate can be an angry blockade if the person on the inside keeps it shut. No amount of love, change, or words will be pleasurable to Sharon until she risks opening herself to Dennis' love – she needs to open the Gate by recognizing his goodness and receiving some warmth with pleasure to allow sweet intimacy across the Threshold. The harder Dennis tries to force his way through with explanations, excuses, arguments, bribes, or attacks – his codependent habits – the more solidly Sharon will keep the Gate locked

156

with her unforgiving anger. He needs to relax and offer patience and presence until Sharon recognizes him as a good guy with whom she wants loving contact – which opens the Gate to potential intimacy.

The Castle archetype permeates the myths of all cultures. Often a soul is locked in a citadel – usually a feminine soul, but not always – desperately needing a savior. A masculine force outside offers both healing and possible threat. Should she open the Gate? Can she trust enough to open the Gate? Trust is hard to come by when you're locked in a fortress.

At the Threshold, multiple forces meet. The masculine can become more trustable with presence, patience, and compassion; or more frightening with alarm, anger, or collapse. The feminine can accelerate love by surrendering to clean masculine presence, or refuse love by clinging to amplified anger and hostile stories, thus keeping the Gate locked.

Sharon can decide to open the gate to welcome Dennis – risking further hurt, but increasing her chances for love fulfilled. Doing so challenges Dennis to step up with compassion and affection, and resist angry, hurt impulses (like saying, "It took you forever to open the damn Gate!"). A powerful measure of masculine depth is how well a man recognizes mistakes and emotional violence in himself, and immediately adjusts to love before, during, or after the violent expression.

I tell them, "You two are at the Threshold. Sharon, I invite you to open the Gate and receive Dennis' best efforts. All you have to do is recognize your need to feel loving contact with him, and feel pleasure at his best efforts. Dennis, this is your chance to be a hero. Be excellent for her and yourself. If you do this, the Gate opens and the Threshold is alive with intimacy."

They look willing, but uncertain. I go on, "Repair of injuries needs affectionate connection, and then a little bit of progress. Look each other in the eyes and transmit affectionate connection."

They do this and smile, and Sharon giggles a little. I take a deep breath. This is a hopeful sign because couples who allow even tiny amounts of pleasurable contact do much better.

I turn to Sharon, "It's more difficult for you. Dennis lightens up when you kiss him and love him. He's always open to your affection. When your Gate is closed and Dennis is making his best efforts for both of you, you need to decide to receive love even when you think you don't want to. You need to actively open the Gate to your Castle. This allows him over the Threshold."

Sharon's face softens as she looks into Dennis' eyes, "I'll try."

Dennis visibly lights up as he reaches out to touch her knee, "I'll do my best to help."

This is a beautiful moment. If you're locked up in a Castle with someone who loves you on the other side, this is exactly what everyone (you, your partner, your family, your friends, or your therapist) wants – lovers resolving injuries into deeper love. If someone you care for is locked up and needs to open the Gate to create the possibility of repair, this is exactly what everyone wants – lovers resolving injuries into deeper love.

The Castle, the Gate, and the Threshold offer powerful myths of liberation – it's almost always a good idea to open the Gate and cross the Threshold courageously in service of love.

You'll notice that Sharon didn't particularly feel like opening the Gate, which reflects another central skill of dialed-in marriage, reaching for love when you don't feel like it.

Do it when you don't feel like it

Greg and Katy are in their early forties, sitting across from each other in my office, visibly uncomfortable with the conversation. They've been discussing each other's faults for about four minutes and we're all getting progressively more bummed out. I figure it's time to interrupt.

"Can you two feel how depressing this conversation is?" They both nod their heads. "So let's change this to something that works. You'll never get to love with critical, angry talk about problems. If you want to make progress, you have to at least shift to mutual respect, and ideally *affection*."

Greg brightens up, but looks skeptical, "That sounds fantastic, but how do we get there?"

I immediately feel lighter. This is the first positive move either has made this session. "Well, first of all, don't you feel a little better right now?" Both nod. "That's because we stopped talking about problems and complaints and started talking about affection. So, Greg, make a positive overture. I suggest you go over and touch Katy with a little tenderness – you know, warm expression, a hug, like that." Katy smiles for the first time in the session. Some people are actually so distressed by suggestions to touch affectionately that they can't stand the idea, but not Greg and Katy. They both like affection and – typically for couples – bitterly blame the other for it not happening more.

Greg slowly rises and approaches Katy as they maintain eye contact. He pauses briefly at about three feet away and looks intently into her face, searching for evidence of welcome or rejection. She seems open so he moves closer and hugs her for about ten seconds while I make approving sounds. He then sits down. Both of them are smiling nervously and a little awkwardly, but clearly the energy in the room is more positive. Then I ask Katy to do the same and she does, with similar results.

As they look back at me I capitalize on the moment, "I suggest you each do this at least five times a day." Katy turns to me and protests, "What if I don't feel like it?"

I'm briefly distracted by all the times I've heard this question over the last forty years. I take a deep breath, smile, and look into her eyes, "*Especially* do it when you don't feel like it."

Relationships are little ecosystems that need nurturing – like gardens. We're often enlivened by our partner's love and guidance, and are usually moved to give in return. But when caught up in life, responsibilities, and waning romantic infatuation, people can get lazy. This is especially true when couples don't have effective mechanisms for processing irritations, or good skills to repair inevitable marital ruptures. If you don't effectively tend the marital garden, it can become dry, barren, and neglected.

In spite of myself, I start a *Therapist in the Wild*-type (TIW) rant (if you haven't visited my website at www.drkeithwitt.com, this is a video series of brief intense messages I offer periodically). Giving myself permission in my web series to get on a soapbox for a few minutes each episode has added TIW rants to my clinical repertoire. "You brush your teeth when you don't feel like it. You go to work when you don't feel like it. You put up with your demanding/sick/distressed/obnoxious children when you don't feel like it – even force yourself to love them and help them, when all you want to do is have them shut up so you can get some sleep! So, *love each other when you don't feel like it!*"

By now both Greg and Katy are laughing. Katy answers first, "OK, OK. I get it! I'm game if Greg is."

Greg gets a little more serious, "I have a feeling if we do it when we don't feel like it, we're going to feel like it a lot more."

Katy and I sit in quiet admiration for Greg's wisdom. When people reach for love, quality insights often show up.

I smile and give them one more *Therapist in the Wild* line, "For now, my work here is done."

But what about when the same negative patterns show up again and again?

Consciousness came to humans with a price. Our animal drives didn't stop when we became self-aware – they became enormously more variable and complex. For example, only we humans have *genetically driven instincts* to adorn our bodies with garments and jewelry, create art, and think in metaphors.

We are social animals, we *must* relate. We have difficulty being in the presence of another without creating some kind of social contract. Try sitting in a waiting room with another person without making *any* connection – it's impossible. At the very least you'll feel a subtle exchange of acknowledgement and social positioning (leaning towards or away, greeting or not greeting).

We also hardwire habits quickly from behaviors. Each time we relate in a certain way – for instance, offering love to anger, or offering anger to love – *we are more likely to go there again.*

Repetitive interactions co-create powerful, demanding relational patterns, driven by evolution and shaped by self-awareness and culture. Most of us automatically offer welcoming smiles when being introduced – an engaging habit of social communion. Some of us instinctively tense and defend when criticized – usually a separating, self-defeating habit. As such patterns are repeated, they constellate into forms which self-reinforce until they become reflexive ways of perceiving, thinking, and responding.

The habits that dominate our waking and sleeping lives (yes, we have habitual patterns even in our dreams) are almost all *relational* patterns with ourselves, others, the world, memories/fantasies/anticipations, and with the stories we automatically generate about all experience. *Each repetition* reinforces itself in our nervous system, making us more likely to relate that way again in similar-feeling situations.

The shorter answer to, "What's the deal with creating the same negative patterns?

It happens, but if we keep reaching for deeper love and more self-understanding, we can transcend almost any toxic habit.

The longer answer?

160

Most of us try to love well, and it's easy to feel like a failure if things don't work out or end badly. We all suffer *some* romantic shame or regrets. I've wished so many times that I'd spent the afternoon at Laurie Garretson's house when I was 17 and she asked me in on my way to get a neck X-ray. She was my first hot kiss, and there would have been a lot more of them if I'd had the wherewithal to blow off my doctor's appointment.

In such remorseful moments, I try to remind myself: *"Lighten up! It's all about effort and progress. Keep moving towards love."*

People hardly ever get intimacy right the first few times. Think about it.

- Are *you* with the first person you fell in love with?

- Are *you* blissfully happy with your spouse and have no doubts whatsoever about your marriage?

If the answer to either is "yes," then God bless you both! The rest of us usually have to get our asses kicked more than once before we start getting into healthy, stable relationship territory.

In one study, a thousand people were asked if they'd ever been dumped by someone they *really* loved, or had dumped someone who *really* loved them. *Over ninety percent* said, "yes" to both questions. Committed intimacy always involves some suffering. When it comes to love, we get the bad with the good.

For instance, each of us is genetically programmed to lust after desirable partners, fall in love with a special person, attach with that person for around four years, and also either cheat or break up to search for new love interests. Culture and consciousness profoundly affect (and moderate) these drives, but they can't be safely suppressed or ignored – we need to work with them to create satisfying relationships.

As we mature, we can integrate our drives with our developing values and learn to connect closer and sweeter. *Satisfying* long term monogamy is possible, but challenging – it needs depth, courage, and willingness in both partners.

I so admire couples who keep improving love – and transcendent love *as an ideal* is ubiquitous. Myths, books, records, and anthropological research reflect the human fascination with enduring, lifelong love – history, literature, mythology, and art is rife with such inspiring romantic tragedies, comedies, and rhapsodies.

The problem is, if both partners can't keep love growing, genetically driven ancestral voices start demanding lust, infatuation, attachment, cheating/separation, and then moving on.

The bottom line?

What's the bottom line? If we don't get better at *recognizing* good partners, *being* a good partner, and *growing* in relationships, we're at risk to be overwhelmed by our social/sexual drives.

Myths – enduring cultural stories – also reveal archetypal forms of catastrophic and tragic human bonding. Examples are Paris and Helen recklessly swept up in romantic infatuation leading to the fall of Troy, the Greek God Cupid ravishing and deserting Psyche, or Gilgamesh spending much of his life driven by regret and loss of his best friend. These epics reflect genetic mandates, ancestral voices sung through emotion and impulse – evolutionary choirs guiding and driving us.

HOW TO GROW BEAUTIFUL RELATIONSHIPS FROM TOXIC PATTERNS?

Most people are self-aware enough to notice patterns like, "I always feel hurt and leave," or "Someone cheats and dumps me." Everyone wants to break out of painful cycles, but it's hard to figure out exactly what to do.

The bad news about repetitive problems is they demand attunement and attention in order to transform – destructive relational habits usually need our conscious focus to change.

The good news about repetitive problems is that they point *specifically* towards necessary work of attunement and adjustments from clueless, to mindful, to dialed-in. Examples might include:

- If you keep being cheated on, whom are you choosing and how do you attune to lovers?

- If you keep losing interest and leaving, why aren't you fighting harder for love with someone you've opened your heart to?

Exploring these questions can resolve such patterns, and also lead to deeper maturity on our interpersonal and psychosexual lines of development.

It starts with whom we choose

Who do we seek out for intimacy? We've already discussed how couples researcher, John Gottman, believes that at birth, we begin generating "love maps" of whom we'll be drawn to. I agree with him. This speaks to the mysteries of romance.

More specific principles are revealed by social research and the wisdom traditions. For instance:

> • Men tend to prefer women around three and a half inches shorter, while women tend to prefer men around three and a half inches taller.

> • On energetic levels, the feminine opens to trustable masculine presence, while the masculine offers an unambiguous claim ("I want *you*.") that can magnetize feminine radiance and surrender.

> • On defensive levels, we are drawn to complementary wounds (the alcoholic drawn to the co-dependent helper, or the victim to the persecutor).

> • All these perspectives grow through developmental levels, beginning with me-first selfishness, developing towards we-first mutuality, and ultimately reaching for love-first what-serves-love-right-now kindness and connection.

This last point about developmental levels is huge. If we know we grow through levels and that effort-and-progress growth mindset standards are superior, we can become more patient with ourselves and our partners at whatever level we happen to be functioning from.

Commit to effort and progress, and eventually the worst "*find a partner, fall in love, somebody cheats or acts badly, painful drama, messy breakup, start all over again*" pattern starts moving towards sturdier love.

So, that's the deal with repetitive negative patterns. They exist. They are strong and destructive. But, we have gifts and resources.

With effort and progress, some good always happens, so focused intent and assertive action usually yields growth. On an even brighter note, love is so powerfully programmed into our genes that – if we commit to change for the better – miracles are possible.

163

I've observed countless courageous people over the decades transcend the most toxic relationship patterns to create sweet, stable love. We all are capable of loving better. We can transform negative patterns into positive growth.

DIALED-IN MARRIAGE IS A LIFELONG PROCESS THAT REQUIRES WE

If you want more strategies and tactics to create and sustain dialed-in marriages, check out my blogs on drkeithwitt.com, or take almost any relationship book to heart. Diverse methods of giving and receiving loving influence seem to work well if people decide to practice them.

Let's move forward in the family life cycle a little. What about parenting? Most parents want to do super-right by their kids. How do we become superior parents?

Let's find out in Chapter 9: Dialed-in parenting

Chapter 9: Dialed-in Parenting

If you're reading this chapter, you're probably already a parent (if not, good for you! You're interested in one of the most important human skill sets – dialed-in parenting). If you have a child, you know the intense hunger for your kid to thrive – to be happy, healthy, successful, and to love well.

Remember the fourth of the Five Stars from Chapter 7? *Is this person – or would this person be – a superior parent?* A superior parent does his or her best to cherish and protect children, and commits to a lifetime of becoming a better parent. Effort and progress over a lifetime, growth-mindset parenting, is the gold standard for increasing your kid's chances for a rich life.

Dialed-in is awareness with acceptance and a caring intent, on purpose, with compassionate judgment, in the present moment, informed by Integral understanding. Our purpose around kids is to be superior parents. Integral understanding involves intense curiosity about each child's interior – the subjective feel of their universe – plus sound principles, and beautiful, good, and true practices for optimizing development.

When my children, Zoe and Ethan, were three and six, we created a world together that would grow for many years. Each night I'd tell them a "Chloe and Nathan story" about a brother and sister who lived with their parents in a magic kingdom. The story always began with each kid telling me what they wanted in the story that night. "A witch," said Zoe. "A dragon," said Ethan.

When we started home schooling with a group of other families, all the children would gather together for Chloe and Nathan stories at sunset when we camped, or at other social occasions, and I would ask them, "What do you want?" "A giant spider," said Clancy. "A mountain of ice," said Marina. Almost always it was a different story; hundreds of different stories, with a few favorites repeated over and over.

For many years, the Chloe and Nathan universe expanded and grew through countless adventures. In those years, the children and I created monsters and heroes and magic kingdoms. We lived the stories together, lost in drama, laughter, epic quests, self-discovery, and beauty, truth, and goodness. As a parent and guide, I did my best to use the stories as vehicles to transmit principles of courage, ethics, love, emotional self-regulation, and community.

My favorite character was Loki. Named after the Norse warrior/ trickster god, Loki was a bridge between worlds – a favorite archetype for therapists. He always carried a bag endlessly full of oranges, and could endure any physical catastrophe and magically rise to function again (somewhat like the cartoon character Wile E. Coyote, who was modeled after the Native American trickster, Coyote). Loki lived half in the rainbow country (the subtle dream realm of magic and infinite possibilities), and half in the gross realm of Chloe and Nathan's kingdom of Cambria, in a big white house with their parents, King Frank and Queen Susan.

During that time, I had the following conversation many times with Ethan and Zoe. One of them would ask, "Daddy, does magic really exist in this world?"

They got that the Chloe and Nathan world was in our imaginations, and that magic existed *there*, but they longed for such magic to exist *here* in Santa Barbara, in our house.

I'd always answer, "Absolutely magic exists in this world. The magic of this world is that we love each other."

Looking back on the Chloe and Nathan years, I know that the children and I were co-creating archetypes of love, peace, meaning, devotion, and transcendence in forms that resonated with everyone's different developmental levels (Chloe started dating in one of the last stories). The homeschooled kids kept asking for Chloe and Nathan stories well into their teens.

Developmentally, children up to around age six or seven live in a magical/mythical world, where Santa Claus and the Easter Bunny can *actually* exist, and adults can do anything. As we grow into conformist grade-schoolers, we learn that Mom and Dad can't actually *do* magic, and that there are concrete explanations for most mysterious phenomena. As adolescents, we learn to think critically, and are given scientific explanations for almost everything. The *beautiful* and *good* – Integral's Upper Left and Lower Left Quadrants – often get short shrift in science-based education (Integral's Upper and Lower Right Quadrants), though that seems to be changing in the 21st century. Most of us are left to rediscover, as adults, that the world is not neatly or simply explained, and that we have yet to find the outer boundaries of human potential and understanding.

We all drive the powerful Ferrari of human consciousness, filled with capacities we sometimes can only dimly sense, if at all. Most families, cultures, religions, and traditions have their equivalent of Chloe and Nathan stories to transmit the magic, mystery, and power inherent in consciousness symbolically to egocentric, conformist, rational, and pluralistic worldviews – which encompass around ninety-five percent of humanity. We each exist at the center of our own universe – characterized by our own unique perspectives and ongoing creations – interwoven and co-created with others' universes. As we grow, we don't lose the ability to make miraculous things happen, we just stop noticing how miraculous our daily manifestations really are.

I meant it when I told Ethan and Zoe that the magic of this world is that we love each other. This, like most of my parenting messages to their developing worldviews, was designed to make sense when they got older and more discerning. Dialed-in parenting accesses as many channels as possible for guiding and delighting children, and truth complements truth, even when we speak metaphorically. The challenge is to have every action, every expression, reflect something your kids would approve of if they remembered it as adults – a great standard for dialed-in parenting. In this chapter we'll attune to ourselves and our kids, and then explore some beautiful, good, and true perspectives of development and family systems to help kids thrive at every age.

As usual, it all starts with attunement

Let's attune to ourselves right now. Deep breaths, awareness of sensation, emotion, thought, judgment, and desire, with acceptance and caring intent.

Now attune to your children, wherever they may be at this moment. What are they doing? What might they be sensing, feeling, thinking, judging and wanting? Feel all this with acceptance and caring intent.

If you have a co-parent, attune to him or her.

MOST IMPORTANT EXERCISE EVER

Pay special attention to the taste, texture, and feeling of being in and out of attunement with yourself, your kids, and your partner. Whenever you feel yourself slip out of attunement, adjust back into attunement, using the processes we explored in Chapter 1.

If you practice, you'll increasingly notice when you're *not* attuned, and then automatically reach for dialed-in.

This is one of the *most important parenting skills*, because when you can't attune, no amount of knowledge helps you deal with your child – it's like trying to explain relativity to your cat.

Kids' worlds are different from adults' worlds

Adults can forget that kids have immature nervous systems. Immature brains have to develop, in order for kids to observe themselves, or to empathize in complicated situations.

Children are genetically wired to crave attuned parents who consistently empathize with their immediate experience of themselves and the world.

Kids' worlds are not the same as the ones we walk around in. A four-year-old can firmly believe in monsters and angels – they can be *real* to her.

Brain wave frequencies, measured in hertz (cycles per second), partly reflect our states. Adults spend a lot of time in mellow alpha, 8-13 hertz, and more variable (can feel better or worse) beta, 13-30 hertz. Grown-ups only enter theta, 4-8 hertz, when dreaming or in certain deep meditations. Children are in dream-time theta *almost all the time* until age six. Yes, kids live in their own dreamlike worlds.

The curse of knowledge

It's easy for parents to attribute adult motivations to kids; it's called *the curse of knowledge* – the assumption that others understand what we understand. Kids' worlds are driven by powerful states they are consciously unaware of, and sometimes unable to soothe.

I can't tell you how many times some parent has complained about their infant/toddler/grade-schooler/teen *deliberately* messing with them. "He *knows* yelling in the car drives me crazy! I've told him a million times!" "She always walks in just when I'm going to take a nap. She can't bear to let me have time to myself!" "She argues just to argue! She enjoys making me mad!"

Sorry, these are normal (unfortunately), clueless, paranoid beliefs, because kids just do what they do, and often have *no* self-awareness or other-awareness. The *last* circuits in the brain to fully mature (at age *twenty-six*) are the empathy and self-awareness circuits in the frontal lobes.

Meanwhile, since we all have mirror neuron systems that share emotions and motivations when we connect, kids are absorbing expressions, tones, beliefs, and defenses from us *all the time*.

Anxiety

"Oh no!" you might be thinking, remembering when you were a nasty, neglectful, or selfish parent. "I've totally screwed up my kid!"

Relax! Kids mostly absorb the good stuff, because almost all parents want their kids to do well, and usually project that to their children in word, expression, and deed.

There's no way I can adequately transmit everything you need to know about parenting kids from conception to adulthood in one chapter (even if I *knew* everything you need to know).

What I will do is list foundational characteristics of dialed-in parents, like self-care and personal integrity. Then, we'll follow my son, Ethan, and daughter, Zoe, from conception into their twenties, with dialed-in parenting tips for each stage (many I wish I'd known better at the time!).

Development never stops, and that includes developing as a parent. I challenge and entreat you to commit to lifelong parental growth.

How?

To start with, you can consciously mature through meditation, mutually satisfying intimacy, education, growth mindsets, turning crises into growth opportunities, personal development work, and receiving influence.

Since our purpose is to be superior parents, and purpose is guided by principles, let's start with six principles of dialed-in parenting.

Six Principles for Dialed-In Parenting

1. Put on your oxygen mask first: Take care of yourself physically, psychologically, socially, sexually, relationally, and financially. Be a healthy model – kids absorb good habits.

2. **Commit to non-violence:** Learn how to recognize and regulate your innate tendencies to emotional and physical violence, usually more towards yourself than others. Violent impulses call us to action, but we can choose compassionate action to create less violence and more love.

3. **Don't be a hypocrite:** Clarify your values and live your values. Children are ultra-sensitive to hypocrisy. Model integrity or lose credibility.

4. **Accept full responsibility:** The buck stops with you when it comes to your child's welfare. No excuses. If problems arise, it is your responsibility to address them so your child feels cherished and protected.

5. **Take care of your marital love affair:** Sex matters! Committed marital intimacy often needs conscious

sexuality. Learn how to talk and touch with focused intent to expand erotic/intimate bliss, and never stop practicing.

6. **Educate yourself about good parenting:** Gather basic knowledge about how to support your child through every developmental milestone. Learn details about the worlds your child inhabits from conception to adulthood, communicate interest and appreciation, and keep helping those worlds become more beautiful and enjoyable. Remember, these worlds shape your children as your children shape them.

These six principles are lifelong projects, and that's what superior parents do, dedicate themselves to lifelong development to support their kids doing the same.

Make mistakes

A big part of being a superior parent is making mistakes. You'll use a bad tone, let your toddler run out of sight in the park, yell at your wife in front of your five-year-old, blow up at your daughter for refusing to wear her jacket, or some other mindless mistake.

Mistakes are priceless *if you notice them and grow from them.* Each mistake becomes an opportunity to become more expert and model growth-mindsets to your kids.

Mistakes are catastrophically clueless if you refuse to acknowledge them and blame others!

Don't do that!

Ignoring or mindlessly denying mistakes is a horrible habit, because you're practicing being clueless! Each time you engage in a behavior, you wire it more deeply into your neural architecture – good news for healthy habits, awful news for unhealthy habits.

Infants are born with instincts to share, care, be fair, and to self-transcend. These are hard-wired social drives to grow and be in harmony with other humans.

Families are little cultures, like little nations that have their own social organizations. Research shows that healthy families distribute power through growth hierarchies which care, share, and are fair, rather than dominator hierarchies where individuals are controlled through fear, shame, and intimidation.

Growth/Dominator Hierarchy

Throughout human history social systems have been designed from two basic models – dominator hierarchies and growth hierarchies. Dominator hierarchies corrupt the human desire for satisfying social status, creating societies where the few dominate the many – think the old Soviet Empire, and North Korea. Dominator hierarchies tend to produce poverty, unhappiness, and psychologically stunted individuals. Growth hierarchies – also known as liberation hierarchies – are designed to help each individual thrive and contribute in a just society. They tend to produce wealth, happiness, and psychologically healthy individuals. Think Northern Europe, Canada, and the United States at its best. Dialed-in consciousness naturally encourages all nations, tribes, and families to be growth hierarchies.

What does a growth hierarchy look like in a family?

- Mom and Dad are in charge, and visibly respect each other's opinions and values.

• Kids have rules and boundaries based on fair standards, and are always treated with respect, even when being disciplined.

• Other people and opinions are welcomed into the family as value added. Families are systems, and when they welcome outside input, they become *open systems* rather than *closed systems* which avoid outside input and scrutiny.

• Distressed kids are *never* allowed to dominate a family – you don't give in to shrill demands, crazy behavior, or children who raise emotional intensity to have influence.

• Boundaries are set with the explicit goals of fairness, caring for others, and supporting each member's development. Remember the standard: "If twenty-five years from now my son saw a video of me disciplining him right now, would he approve of my tones, tactics, and behaviors."

Let's follow Ethan and Zoe from conception to now

My kids, Ethan and Zoe, are now 28 and 25. Rather than just talk abstractly about how boys and girls develop, I'm going to use stories about them (they both said it was OK).

Given the infinite variability of humans, arguable each boy and girl is unique, but there are milestones and processes shared by most children, and knowing them guides us in being dialed-in parents.

First, spirit infuses matter

When an egg is fertilized, a little electromagnetic field comes into existence and lasts until death. I like to think that this field is a carrier wave for Spirit to infuse matter.

From conception to birth, a baby's universe is Mom, and so we want Mom to be healthy, happy, and well nourished. If a mom chronically stresses out, especially the last three months (third trimester) of pregnancy, her baby is likely to have emotional regulation problems, kidney problems, and compromised puberty.

So, if you're pregnant, do what it takes to stay happy and well-nourished! If your partner's pregnant, do what it takes to help her stay happy and well-nourished! Remember principle four, "Accept full responsibility." No excuses, just do it!

Birth is a big deal

You will remember the birth of your children for the rest of your life, and (scary thought) your spouse will also remember how *you* handled yourself and dealt with the situation. Find an OB or midwife you trust, and follow their advice – they are advocates for your child's welfare.

Ethan was born in Santa Barbara Cottage Hospital, and Zoe was born at home in our living room. I remember each birth vividly.

We wanted a home birth with Ethan and had chosen a midwife. Becky's waters broke, and we got ready. Unfortunately, Becky couldn't progress past a certain point, and, twenty-four hours later we were in Cottage Hospital with a very cool OB named Dr. Green. Becky was given IV pitocin (a hormone to speed up delivery) and out came Ethan. We took him home that night, against medical advice (AMA), and he slept through the night for the last time in two years.

Zoe was born in our living room in a happy group of two midwives, three friends, and my good buddy, Michael Petracca, to play with Ethan while I attended to Becky. Becky was sitting in a birth chair and out came beautiful baby Zoe.

Every Zoe birthday we'd put a chalk circle on the floor where she was born and thank all Spirit everywhere for adorable, brilliant Zoe.

Babies need love and attunement

Get enough help (from work, family, friends, partners, all trustable people) so you can love and attune to your baby most of the time. Children who get the attention, space, and connection they need become what's called *securely attached*. When you attune to them, infants let you know what they need with smiles, cries, eyes, and a zillion other non-verbal signals.

174

Securely attached kids are confident that there is a just, attuned caregiver available all the time. Read almost any baby book, especially books on "Attachment parenting," for priceless knowledge.

Five S's

One of my clients brought her four-month-old Mitch into our session, and told me her husband had a genius for soothing him. "Last night Mitch wouldn't stop crying, so I handed him to Allan, and he calmed down like magic. I asked Allan, 'How do you do that?' and he said, 'The five S's from 'The Happiest Baby on the Block' – sucking, swinging, shushing, swaddling, and sidelining [holding a child sideways].'" I wrote these down and continue to be amazed at the wealth of wisdom available in this culture.

Secure attachment happens when *you,* the parent, are **present, contingent,** and **marked,** so your baby feels **known, accepted,** and **protected.**

> **Present** is being there when baby needs you. In some tribal cultures, infants don't leave adult arms until six months old. It doesn't matter how great a parent you are if you're not there when baby needs you.

> **Contingent (also congruent)** is when your expressions and tones fit with your states of consciousness and harmonize with your baby's states. Attunement registers powerfully in baby brains, and they want you to be there with acceptance and caring intent. Remember, there are mirror neurons in your baby's cortex which recapitulate your states of consciousness as you feel theirs through your mirror neurons. Babies can tell if you're pretending to be loving when you actually want to yell at them. It's OK to be mad – just notice it and tell your child in a kind

tone, "I know you don't like it that I'm mad, but I know you're not doing this on purpose and I'm getting over it." Children whose parents verbally monitored feelings in these ways – "You're feeling happy!" "You don't like the cold counter!" "I know the loud noise scared you." – were better able to identify and soothe their own feelings *years later*. Apparently, telling your children how they feel, helps them create brain circuits dedicated to emotional self-awareness and self-regulation.

Marked is baby-talk, where you add a little extra emphasis of tone and expression when you talk to your infant or toddler. "Oh! You're *mad!*" with an exaggerated angry face and slightly amplified tone, tells the baby that you are empathizing, not really mad yourself. These subtle emphases are called "marking" your tones and expressions, so your child feels attuned to, rather than threatened.

When a parent is present, contingent, and marked, kids tend to feel *known, accepted,* and *protected:*

> • **Known** is that sense of someone else *gets* you – knows your inner experience. *You don't feel alone.*

> • **Accepted** is that sense of being held and approved of, no matter what your state. If an infant wants holding, and is crying or screaming, the holding communicates, "I love you no matter what."

> • **Protected** involves baby feeling safe in your arms from the world *and from you.* Baby's nervous system thus knows that when you're around it doesn't matter how chaotic the world is, or how distressed you are, baby is safe.

Present, contingent and marked, to help her feel known, accepted and protected.

Toddlers need approval, disapproval, play, and patience

Donald Winnicott, a developmental psychologist, called the toddler years the "play space," and the more playful the feeling is to the thousands of yes's and no's, the better.

A normal American toddler hears the word "no" every eight minutes from age ten months to seventeen months. At ten months, kids start to walk, realize they need to seek out mom to soothe them when they're upset, and begin feeling shame emotions when disapproved of. That "no" every eight minutes often results in unpleasant shame feelings of distress, slack face, weakened chest/shoulder muscles, looking down, blushing, and freezing.

When mom picks up an ashamed toddler and comforts him, a securely attached kid regulates back to happy arousal in about ten seconds.

These (approvals-feel-good, disapprovals-feel-shame/bad) processes are central to learning culture and being a happy pro-social human being. That means *we need to appropriately shame our children.*

Yes!! Dialed-in parenting does not pretend that shame and shaming is bad. Dialed-in parents realize that shame, like other developmental forces (such as the will to compete, dominate, defend, or avoid), need to be used to help our children grow. How?

> • Disapprove respectfully, but unambiguously. "No!" firmly with disapproving expression or gesture usually does the trick.
>
> • Pick your child up and love him as soon as he's stopped the forbidden behavior (dumping out the flour, tipping over the lamp, playing with the horse poop, kicking his baby sister – you can finish the list in your spare time, and, if you're like most parents, it will be a *long* list).
>
> • Remember, securely attached kids shift back to happy after about ten seconds of love and approval, and they have experienced *a little bit of social learning.*
>
> • Repeat this process endlessly for the next eighteen years.

Language brings self-aware consciousness, and now *We* can *talk*

From age eighteen months onward, kids' brains explode in capacities for language. In an astonishingly short time, children learn vocabulary, grammar, syntax, and many rules of conversations. In an educated household, a child has a vocabulary of over a thousand words by three years old – as many as adults possess in some uneducated households. With language comes "me," "you," and "we" as conceptual realities – your child has interior representations, anchored in language, of self and others.

Now we can explain and interact – what a relief! It was so hard for me not to be able to ask my kids what they were feeling and thinking as toddlers. I had to guess and feed it back to them – good for them, but often frustrating for me.

Emotional coaching and dismissing

John Gottman discovered that parenting styles tended to group into two different *types:* emotionally coaching parents and emotionally dismissing parents. These types are like growth and fixed mindsets; they can be changed with effort and it's a good idea to change to emotional coaching because, in general, it's better for children.

Emotionally dismissing parents don't pay much attention to emotion and, when they do, it's some version of, "Suck it up!" They believe kids should behave, follow instructions, and have little patience for kid fears, angers, sadnesses, or complaints.

> • Four-year-old Arnold complains about his six-year-old brother, "Johnny hit me!" Mom responds, "Too bad. Clean your room."

> • Seven-year-old Sally starts to cry because her friend, Emily, cancelled a sleepover. Dad is impatient, "Stop crying! You have to go to school."

> • Three-year-old Sara can't go to sleep, "I'm afraid of the monster in the closet." Mom is tired and sick of explaining, "There's no monster in the closet and I don't want to hear about it anymore!"

We all need a little bit of emotional dismissing. Sometimes, we do need to suck it up and carry on – finish our homework, get up from a fall playing soccer and get back into the game, or stop complaining and empty the trash. In general, though, emotional coaching seems to be better for emotional, social, and intellectual development. Emotionally coaching parents pay a lot of attention to children's feelings. They recognize emotional spikes as learning opportunities. They attune to themselves and their child, wait till the kid can talk, identify and validate the emotion, but have judgments and boundaries about behaviors. Problem solving and limit-setting naturally flow from these states.

Here are the same kids from our above examples with emotionally coaching parents:

> • Four-year-old Arnold complains about his six-year-old brother, "Johnny hit me!" Mom responds, "I'll bet you're mad at Johnny." "Yes!" says Arnold. "What happened?" asks Mom. "I took his tractor without asking," Arnold confesses. "Well, he shouldn't have hit you, but you know how mad he gets when you take his things."• Seven-year-old Sally starts to cry because her friend Emily cancelled a sleepover. Dad waits till Sally calms down enough to talk (emotionally coaching parents tend to be attuned to when their children are too upset to relate, and when they've dropped back into social engagement where they can now understand, speak coherently, and be likely to receive influence). "You're frustrated and disappointed because Emily couldn't do the sleepover." Sally has stopped sobbing, and answers, "Yes. She promised!" and more tears well up at the thought of the broken promise. Dad is loving and patient, "Why did she say she had to cancel?" Sally responds with, "Her brother got sick and her mom doesn't want other kids around." Dad nods, "Sounds reasonable to me, but I know you love staying at her house. Maybe you can sleep over next week after her brother gets better. We need to get you to school now." Sally nods hopefully, "Maybe. I'll ask her today if we can do it next week."

• Three-year-old Sara can't go to sleep, "I'm afraid of the monster in the closet." Mom sits down on Sara's bed, "You're scared of the monster in the closet?" Sara nods. "What does it look like?" Sara explains, "It's like a big crocodile!" Mom nods seriously, "I hear they need lots of water. Maybe we should bring the hose in and water your closet to keep it happy." Sara laughs, "You'll get my shoes wet!" "Good point!" says Mom, "Maybe it can stay in the bathtub."

Yes, emotionally coaching requires more patience and depth from parents. Still, it is clearly the more dialed-in parenting style.

Different ages have different worldviews

Dialed-in emotional coaching takes into account the different worldviews kids have at different ages. You'll notice that Mom didn't waste a lot of time with magically thinking three-year-old Sara – she identified the emotion and then let the conversation alter Sara's state. Dad did problem solving with seven-year-old Sally that satisfied her grammar school black-and-white sense of justice, by suggesting that the promise of a sleepover could be kept later. Four-year-old Arnold got a dose of family rules and eye-for-an-eye justice when Mom put together his unilateral expropriation of Johnny's tractor with getting hit by Johnny.

Emotionally coached kids have better emotional self-regulation, better math and reading scores, better concentration skills, less conflict with a best friend, and are evaluated as more socially competent than kids from emotionally dismissing families. These effects lasted to age fourteen in one study.

Even more significantly, a discrepancy between parents in styles – for instance, an emotionally dismissing Dad trying to parent with an emotionally coaching Mom – predicted divorce more than almost any other single variable.

Luckily, emotional coaching has expanded into a cultural standard, with most parents, preschool and elementary teachers, dance and martial arts instructors, music teachers, and almost everyone else who works with kids agreeing, whether they know the term "emotional coaching" or not, that emotional coaching is generally the way to go.

What about when you think he's too harsh, or she's too easy?

Good parents, even emotionally coaching good parents, still disagree about parenting. There was an eight year period in our family where three-fourths of Becky's and my arguments were about parenting, mostly parenting Zoe who, like me, was born emotionally reactive, and needed extra guidance and support with feelings, beliefs, and reactions. Becky and I eventually helped each other be better parents by taking each other's parenting points seriously and working to improve. For example, my tones became more patient and kind, and Becky got better at setting limits when they were required.

Parenting – Easy and Hard Children

Parents with more than one child usually tell me that one of the kids is harder to parent at one time or another. In other words, if you have two kids, one of them is likely to be easier or harder at any given age – sometimes for different parents, as in it's easier for Dad to parent little Emily than Mom, or vice versa. Nothing is more insufferable than those lucky parents with two easy kids – confidently secure in their superior parenting and eager to share their wisdom. My daughter was more difficult for me to parent than my son, but raising Zoe – who's currently doing great – taught me humility, a priceless gift, and she and I have wonderful conversations these days about everything, including her development and my strengths and weaknesses as a parent. Therapy works! If you have problems with your kids, go sooner rather than later, because children are learning constantly, and the sooner you interrupt negative habits in yourselves and them, the easier and quicker everyone changes.

If you and your spouse can't agree on how to parent one of your children, find a good therapist and have sessions until you feel dialed-in to your child and each other most of the time. Gottman's divorce data from parents who had conflicting coaching/dismissing styles was for couples who didn't receive therapy.

Play is necessary and complicated

Play has changed dramatically since the 1950's and 1960's when I grew up. TV and other screens are ubiquitous, most toys have computer chips in them, are modeled after TV characters, and get heavily promoted on kids' shows (until the 1980's, the U.S. government didn't allow such advertising). Kids spend less time outdoors, engage in less unstructured play, and games are much more supervised by adults.

Schools have radically cut back on recess, and the kinds of games kids used to make up with balls, blocks, and other objects have faded, as have the multiple aged play groups, where older children initiate younger ones into games.

Interestingly, games where children voluntarily follow rules, engage in roles, and share spontaneous creativity ("Let's play Cowboys and Indians – you be the cowboy and I'll chase you!"), increase self-regulatory skills – they boost *willpower*. Willpower is more correlated with adult success than IQ, SAT scores, or GPA.

Apparently, play is super important to development and happiness. Finland – whose kids routinely score higher on standardized tests than *any other country in the world* – has recess after every class through Junior High School. Not surprisingly, Finland – along with most other social democracies in Northern Europe – also routinely ends up as one of the happiest nations on Earth, according to U.N. happiness surveys.

Don't touch the floor and the monster game

Becky and I were all over the play thing when we were raising Zoe and Ethan:

- We wanted them in nature, and had outdoor easels, big toys, fruit trees, berry patches in the back yard, and huge trees with ropes and a rope swing in the front to lure kids outside.

• We wanted them imaginative, so we had ambiguous toys like blocks, costumes, puppets, various sized wooden boxes, and lots of balls and props to create games and pretend universes.

• We wanted the house to support development, so we remodeled it using the Pattern Language principles of Christopher Alexander to have a parents' realm, a kids' realm, and common areas, all with cheap furniture that we wouldn't mind being stained and scratched by art projects and careless kid mistakes.

• We welcomed other kids and families into our house – we had an open system that invited input from the outside.

• We bought countless books, and read to the kids daily till Ethan went away to college.

• We wanted them to have friends with growth mindsets and liberation hierarchies, so we found a group of likeminded homeschooling families with whom we camped, hung out, explored the world, and had parties. This was especially important during pre- and grade-school years, when kids' primary identifications are with family and tribes of families.

A couple of games I remember with affection are Don't Touch the Floor and The Monster Game.

Don't Touch the Floor was a game Ethan and Zoe created that they could play together even though Ethan is three years older. They'd try to move around the house together without touching the floor, using all the furniture plus cushions and pillows they'd scatter strategically.

The game was played inside (even in Santa Barbara you can't play outside all the time), but was active. It was both competitive in ways that evened out the three-year age difference (you "lost" when you touched the floor), but also cooperative in the sense that it never caused arguments, and created endless mechanical problems they had to instantly solve, sometimes cooperatively.

According to current play research (and there's a lot of it!), voluntary, creative activity that involves setting up problems and then solving them, is one definition of play, and taking turns and cooperating with other kids in such games is particularly good for social development.

The Monster Game arose from Becky and me trying to figure out how to understand and deal with destructive shadow, the dark unseen aspects that all of us have, to varying degrees. Like many families, we had encountered craziness and abuse from disturbed adults, and you can't have theoretical discussions of such things with young kids.

So, we played The Monster Game. It was in the evenings, after dinner when we all still had energy to run around, and a little time to play before stories and bed.

The kids were four and seven. We'd take turns being the monster, who had to cover his or her eyes, and count to sixty. Everybody else would hide in all the nooks and crannies of our big house with lots of closets. Then the monster would slowly hunt through the house until they found someone, and grabbed at them making "Grrr grrr!" monster sounds. The caught person would take off with the monster in hot pursuit, everyone screaming happily, back to our family bed where we'd all tumble together, safe. The monster was now transformed into Zoe, Ethan, Daddy, or Mommy again, and it was someone else's turn to be the monster.

We wanted our kids to express the hunter and hunted sides, the attacker and attacked, in an atmosphere of play and love. I believe this set them up for future run-ins with shadow, and so far that's proven the case, in that both Ethan and Zoe have a fine understanding of violence in themselves and others, don't allow it from others, and challenge it when they direct violent thoughts or impulses at themselves.

Also, rough and tumble play with strong dominant parents--parents who firmly cool it before anybody gets hurt or distressed--is associated with emotional regulation and social maturity throughout childhood and into adolescence.

Childhood is not that long

Kids are teenagers before you know it – ask any parent with grown children. We have a limited window to make lifelong impacts on physical, emotional, social, sexual, and professional health. Play impacts everything. Clueless play is: give the kid a screen when they want it. Mindless play is: leave them alone if they're not causing problems and hope for the best. Mindful play is: consciously arranging play to be fun, fair, and healthy. Dialed-in play keeps reaching for expanding and strengthening our child's current worldview, and prepping them for the worldviews to come.

From ten to thirteen, kids' thoughts and opinions expand

As children enter adolescence, their brains go through a critical period of generating lots of new circuits (neurogenesis), while unused neurons die and are excreted (apoptotic cell death). Where previously they thought in mostly black-and-white, concrete terms, teens now can be more relativistic – they can see more than one side of an issue. This ability to manipulate the forms of the world in their minds is called formal operational thinking, discovered and popularized by the French cognitive scientist, Jean Piaget.

This is often when kids start questioning family rules and parental behaviors. "Why do I have to go to bed at 9:00?" "You told Aunt Clara we were busy Saturday, but we're not!"

When Zoe was eleven, she came back from a DARE (Drug Abuse Resistance Education) class one day and asked me, "Daddy, are you an alcoholic?"

Always ready for an emotionally charged dialogue, I sat down with her, "Did they talk about drugs and alcohol in your DARE class today?" She nodded. "And you're worried that, since I drink, I might be an alcoholic?" She smiled at my understanding, "Yes!"

Luckily, I have a lot of information about addiction, and knew this was a teaching moment. "Zoe, there are three types of drinkers. Type One is like your mom. She doesn't care much for drinking, and can make a beer last a month. Type Two drinkers enjoy drinking, but have rules they follow that they hardly ever break. I don't drink during the work week, and never have more than two or three glasses of wine on the weekend. Type Three drinkers drink more over time, often can't say 'no' to the next drink, and drinking ends up ruining their lives. What kind of drinker do you think I am?"

"Type Two." Zoe said promptly.

I probed deeper, "What kind of drinker do you think you'll be?"

Zoe, honest like everyone in our family, thought for a minute and then said, "I don't know. Maybe I'll never drink."

"Right," I said, "But if you do, you'll find out if you're a Type One, Two, or Three, and if you're a Type Three and become an alcoholic, then what?"

Zoe looked thoughtful, "I guess I'd have to stop."

These relativistic concepts made sense to her more formal operational mind. At age eight, the same conversation would likely have been confusing to her more concrete, black and white thinking style.

At fifteen, kids' nervous systems are alert for models to grow towards

Look in any teenager's room, and what do you see on the walls? Yes, I know that everything is chaotic, and there are all kinds of weird objects scattered haphazardly around, but you'll likely see big posters of beautiful, iconoclastic, or successful young adults. It might be athletes your kid admires – football, soccer, volleyball players, or dancers, or actors/ musicians/artists like Taylor Lautner, Dakota Fanning, Emma Watson, Taylor Swift, or Justin Bieber. At around age fifteen, our nervous systems are alert for models for us to grow towards. Genetically, we are wired to become adults by both wanting to hang out more with other teens than with older or younger age groups, and by admiring and emulating people who embody traits or characteristics we admire.

At around fifteen, I decided to become a therapist and a martial artist, inspired by my therapist Joe Ericson, and by Tsutomu Ohshima, the senior teacher of Shotokan Karate.

These were not conscious decisions; I *discovered* that I hungered for these identities, and dedicated the following years to becoming the best therapist and martial artist I possibly could become. (In later years, when my wife and son met Dr. Ericson and Mr. Oshima, they marveled at how similar my voice, movements, and values were to these two men, whom I stopped having contact with in my early twenties.)

My parents were completely supportive. They had no idea really why their son Keith decided to be a psychologist and a martial artist, but they respected my choices and helped me progress. They did the same with my older brother Gary (who became first a Marine, then a District Attorney, and then later a Superior Court Judge), and my younger brother Earl,

186

who earned his doctorate in Physics at Cal Berkeley, and has spent much of his career analyzing simulated atomic explosions in the atmosphere.

Even more interesting to me, my parents stayed together over sixty years till my father's death at ninety, and they both gave up drinking alcohol in 1965. My brothers and I have all stayed married and faithful to our wives in the intervening years, and no one in our families has developed alcoholism or drug addiction. Apparently, my brothers and I chose our parents as models for commitment, fidelity, and sobriety.

Parenting becomes more collaborative with teens

Rather than instruct, inform or direct teens about values, I've found it more effective to challenge them to be true to their own values. I encourage parents to collaborate first, and then set boundaries in areas that teens demonstrate they have inadequate control.

Where you can just tell your six-year-old to finish his homework, you can't order your seventeen-year-old to study hard for her SAT exams. If she doesn't have a value of studying hard, you'll probably help her more by discussing what her values are, and what makes it easier or harder to embody them. Therapy is priceless in situations like this, and I recommend it highly if your kids are willing or interested.

Development is collaborative from conception onward – even babies influence how they grow with their temperaments and rapidly forming personalities – but, development needs to be *especially* collaborative with teens and young adults who now have most of the power in determining their futures.

Even with out-of-control teens – drug addicts, hostile or oppositional kids, anorexics, or the sexually reckless – I'll discuss with them how their parents might have to hospitalize them, or send them to therapeutic boarding schools, if they can't gain control over their lives.

Such mutually respectful, age-appropriate dialogues about *any* aspect of life are characteristic of dialed-in parents.

What about truma?

We do our best to protect our kids, but trauma happens. Ten percent of boys and 20% of girls have some sexual trauma perpetrated by a teen or adult during development. Injuries, surgeries, car wrecks, parental divorces, losses of friends, family members, pets, or houses are among the many potential sources of childhood traumas.

What do we do then?

Dialed-in parenting draws from the "true" when it comes to such questions. In American society, there are tendencies to ignore or deny trauma, a kind of cultural emotionally-dismissing attitude, "All you did was break your leg. It will get better, so stop complaining!" Or even worse, the tendencies of adults to not believe children who describe sexual abuse – which led to the mandatory reporting laws which make it illegal for therapists, teachers, nurses, or doctors to not report the *possibilities* of physical or sexual abuse when evidence comes their way.

Traumas need to be acknowledged and eventually discussed when the hurt person is ready. Therapists are trained to help families with this, and, when there's a possibility of trauma, it's a good idea to check in with a professional.

DIALED-IN PARENTING FOREVER

Superior parents keep improving throughout their lives. As our kids become adults, respecting them, being interested in their lives (both their interior feelings and thoughts as well as their life experiences), and being available to support and help them, continues to influence adult children profoundly.

Believe me, I have encountered people of *all ages* either thanking God for their dialed-in parents, or wishing their clueless or mindless parents were more dialed-in.

"This all sounds fine," you might be thinking, "But it's hard to change habits that get so ingrained."

It *is* hard to change habits, and that's what we're addressing in Chapter 10: Dialed-in Habits.

CHAPTER 10: DIALED-IN HABITS

What is a habit?

A habit is a pattern of self-reinforcing processes. Habits are unconscious tendencies for us to do, say, think, or feel certain specific ways when we're cued by sensations, events, sounds, smells, memories, or any other experience that our nervous system determines needs a response. Each repetition of a habit strengthens it a little bit, so that over time it becomes almost impossible to do anything else when a habit is cued – great for healthy habits like brushing your teeth after meals and being kind to friends and family, horrible for unhealthy habits like smoking, impulsive cookie eating, and using mean tones with your children when you're tired.

One Princeton study found that people spent 40% of their waking hours in habitual behavior – not conscious decisions, but *habits* determined what they did, said, and thought. (I think the figure is closer to 60%, but I'm too lazy to do the research to find out if I'm right.)

Most of us underestimate the number of habitual choices we automatically make. A good example is food-related decisions. People were asked how many they made in a day, and most people guessed around 14. When the same people were observed throughout the day, the researchers found that they made an average of 227 food-related decisions.

You walk into my office and say, "Hi Keith!" I say, "Hi, good to see you!" Very little conscious choice went into either of our greetings, we just did our habits.

We habits – dancing with each other on multiple levels, your habits of relating organizing with my habits of relating – naturally form when people interact. Complex systems seek coherence, human relationships on every level are complex systems, so our habits of relating self-organize into coherent shared habit patterns.

Each time we engage a habit, the neural networks involved attract oligodendrocytes – cells dedicated to myelinating activated circuits by wrapping the neurons involved in fatty sheaths of myelin. A heavily myelinated circuit is *one hundred times* faster than an unmyelinated circuit, so myelin radically increases bandwidth and signal strength.

Habit circuits are heavily myelinated, and with each repetition, oligo's (my favorite hip name for oligodendrocytes) start myelinating the neural networks, and we're a little more likely to do the same dance again in similar circumstances.

Healthy and unhealthy habits

Suffice to say that habits guide our lives and, as we all know, there are *healthy (good)* habits and *unhealthy (bad)* habits. All involve combinations of "I will," "I won't," or "I want."

Healthy habits help us be more vibrant, socially successful, happy, and personally fulfilled. Brushing your teeth (*I will*), smiling at your kids (*I want* to be a superior parent), telling the truth (*I won't* lie), stopping after the first or second beer, using your turn signals when driving, and acknowledging mistakes are all healthy habits.

"I will," "I won't," and "I want" all involve willpower, which can be cultivated with practice. If you challenge yourself to five minutes of walking outside every day ("I will"), or refusing to eat pastries at work ("I won't"), or consciously keeping your eyes on the road ("I want" to be a safer driver), your willpower will increase. In fact, consciously practicing mostly healthy habits increases willpower.

We all know some foundational healthy habits that create happy fulfilled lives:

- Get enough sleep so you're not nodding off during the day, usually seven to eight hours a night.

- Eat healthy kinds, portions, and combinations of food consistently.

190

• Enjoy your pleasures, but don't practice addictions. If you discover yourself compulsively engaging in unhealthy behaviors, seek and receive help to change.

• Create and maintain satisfying relationships.

• Exercise regularly.

• Cultivate an optimistic attitude towards life.

• Interrupt stress cycles often (hourly, if possible) with deep breathing, gratitude, exercise, fun, play, intimate contact with people you love, or anything else that lightens you up in a healthy way.

• Meditate, attune, or otherwise engage in regular contemplative activities.

• Live your principles.

• Cultivate growth mindsets and transform fixed mindsets when you discover yourself practicing one.

• Make work satisfying by choosing jobs that fulfill you, or by working up to your personal standards of excellence at whatever job you have.

Unhealthy habits challenge our physical resilience, screw up relationships, generate painful misery, and lead to failures in behavior, confidence, willpower, and self-image.

We all know unhealthy habits when we see them:

• Automatically blaming others.

• Automatically attacking ourselves.

• Regularly eating the wrong food or too much food.

• Smoking cigarettes.

• Drinking alcoholically (or practicing any addiction, since addictions – even apparently "healthy addictions" like exercise – involve acting compulsively and losing our choice to be different).

- Ignoring facts which disagree with preconceived notions.

- Fixed mindsets.

- Violating your own principles.

- Violence in almost any form, both emotional and physical. Martial arts, football, sports, or performances (*Who's afraid of Virginia Wolf, for* example) are play, so they don't register in our nervous systems as real violence – because they are voluntary, cooperative, and participants generally have mutual respect. They can still be dangerous and risk real violence – a fight on the field, or an intentional sideswipe in a NASCAR race, for instance – but generally in themselves are not violent.

FAVORITE UNHEALTHY HABIT EXERCISE

Think about your favorite unhealthy habit. What's the bad habit you practice the most? You don't have to tell anybody. "I'm attracted to big toes – I can't stop staring at them." "I eat too many cookies." "I never use my turn signals."

I want you to observe yourself in your mind doing that unhealthy habit… but observe yourself with acceptance and caring intent. Be interested. "Wow! I eat too much dessert after 8:00 pm, but never before 8:00 pm." "I always drink too much when I go out with my friend, Jim… that's interesting." If you can consistently observe yourself with compassion and caring intent, something will start being different. Just self-observation creates change, because you're observing what cues your habit (going out with Jim), your state of consciousness which says, "Yes!" to your bad habit, and the consequences of repetitively doing the same unhealthy behavior.

Everyone has some unhealthy habits, and a growth mindset is the way to address them. Effort and progress over time dissolves most bad habits (or turns them into good), and as added bonuses amplifies willpower, and increases maturity on multiple developmental lines such as the integration-of-defenses line, the self-line, and the moral line.

Willpower matters

Most people associate ending bad habits and creating good habits with willpower, and they're right – willpower matters.

What's more, willpower is a stable trait that can be measured in preschoolers, and stays stable (in the absence of interventions) into adulthood.

Roy Baumeister in his excellent book, *Willpower,* chronicled how four-year-olds who could resist eating a marshmallow better than other kids had higher achievement, better SAT scores, better jobs, and happier relationships as adults. As I mentioned in Chapter 9, willpower is a better predictor of success than GPA, college entrance scores, or IQ.

Willpower can be broken down into "I will," "I won't," and "I want." I call these the "Big Three," and the more we practice the Big Three, the more willpower we will have.

- "I will" (exercise daily, eat vegetables with each meal).

- "I won't" (swear, flirt with the cute manager down the hall, buy whatever I want when I'm shopping).

- "I want" (to be slimmer, kinder when I'm frustrated, more attentive when I'm talking with my wife).

One method some people use to boost willpower is with willpower challenges like keeping a bowl of candy around that you *never* let yourself eat from. Willpower grows with resolve, compassion, and self-care.

Unfortunately, willpower falters with:

- Fatigue.

- Sleep deprivation.

- Low blood sugar.

- Decision overload – after you've made a bunch of decisions, your willpower weakens.

- Cluelessness and mindlessness.

Culture is shared habits

Culture is largely shared habits of groups of people, developed over time, held in place (or challenged) by the beautiful, good, and true validity standards. We observe ourselves and others practicing or not practicing cultural habits, and will disapprove of violations, and approve of the cleanest expressions (in our opinion) of cultural values. These "cleanest" expressions aren't necessarily healthy. Many colonial or fundamentalist cultures of the nineteenth and twentieth century objectified human beings – slavery and racism in the U.S, anti-Semitism in Nazi Germany, apartheid in South Africa, etc.

Examples of current American habits include:

- Wearing clothes when you go to the mall. You will be heavily disapproved of (by most) strolling naked through Macy's.

- Not screaming public profanities when frustrated.

- Saying "Hello," back to someone who greets you.

- Driving on the right side of the road.

- Watching television.

Habits can be learned instantly

If we don't naturally develop or absorb habits through our family, culture, or circumstance, we mostly need to learn and systematically practice them – it usually takes time to develop a new habit.

But there are exceptions.

We all know how traumas can create habits of worry, rage, terror, or obsession – Post Traumatic Stress Disorder (PTSD) is a condition that can be programmed instantly into your nervous system by one horrible experience like an assault, a car accident, or a catastrophic loss. Contrary to some people's understanding, PTSD is a relatively rare response to a shocking bad experience. Most of us have built in resilience that protects and guides us through trauma, usually combinations of inner resources and connections with caring others.

On the other hand, sometimes a lovely experience can shock us so much, we automatically change. This happened to me once when Becky went to a therapy session about twenty-five years ago. I asked her what she worked on and she replied, "I worked on loving you better."

I was shocked by how sweet and generous this sounded, and at that moment resolved to do the same, and have ever since. That one moment created a new habit of working on more consciously loving Becky better every day.

Habits and genetic predispositions

Habits can cause problems when they're at odds with genetic predispositions. Culture scrambles our neurobiology when it promotes habits that deny or suppress biological drives, a classic result of not cross-validating "good" standards with "true" research.

Take gossip for example.

We frown on gossip and enjoy gossip

Almost everyone enjoys gossiping, but American culture tends to frown upon gossip.

Are *you* comfortable with *enjoying* gossip? Most of us have gossiped, and will enthusiastically continue. We know in our deepest hearts that, even though culture paints a faint "ick" patina on gossip, everyone indulges.

Studies suggest that up to 70% of human conversation is about *someone else*. We are *hard-wired* to gossip, so a dialed-in approach is to *gossip well – to practice healthy gossip.*

Dialed-in helps us refine "good" standards. With gossip, a better standard might be some version of, "It's natural and OK for me, you, and anybody to gossip – let's try to gossip with compassionate understanding."

Culture gives the priceless gifts of tradition, social order, and accumulated wisdom. As we understand culture more deeply, we'll always find more caring versions of values and share them with each other. This is one engine of healthy cultural growth.

The Universe is a conglomeration of habits

People aren't the only ones with habits. Objects have self-reinforcing processes (rocks have habits of slowly disintegrating in air and water, for instance). Since the whole universe is organized according to complexity theory, each new level of complexity creates new habits, waiting to be energized, embodied, and processed through time until they become included in new, more complex habits – evolution is basically habits building on habits.

Physics

If time is a habit, how can time be included and transcended in an evolutionary flow?
Endel Tulving pointed out in the 1980's how human beings engage in "mental time travel," each time we remember the past or anticipate the future. Dean Radin wrote a great book called "Entangled Minds" demonstrating possible effects of focused intention in the past and future. Stephen Hawking thinks a time machine could be constructed out of wormholes. These realities and possibilities have already evolved the habit of time.

In the beginning was the Big Bang,

BAM!!!!

The universe exploded into being, and immediately cosmic habits existed. Gravity, speed of light, electromagnetism, chaos theory, and the periodic table all came into being at once.

This last example, the periodic table, is particularly indicative of how some cosmic habits came into existence as potentials. At the point of the Big Bang everything was just plasma – there were no elements, but the eventual forms of the elements and the organization of those elements into the periodic table already existed, waiting to be manifested as oxygen, iron, gold, uranium and all the rest created by the first stars.

Maybe in other universes there are different cosmic habits, but in this universe the ones we have will remain patterns of self-reinforcing processes – cosmic habits – till the end of time.

Let's fast forward to life. Prokaryote organisms, the first tiny living cells which had no organelles (mitochondria and other tiny organs inside them) populated the oceans of earth, and life became a habit.

As it turns out, almost all life on Earth is carbon-based. Life could have been silicon-based, but it wasn't. Carbon-based life became a habit on this planet. There might be other kinds of life elsewhere, but on this planet carbon-based is a cosmic habit.

When more complex eukaryote cells (which have organelles inside them) got established, eukaryote cells became a habit of nature, and became the building blocks of all that followed.

Evolution

DNA, RNA, chromosomes, how did those habits happen? I don't know, but my hypothesis is that there were a couple of worms within a cell – worms that originally started out as parasites. Out of countless billions and billions of worms living and dying in cells over hundreds of millions of years, all of a sudden, wham! One worm started passing on traits to a cell, and then two twined together to change and amplify characteristics. RNA, DNA, and chromosomes then forever became a habit of life on Earth.

Sexual dimorphism radically accelerated evolution

Fast forward to male and female – sexual dimorphism – into fish, reptiles, birds, mammals, primates. Now, *each generation,* a male's genetic history blended with a female's to create new characteristics, all with some potential to become new habits.

Part of dialed-in is realizing we are each constantly influenced by thousands of genetically based habits evolved over a billion years to help us survive and thrive.

Social learning was another evolutionary turbo-boost

Mammals and birds became able to pass on social learning, self-reinforcing *social* habits. Humans could *remember,* then *speak* and remember, then *write* and speak and remember – each advance amplifying the number and intensity of habits we could generate and weave into our biosocial environments.

We have habits of attention and talking, habits of listening and processing information, habits of wanting and resisting, habits, habits, habits. We're all habiting simultaneously, naturally, and generally not thinking about it. Why? It's habitual! It mostly happens non-consciously.

Individual development and complexity

Individual development goes from stable habits, to disruptions and disorganization, to stable new complexity. Each level of organization is a series of habits. Those habits guide us until they're destabilized, and then we either regress or form another more complex level of habits.

We see this in human development:

- Infants happily progress through rolling to crawling and more interactive relating, but they often get a little bit fussy around the age of one. Why? Because the habits that had been sustaining them crawling around and so on (not to mention the way that they'd been relating to mom as infants, not really conscious of being separate from her) aren't working anymore, because of brain/body development and social learning. They're standing upright and staggering around, learning to walk, which becomes more interesting than crawling. Habits of crawling and not being as consciously aware of the need for mom when upset are disrupted, and kids can get crabby until they stabilize into new, more complex habits of relating and moving through the world.

• This also happens at age two as kids develop language.

• It happens at the ages of four to six as kids develop a sense of themselves at the center of their own autobiographical life histories.

• It happens at age eleven with relativistic thought, fifteen as nervous systems reach for adult models, nineteen with instinctive striving for autonomous identities, twenty-six with fully mature empathy and self-reflection circuits, and periodically throughout all subsequent critical periods.

Habits often start non-consciously

Almost all of our habits first grab us non-consciously. Mostly our brain reads the world and lights up a habit within about 50 milliseconds (msec). If we're aware of habits at all, we catch them starting 300 msec, 500 msec, maybe one and a half seconds. If we practice attunement – aware with acceptance and caring intent of body, emotion, thought, judgment, and desire – we can become progressively more mindful and consciously aware of habits as they arise.

Aware, we have choices!

Integrally-informed choices rock – they lead us to *dialed-in.* Dialed-in can create *magnificent, brilliant* new habits!

> **One cool bit of research** – the most important time interval in starting a new good habit is the first thirty seconds. If you can *begin and sustain for thirty seconds,* your chances of continuing skyrocket.

> **Another cool bit of research** – If you're stopping smoking, drinking, drugging, overeating, or destructive sexing, you benefit from having a plan when the craving comes. Smokers with a plan (call a friend, drink a cup of tea, or walk around the block) were *twenty-five times* more likely to resist smoking when they had the impulse.

Keystone habits

Some new habits, called *keystone habits,* have unexpectedly far reaching consequences – their effects can ripple through your life, improving seemingly unrelated areas.

Charles Duhigg, in *The Power of Habit,* specifically mentions regular exercise and food journaling (writing down everything you eat – even if it's only for one day a week) as powerful keystone habits.

Regular exercise tends to cause people to:

- Eat better.

- Be more productive at work.

- Smoke less.

- Be more patient.

- Feel less stressed.

- Spend less money impulsively.

Food journaling apparently results in people:

- Losing twice as much weight in six months as other weight loss methods.

- Discovering patterns of eating that make it easier to improve.

- Planning future meals to be healthier.

One of my favorite examples of keystone habits was conducted on men with histories of emotional or physical violence with their domestic partners. Researchers had these guys eat with their non-dominant hand (their left hand if they were right-handed) for two weeks, and domestic violence plummeted.

How could eating with your non-dominant hand be a keystone habit? I suspect it was because eating left-handed forced self-observation, and amplified, "*I will* (eat with my left hand)" and "*I won't* (eat with my right hand)" willpower. Perhaps this combination of increased self-observation and extra willpower translated into less yucky violence, because most of us, deep down, don't want to hurt others.

Relational keystones and social contagion

In relationships, changing a keystone habit will tend to upset your social system, because we matter to each other. When you institute a cascade of new behaviors, your culture of intimate relationships is disrupted and has to reorganize. You and your family are an intimate interdependent *we*, who influence each other with healthy and unhealthy habits – so cultivating good habits helps everyone who knows you.

Take smiling, for example. When we smile, even when we force a smile when we don't feel like it, pro-social areas in the frontal cortex of our brains associated with better moods get activated. If you force yourself to smile every ten minutes or so, your mood will improve. If I look in your eyes as you smile, mirror neurons in my brain associated with action – motor neurons – will fire in sympathy, I will feel like smiling, and my mood will be slightly elevated.

So, are habits contagious?

Yes, for better or worse, social contagion is a powerful force in groups:

- If your social group smokes, you're more likely to smoke.

- If your social group is obese, you're more likely to be obese.

- If your social group has healthy habits, you're more likely to share them.

This is not a bad thing. We want to upset our social systems in good ways. I used to get mad at my kids for not valuing my (what I thought was *great*) advice. "Come on. That's good advice! Follow it!" You can imagine how well *that* worked out.

So, I learned to be kinder and more patient. When I started getting mad or frustrated, I tried to shut up and be nicer. This proved socially contagious. The kids started becoming kinder and more patient with *me*.

Creating healthy new keystone habits will often result in unexpected positive differences for you and the people around you.

How do you identify potential keystone habits?

One way is to use your imagination. Imagine some new habit that, if you practiced it regularly, you'd think, "That would be so wonderful!"

For instance, when talking to practicing addicts, or people who have given up on improving important areas, I've often had variations of the following exchanges:

> *"What would it be like if you didn't feel like drinking?"*
> Tears sometimes well up, *"It would be a miracle!"*
>
> *"What if you didn't feel like doing cocaine?"*
> Hope and confusion, *"I can't even imagine."*
>
> *"What would it be like if you got enough sleep?"*
> Wonderment, *"I would love so much to get enough sleep!"*
>
> *"How would you feel if you exercised five times a week?"*
> Joyful incredulity, *"Oh, God, that would be so great!"*

Your imagination can let you know volumes about what would up-level your life. The activities that evoke such powerful, grateful, feelings in fantasy quite likely reflect potential keystone habits that could deliver unexpectedly wonderful outcomes.

Slowed breathing and regular exercise – potential healthy keystones for all of us

Heart Rate Variability (HRV) is a sign of how sensitive your heart/brain system is to the present moment. It's a measure of how effectively your Vagus nerve slows down and relaxes your heart rate. The Vagus is the tenth cranial nerve connecting your brainstem with your heart. Since most of us are safe most of the time, high heart rate variability means our hearts beat relaxed and harmonious most of the time, attuned to the world and secure in our safety.

HRV is *highly correlated* with willpower, the ability to reflect and act consciously in the face of habitual drives, needs, impulses, or emotions. Alcoholics in recovery with higher HRV were less likely to relapse. Higher HRV is associated with lowered stress responses, as well as decreased depression. Some neuroscientists consider HRV to be the single most revealing measure of general good health.

Regular exercise as panacea

Regular exercise is another miracle habit – a classic keystone. Most health researchers agree that regular exercise is the closest we've come to discovering a panacea – a cure to all ills.

Not only does regular exercise increase HRV, lower blood pressure, and improve your mood, but people who exercised regularly were less likely to eat junk food, more likely to eat healthy food, and more likely to save money. They watched less television, procrastinated less, arrived

203

> ### Simplest technique ever for increasing
> ### Heart Rate Variability
>
> *Count your breaths for one minute. I just counted twelve – one breath every five seconds. Now extend your inhale and especially your exhale (it's much easier to extend your exhalations to completely empty your lungs of air) until you are breathing four to six times per minute – around once every twelve to fifteen seconds. Slowing down your breaths increases heart rate variability and boosts willpower. Two minutes twice a day of this practice can become the habit that adds years to your life.*

more on time for appointments, and felt increased control of their emotions. These effects happened both in the short term (fifteen minutes after exercise) and in the long term.

One set of studies actually showed five minute intervals of exercise having larger effects on mood and self-control than more extended workouts; and exercising outside in nature was better than inside.

Attunement can be the greatest habit ever

All meditative techniques, including slowed breathing and attunement, increase willpower, and stimulate growth of both gray matter (new neurons) and white matter (more myelin and energy generating glial cells) in our brains – especially in the executive control centers in our frontal lobes. Changes can be measured using fMRI brain imagery technology after only ten meditation sessions. Brains actually *grow and change* shape when we meditate.

Practice attuning to yourself, others, and the world consistently, and you naturally go into attunement when not otherwise occupied. This is why I suggest you attune all day in different situations and with different people. There's lots of research that shows that learning accelerates when we mix up the content of what we're studying, the place we study, and the states of consciousness we're in while trying to learn new material or practice new habits.

We have habitual states of consciousness – attractor states

You get up early and climb into the shower. The water runs hot and silky over your body, relaxing as you shampoo and soap. What are you usually thinking and feeling?

- If you're a naturally "up" person, the coming day looks pretty good.

- If you're a depressed person, the world weighs you down with obligations, shameful failures, and certain disappointments.

- If you're an angry person, you're ruminating on injustices and personal slights, with lots of nasty stories about jerks who did you wrong.

- If you're an anxious person, you're dreading the day. Why? Because that's what you do – worry.

If we could choose – you know, press an "Up," "Down," "Angry," or "Anxious" button with instant results – we'd all press "Up." Sadly, most of us have *habits* of spending too much time anxious, angry, or depressed – feeling powerless to change.

But there's hope! *We can train our brains to develop new feeling habits to shift from bummed to grateful.*

How can we liberate our "up" selves?

The first step in lightening up is accepting and managing our darkness. A big part of the price of feeling better turns out to be acknowledging and helping the depressed, angry, and anxious parts of ourselves. For instance, you could confidently tell yourself, "Yes, I'm seeing the world through gloomy glasses, but I know it's a brighter place."

Now that you've recognized your dark outlook as an unhealthy habit of attention, you can focus on gratitude and positive anticipation. Socrates really nailed it with, "Know thyself," but could have added, "Practice habits of optimistic explanatory styles." In fact, Aristotle did get this. He suggested happiness involved learning and practicing virtuous habits.

The key is *practice*. Generate gratitude and positive explanations for yourself and the world, and maintain those states as much as you can. For instance, what are you grateful for right now? Your husband; wife; kids; friends; spiritual path; job; country; health...? *Find what you're grateful for, feel gratitude in your heart, and practice it all day long!*

Attractor states and default modes

Where do you naturally go in your thoughts when there's not much else happening? Sometimes I space out looking at clouds, sometimes I gravitate to whichever client is in the most trouble, or sometimes I'll start thinking of next Sunday's game between the Patriots and the Broncos. Those habitual places my brain takes me are called *attractor states.*

When you're up early in the shower with not much else on your mind, your brain coasts into rambling about the present, past, or future. These brain states, called *default modes* by neuroscientists, arise from brains constantly scanning everything inside and outside us, and associating – all the time generating habitual emotions and beliefs.

We often get out of the shower, get dressed, head out, and throughout the day ruminate about problems and solutions (which can be attractor states) – after all, in the wilds where we evolved, survival came first, and you couldn't be too careful. Fortunately, most of us don't live where death can lurk behind any bush, so we don't need to constantly be as vigilant for life threats (though driving, walking across the street, or engaging in any sport or physical activity involves hazards).

More commonly, default modes drift from one story to another... about the breakfast table, the afternoon tennis match, the way the light shines through the dust, "I wonder how Zoe's doing?" "This jasmine smells so good," – stuff like that.

We can harness our neurological tendencies for habitual states of consciousness like attractor states and default modes.

Since mostly we *are* safe and secure in almost every moment, we can practice *feeling* safe – consciously noticing how fine everything is right now – until *that's where we naturally go.* We can train our brains to be habitually more "Up."

Dogs are so lucky

Humans exist simultaneously in the past, present, and future, and can imagine things. This, of course, is a magnificent blessing, but it also tends to make us worry and get defensive, because we can *remember, anticipate, and imagine.*

Animals rarely have anticipatory anxiety. Your dog is not worried about prostate cancer or flesh eating bacteria, and is not fuming about the neighbor who yelled at him yesterday for barking. Your cat could care less about bankruptcy tomorrow.

You can worry or take offense at *anything real or imagined.* Since brains instinctively try to solve problems, real or imagined threats cause your brain to go into worry/must-solve-the-problem mode – in other words, *anxiety.*

Each time we create a brain state, it's more likely to be recreated. If we create it enough, we automatically go there in certain situations – it becomes an *attractor state.*

Cats and dogs don't waste time on such visions. Human speculation can amplify and elaborate our ancient mammalian defenses. We have problems when our super-powerful brains fixate on ludicrously low-probability events, generating surges of anxiety and fight/flight arousal – not fun, and bad for your health. For instance, you'll never enjoy swimming at the beach if you obsess about shark attacks, one of the lowest probability threats around.

It's good to be prepared

It's good to be prepared, but not to have anxiety, depression, or killing rage as attractor states. Let's look at the light side of attractor states – the possibilities of using them to create habits of feeling *stoked and satisfied.*

Psychologist Donald Hebb wrote in 1949, "Neurons that fire together, wire together." The more we activate certain states, the more likely they are to become attractor states and default settings for our brains (the physical mechanisms involved in neurons that fire together wiring together is the myelination process that's activated every time we switch on a neural network). So, it's going to pay off big time if we can practice amplifying caring, joyful, habitual states enough for them to become attractor states.

What are tested methods to increase and amplify caring, joyful habitual states?

- *Contemplative practice* – attunement, meditation, centering prayer, yoga, journaling, self-reflection, etc.

- *Cultivating compassion* – remembering most people want to be good, but some are better at it than others. Let's do our best to forgive and grow from our own and others' imperfections.

- Interrupting anxious, depressed, and angry states, and practicing gratitude for who we are and what we've been blessed with.

If we consistently evoke such practices, thoughts, and emotions, we can eventually *naturally – automatically* – go there.

Twentieth century psychologist and visionary, William James, thought a new habit could be programmed if practiced daily for twenty-one consecutive days. I don't know where he got that number, but it has been adopted by Harvard happiness researcher and author of *The Happiness Advantage*, Shawn Achor. This correlates nicely with neuroscience findings that practicing a positive new habit for thirty days stimulates stem cells in our brains to divide and form integrative neurons with extensions to our amygdala, the brain area that regulates emotions. These integrative neurons have a lot of GABA receptors in them – a neurotransmitter associated with *soothing,* and take up to three months to fully mature.

Joy and gratitude are beautiful attractor states

We can live in progressively more joy and gratitude if we practice them daily. Four practices I particularly like are:

- Each time you go outside, let yourself feel unity with nature.

- Smile ten times a day in situations you wouldn't normally.

- Compliment two people every day.

• Look your partner in the eyes every morning and night, smile, and tell him or her, "I love you," while cultivating the sensation of love in your heart and face.

There really are "Up" buttons, but we have to sometimes push them thousands of times to create new attractor states, new default modes, positive habits of being.

Just trying to be more positive and caring makes us better people, and it feels good to believe you're becoming a better person. If you cultivate joy, love, and gratitude, you're likely to be more generous, insightful, empathic, and healthy – you're building beautiful attractor states. These states support love, optimism, faith, and unity with everything.

What's not to like?

We have multiple brains

We have incredible capacities for learning. This is no surprise, because we have many brains. Neuroscientists have identified at least seven discrete brains, and all of them learn. They include:

• Brain stem – the basil ganglia are especially prominent in learning and enacting habits.

• Limbic area – our midbrain associated with emotions, memories, and motivation.

• Cerebral cortex – six credit card thick layers folded on top of our brain.

• Frontal lobes – the most recent addition to our brains and huge… 27% of our cortex, compared to 17% in chimpanzees.

• Right and left hemispheres – The right includes most habits and an integrated map of the body. The right hemisphere is non-verbal, intuitive, emotional, nonlinear, and processes faster. The left hemisphere is logical, linguistic, linear, and processes slower.

• Brain-to-heart-back-to-brain processing circuits run by the Vagus nerve and central to wellbeing and emotional self-regulation.

All these brains develop habits which are cued by experience and kick in unconsciously.

The talent code recipe for developing new habits

Malcolm Gladwell famously noted that ten thousand hours of practice are required to achieve mastery – habitual excellence – in most fields. Daniel Coyle wanted to dig deeper into why some teachers and places produced so many talented individuals in different areas, so he investigated nine global "hot spots" that produced disproportionate numbers of geniuses and high achievers. Why did Brazil produce so many soccer prodigies, John Wooden so many championship teams, and Argentina so many superlative orchestra conductors? He interviewed coaches, neuroscientists, and champion musicians and athletes, searching for common factors and underlying neurological mechanisms. He compiled his findings in his book, *The Talent Code*, and found that three factors emerged in creating habitual excellence. He labeled these factors *ignition*, *deep practice*, and *master coaching*. Not surprisingly, these factors involve growth mindsets, progressive levels of maturity on important lines of development, and optimal states for learning and changing habits – all cross-validated by beautiful, good, and true standards.

Ignition

Fire in the belly, passionate commitment, and deep soul's purpose are all terms for *ignition*, the overwhelming dedication someone feels in committing huge amounts of time and effort to learning and practicing new habits. We are ignited by heroes such as Nelson Mandela, Peyton Manning, and Taylor Swift. We've already discussed how kids have posters of their favorite athletes, actors, and musicians posted on their bedroom walls – unconscious choices their nervous systems have made of people to grow towards.

Great teachers, loving parents, and master coaches can ignite us to commit to mastering new habit constellations. One gifted teacher, *at any age*, translates into tens of thousands of dollars of added income when the student eventually joins the workforce. What has this teacher provided? Certainly, in many cases, ignition of a passion to excel in some fashion.

Deep practice

To maximize learning of new habits, individuals need to see the habit they are cultivating as a whole, break it up into little pieces, and slow down and speed up time when they practice. This is called "chunking."

Then, they need to practice to the point where they are making regular mistakes, and then correct or be corrected. This "bittersweet" spot has a feel of being on the edge of performance, where control and loss of control meet. Wayne Gretzky, for example, fell frequently during hockey practice. He looked for the outer limits of how fast and maneuverable he could be, and kept pressing that boundary, optimizing his development as a hockey player.

Master coaching

Coyle found that master coaches share four characteristics:

- They develop a "matrix" in their area of expertise that gives them deep and wide understanding of how their particular skill set of habits fit together, and how to move forward *from any spot* into creating more mastery.
- They demonstrate keen perception of how their students function in the present moment, and respond to feedback.
- They utilize a "GPS" system of offering quick, effective adjustments to alter bad habits and enhance good habits. They rarely criticize, and can always take their students a step deeper into mastery.
- They have some quality of "theatrical honesty," empathy, selflessness, and moral honesty when pointing out mistakes. They are truth-tellers who capture the imagination of their students through attunement and pleasure at effort and progress.

Think of the best coach, teacher, or therapist you ever had, and they will have some quality (whether quiet and subtle, or extraverted and extravagant) that inspired you to follow their advice and want their approval.

Habits are ubiquitous

Habits dominate our existence. Knowing this, and noticing ourselves being clueless, mindless, mindful, or dialed-in, we can continually be modifying our habits to better serve fun, joy, love, and health.

Try observing your habits today – see how many of them you can become conscious of. Remember, self-observation alone changes habits to some extent. A dialed-in life harnesses and coordinates our drives and habits to keep growing and living well. Such self-observation also broadens the scope of awareness; it literally gives us deeper consciousness – one of the coolest benefits of living a dialed-in life.

INTEGRAL IS ALL ABOUT MULTIPLE PERSPECTIVES

Understanding the universe as habits is another Integrally informed set of perspectives which can help us live and love well. You'll notice how in each chapter, we're exploring sets of perspectives to help us live and love well. The Beautiful, Good, and True standards we bring to each moment, me-first, we-first, and love-first worldviews, maturity on different developmental lines, and the multiple sexual and emotional dynamics in relationships, are all sets of perspectives that reveal the universe in unique ways, and guide us to joy, health, and intimacy.

The Integral system assumes the universe is too complex to be explained or dealt with using only one set of perspectives, so it organizes multiple perspectives to maximize clarity and impact. They all fit together in a fluid, dynamic matrix that can help us do better in almost any situation.

In our last two chapters we'll explore multiple perspectives about two other central aspects of life: work and spirituality.

Chapter 11: Dialed-in work – what kind of tribal leader are you?

"Being aware with acceptance and caring intent, *on purpose…*"

Work and purpose go well together.

Work can have deep meaning – like being a therapist, doctor, nurse, teacher, police officer, fireman, small business owner… almost any profession where our service has deeper significance beyond just our self.

Work with purpose can come in many flavors:

We can work for someone we respect, and feel the warm sense of being a valued, trusted employee who delivers reliable quality, while enjoying regular acknowledgment and appreciation.

The nature of our work can have a sacred feeling to it, a sense of calling. Being a psychotherapist has always had a luminance to me – it feels like sacred work. But sacred work doesn't have to involve healing or direct service. For instance, I've found most people in the entertainment industry – from the soundman, videographer, or editor, to the producer or lead actor – feel a sense of being part of a creative, magical enterprise larger than themselves on almost any project.

The company you work for – such as Apple, Zappos, or Patagonia – can embody principles like integrity, social responsibility, creativity, and respect. When you feel a member of such a community, something mysterious can click in and sate your hunger for purpose.

We can feel competent, honorable, and comfortable at work selling tires, doing makeup, or running the library at the elementary school.

How do we find purpose?

How do we discern our purpose and choose work that gives us what we most want (or need) to give? More than anything else (other than survival demands for money and security), we want work to feel meaningful. Most of us have asked ourselves, "What was I brought here to do?" or "Is what I'm doing my deepest gift to the world?"

David Deida suggests if we feel the suffering of not living our purpose – if we concentrate on yearning to give our best gifts to the world – guidance will come. His message is to not fight the frustration and hunger to give larger in our lives, but rather to embrace it, savor it, and cultivate it until an opportunity, impulse, idea, or activity shows up that alleviates the hunger.

Give the qualities that people love in you

Arjuna Ardagh (the originator of Awakening Coaching), in an interview with Terry Patten, was asked by a woman in her fifties to help her figure out, "What is it I'm meant to do." He suggested she ask twelve friends and relatives, "What is it about me that you really love, and you get from me more than from other people? You're asking about qualities." He suggested that there would be overlap in the twelve answers, and that together they would constellate a catalog of the qualities people especially loved about her. He went on to suggest that, "Those qualities are basically what you're here to do on the planet."

Here is meaning based on *who we are* more than *what we do*. Ardagh explained, "It doesn't really matter that much what you do with your time, so long as it provides a channel for those qualities to flow." He explained how Americans have countless choices which can confuse us, and distract us from our true natures. He finally concluded "So long as your gifts can flow into the world, you're going to be happy."

Pissed, dissed, blissed, and blessed

Bill O-Handlon is a therapist/writer/teacher who suggests that these four energies can guide us to purpose:

• **Pissed** refers to situations or issues that make us so mad we need to do something about them. I suspect many who work in the environmental movement were originally motivated by how angry they were at environmental degradation and human-perpetuated mass extinctions. Filmmaker Michael Moore reported that, even though he was always frightened before one of his often adversarial interviews, that he remembered how angry it made him that the little guy was being screwed and this motivated him to step up.

• **Dissed** refers to how we be might have been so challenged or put down that we became motivated to succeed. For instance, a disproportionate amount of successful entrepreneurs have dyslexia, a condition that often involves a smart person being miscatorgorized as not that smart as a child. It's easy to imagine such children thinking some variant of, "I'll show them!"

• **Blissed** especially refers to the Joseph Campbell quote when asked about meaning, "Follow your bliss." In general, if some area or activity is so pleasurable you can hardly stand it, there's likely personal meaning involved. Often there's a job there. I love sharing useful life/love perspectives with others, and this has led me to teaching and writing.

• **Blessed** refers to someone believing in us and guiding us through their understanding and confidence. My first therapist, Joe Ericson, told me when I was sixteen that I'd be a good therapist, and when I heard those words a thrill went through my body – I felt blessed. Perhaps, you've had a teacher, parent, mentor, or guardian angel tell you about your special gifts or abilities – perhaps waking you up to possibilities that weren't there before. If so, tell the story to someone you love.

We are called to action by many different energies, positive and negative, pleasurable and painful – pissed, dissed, blissed, and blessed.

215

What about when I have a regular job – you know, OK, but not especially meaningful?

Like most therapists, I'm fascinated with what makes employees and employers happy or unhappy. Over the years, I've found bits of research that seem particularly useful in understanding and dealing with work issues. For instance:

> • The three reasons a valued employee is likely to leave a job are 1) that he or she doesn't think the management structure is fair; 2) their contributions go unrecognized; or 3) they are not included in important information. Notice how none of these have to do primarily with compensation.

> • From middle management up, it costs approximately the yearly salary of an employee to bring someone new into a position.

> • Companies that have more women managers on average have more return to stockholders – they seem to run smoother.

Type One, Two, and Three employees

While vicariously participating in countless companies and professions, helping CEOs and workers at all levels, I've observed how employees fall into three major categories:

> **Type One:** He or she treats the organization as if they're personally responsible for its integrity and success. A Type One makes good decisions, and flourishes when receiving respect and recognition. Type One employees are rare and priceless, and should be retained under almost all circumstances. Professionally, Type One employees spend lots of time in we-first and love-first consciousness, where their natural inclination is to serve

216

the highest good. They tend to have growth mindsets and generally receive helpful influence effortlessly.

Type Two: He or she does an OK job, but screws up occasionally and needs to be supervised and periodically directed back on task. Type Twos form the bulk of most companies' employees, they need consistent, respectful supervision, and are value-added when properly managed. Type Two employees often come from me-first and we-first worldviews, where better communication is sought to answer problems with more or less awareness of their relative abilities (or inabilities) to receive influence.

Type Three: He or she will compulsively cause problems (sometimes even starting lawsuits), create conflict with other employees, and ideally should be eased out of your organization as quickly as possible. Type Threes are extra crazy and usually have a personality disorder of some sort. Type Threes often operate from me-first egocentricism with little or no ability to receive influence – especially when feeling the least bit threatened.

Managers help people grow

I once worked with a brilliant engineer named Kate who was inspired by, "the best boss I ever had." When Kate originally interviewed with this boss, he asked, "What does a manager do?" and she answered, "Help people grow on the job." "Yes!" he exclaimed excitedly "So few people realize that!"

If you are a manager, your job is to get your work done well and to help your people grow.

But people are complicated – how do managers best accomplish these goals?

It begins and ends with attunement

Attuning to yourself and others forms foundation skills for all work. Like parenting, if you can't attune, you might as well forget about giving

217

or receiving consistent positive influence. Let's assume you're a Type One manager. First, you attune to yourself and others, and then what?

Get rid of Type Threes

Learn to cut your losses. Type Three employees are hopeless, so don't waste time trying to help them grow, once you've figured out they have major resistance to change and compulsively create problems – get rid of them professionally and efficiently (if you don't document and follow policies and procedures perfectly, they're likely to sue you for wrongful termination). This highlights the social contract of work – we must be able to do the job or willing to learn to do the job. Unlike parenting where you're committed for the duration, or therapy where you and your client can take whatever time it takes to grow through blocks, work has a bottom line – hopefully, reasonable and compassionate – that must be met for someone to stay employed.

How to find out if someone is a Type Three worker? They show some or all of the following characteristics:

- They make the same mistake again and again in the face of instruction and feedback.

- They are cynical about the company, and resist finding the positives in the business' mission or organization.

- They chronically complain, and often define themselves as unfairly treated.

- When confronted, they defend, attack, make endless excuses and don't improve.

Type Ones are priceless

If you're lucky enough to be managing a Type One employee, give them recognition, responsibility, and respect. They are *personally identifying* with your company's mission, so find ways to turn them loose on tasks and problems.

If you are a Type One employee, understand that your value extends beyond your work product. You'll find yourself naturally organizing your thinking and behavior to embody growth mindsets, and this "effort and progress is beautiful, good, and true," worldview is contagious in most workplaces – especially if the CEO is onboard.

Type Twos are valuable and need attention

Type Two employees need to be regularly supervised and corrected if they are to optimally benefit the company. They will slowly improve and benefit the company, but still make mistakes and push boundaries. Never humiliate, castigate, or unfavorably compare them with Type One employees – the distress this generates can translate into worse performance and slowed growth. *Do* value their contributions, and set up mechanisms to monitor their work so you can tell them what they're doing well and what they need to improve. The more this evaluation/ feedback process is fair and accepted as normal business-as-usual in an organization, the less stress and more productivity for everybody. If possible, set them up with a Type One mentor.

I once worked with a doctor who trained and supervised a group of residents in a high stress medical environment. Every two weeks, he had everyone sit down and go over mistakes and superior decisions of the last two weeks, challenging the group to keep adjusting to improve service and professional development. He created a growth mindset culture in an environment where admitting mistakes was often quite difficult – these were high achieving, superbly educated MDs, not used to making or admitting mistakes, and conditioned by litigious medical America to avoid taking responsibility for potentially costly mishaps. He created an environment that nurtured Type Ones and gave Type Twos the input they needed to grow.

This last example illustrates another phenomenon I've observed in organizations – if you want to change the culture, you need buy-in and participation from your top manager.

Relating and handling

All work involves human relations to varying degrees. Whether you're dealing with bosses, employees, coworkers, or customers, how you socially engage heavily determines work culture and comfort levels on the job. *Relating* consists of cooperative, unguarded conversations that feel mutually respectful and open to influence. *Handling* means implementing strategies to get things done with people you've found you can't relate with. Good relating is value added, but so is good handling of people when you can't relate with them.

Most communications involve relating and handling to varying degrees. If you're attuned to yourself and others at work, you'll notice who you can just be frankly yourself with (relating), and who you seem to need to be more guarded with (handling). Try not to make someone wrong for having to be handled, or yourself wrong for needing to be handled. All relationships involve both relating and handling at different times.

> **Relating** is talk the way I'm talking now, as an equal giving and receiving influence. We're interested in growth-mindsets, appreciating what is, confident of continuing improvement. Relating is more fun and intimate, and naturally becomes the primary mode of discourse with Type One employees. These often include coworkers who seem honest, hardworking, and attuned, and managers you admire who embody the best of company culture.

> **Handling** involves using assertion skills, along with the power structures available to you, to get things accomplished and minimize negative drama.

Handling is the primary mode of dealing with Type Three employees, and is the classic "managing up" position if you are a Type One and your boss is a Type Two or Type Three person. If your boss becomes dangerous in some way (punitive, jealous, threatened, etc.) when you try to relate, you probably need to mostly handle him or her.

Since handling is a necessary form of dealing with Type Two and Type Three individuals, it's good to make it comfortable and effortless. Attunement broadens your view, so you can often see emotional/professional patterns invisible to others – leading you to become more dialed-in with your understanding and social strategies. If you try to relate with someone about *his* negatives, and he often gets crazy to some extent, you're likely dealing with a Type Two or Type Three person, and you need to handle them.

Three examples of handling:

• You tell your work mate he's not meeting deadlines and holding up the team, and he makes excuses, blames others, or complains about how difficult things are at home. You tell him, "I'm sorry it's been so hard. Let's figure out what support you need to meet your deadlines." You'll notice I'm not emphasizing negative work patterns or lack of personal discipline, as I might if I was relating. Instead, recognizing him as a Type Two employee who needs to be handled, I'm enlisting him to participate in progress that doesn't involve him having to acknowledge personal flaws or mistakes, but arranging to modify the work environment to give him better support, while holding him more accountable.

• You tell your secretary he's making too many personal calls at work, and he tells you his personal life is none of your business. You respond, "You're right that your personal life is none of my business, but how you spend your work time is, and you can't make personal calls during work hours anymore." This firm boundary avoids the emotional dynamics seething below the surface, because you happen to know he won't change unless presented with a black-and-white directive. A Type Two employee will follow the new rule (mostly), and work will improve. A Type Three employee will feel abused by the rule, and consciously or unconsciously make you pay for the confrontation.

• Your boss takes credit for your ideas, and when frustrated gets critical and dismissive. You insist that others be present at meetings when he's mad at you, thus changing his state which allows abusive behavior in private, but becomes more inhibited in public (where feeling observed moderates his me-first egocentricism).

221

Relating is direct, while "managing up" is almost always some form of handling

What are common characteristics of relating?

- Relating is direct, as in, "This is what I think is best. What do you think is best?" We're both interested in each other's ideas and opinions, and are willing to influence and be influenced, even to the extent of changing our positions if presented with better ones. We are in a healthy we-first, or even a love-first, moment.

- When we relate, we generally know who makes the ultimate call if we don't agree – me, you, a vote, or someone higher up the ladder. We try to find a solution we both believe in. If we can't, we find people more knowledgeable than us to add new information to the mix, or to consider our different approaches and either give feedback or make the call. In our shared "we" culture, it feels "good" to reach for the best solution/response/ perspective, rather than needing to be right or blindly repeating past actions.

- Mostly, when we're relating we're invested in optimal solutions, willing to be wrong, able to change our minds, and don't take it personally if our opinions don't prevail. We embody and advocate growth mindsets, and naturally reach for the higher levels on developmental lines. If we're primarily in we-first worldviews, we communicate effectively and fairly. If we're in love-first, we naturally support mutual intuitive leaps and insights.

Managing up

We've all heard the term, "Managing up," but what does it really mean? First of all, it means you can't consistently *relate* to a particular person higher than you on a power hierarchy, so you need to *handle* them. Secondly, it means that to effectively accomplish either work or personal goals with this person, you need handling skills.

222

For example:

> **Narcissistic managers** need positive feedback, will avoid giving you credit, and easily blame you when there are problems. An effective strategy is to avoid criticizing them, be willing to offer ideas and have them appropriated, and be very free with compliments about what this person does right. It's also good to have a backup support system if possible for when you become the target of narcissistic rage (which is likely to happen if you are present during – or, worse, participate in – some mistake, miscalculation, or unattractive social spasm of your narcissist boss).

> **Paranoid managers** often have what psychologists call traits of Borderline Personality Disorder. When offended, they want to punish (where offended narcissists just want you to disappear). They might be super-friendly, even inappropriately so, one day, and then think you are the worst employee ever, the next. When handling them, it's good to be impeccable and somewhat distant, avoiding intimate talk, socializing, or any wavering of work boundaries. It's also good to start looking for another job or a lateral move in your organization, before the hammer falls and you become a feature player in some paranoid fantasy.

Erotic polarity at work – a minefield you want to avoid

We all like to be attractive, and attracted, to people we find sexually appealing. Most of us even like people we find *unappealing* to find us attractive, just because it's validating to feel attractive and sexually magnetic. Most of us wear outfits we believe we look good in to work, make sure we're well-groomed, and are self-conscious about our appearance. We mostly like it when others notice us looking good, and we tend to enjoy interactions with people *we* find attractive.

Given the biochemistry of lust and romantic infatuation, these are dangerous forces if we're not dialed-in. Feed an attraction enough, and you'll get caught in a distracting attraction. Feed a distracting attraction enough, and you'll activate a romantic infatuation. If two people feed attraction or romantic infatuation enough, they can cross the border into an affair – fun and healthy between two singles, or a disastrous secret affair if one person is already married or hooked up.

As we explored in Chapter 7, love affairs are extremely forgiving until a certain threshold of intimacy is reached, the romantic infatuation haze begins to clear for one partner, and the demons of jealousy, envy, desire, defensive patterns, and frustrated love come to the fore. Even if your lover holds an equal power position at work (rather than employee or boss), a love affair is dangerous – you're relying on yourself and your lover to not go crazy when love-affair-problems arise (and love-affair-problems *always* arise).

Workplaces are the most common breeding grounds for affairs (pun intended!). Believe me… you don't want to go there!

In California, *one sexual episode,* or *comment,* or *joke,* or *invitation* can cost you and/or your organization tens of thousands of dollars. Most sexual harassment suits *never even make it to court.* When someone makes an accusation, it's almost always easier and cheaper for the lawyers to work out cash settlements than to litigate and explore what really happened. Also, what really happened is often embarrassing to devastating, especially in the case of secret affairs.

Unfortunately, one of the main places people meet lovers is at work, so how to deal with sexual polarities at work?

- Avoid socializing with possible partners above and below you on the power hierarchy.

- *Never consider* a secret affair.

- If you do think about dating someone, first imagine what it would be like if a relationship with them went *way* south. Is it worth endangering your job, or your potential lover's job, to start dating?

- If you do date someone from work, behave *completely honorably.* Lying, cheating, or exploiting in a work relationship colors your reputation like dye spilling into clear water.

Tribal leadership, Dave Logan's super-cool system of optimizing work cultures

Dave Logan and his colleagues at the University of Southern California Business School have come up with the best corporate culture orientation I've ever discovered.

If you're a student of business culture writing, you might notice that it's hard to remember almost anything people write about business cultures. "The three rules for successful businesses," "The seven habits of highly effective people," etc. all sound totally relevant when I read them, but for the life of me, I have trouble remembering (much less applying) them after I finish the book or article.

Not so with Tribal Leadership! This system sticks with you, provides relatively effortless ways to honestly look at you and others in the context of work cultures, and has built-in action steps to progress from less successful (Tribal One) to most successful (Tribal Five).

It's also wonderfully useful in psychotherapy. Check out the following story about Jim, a guy who benefitted immensely both personally and professionally from the Tribal Leadership model:

Jim – mid-twenties, strong and good-looking, strides frowning into my office. He usually arrives bummed out and in a hurry. Jim loves hiking in the mountains behind Santa Barbara, sometimes bulling his way through chaparral and up rock faces with pure power. I know his family to be good people who are worried sick about his alcoholism, which recently resulted in his first DUI (if you work at all with alcoholics, you get in the habit of saying "*First* DUI").

The DUI woke Jim up enough so that he's currently struggling with abstinence and attending AA meetings. Like many addicts in the early stages of recovery, Jim slips periodically, occasionally driving up to the top of San Marcos Pass with a whiskey bottle, drinking it in the moonlight, and talking to the bottle until he passes out. Not surprisingly, Jim suffers clinical depression and has catastrophic personal relationships.

I hand him a cup of tea, asking, "How are you doing?"

Jim gives me a sour look, "It's another shitty day in paradise."

Jim is a classic example of a Tribal Stage Two individual. His life position is, "My life sucks." He believes that others have good lives, and

225

even that he himself *could* be happy and successful. It's just that, on balance, his life sucks.

Tribal Leadership is genius

Dave Logan, John King, and Halee Fischer-Wright are the authors of *Tribal Leadership*, a groundbreaking work on how humans naturally form tribes, and that these tribes develop from primitive Tribal Stage One (life sucks) to advanced Stage Five (life is great). The system forms a practical framework for operationalizing relating and handling with Type One, Type Two, and Type Three employees.

You can tell what kind of tribal orientation someone has by observing what they do and how they talk – literally the words they use. Here are a few details of the *Tribal Leadership* system (for the whole deal, treat yourself and go to www.triballeadership.net; these guys are incredible):

Human groups – from a few to around a 150 people – naturally form five kinds of tribes.

> **Tribal Stage One**, "Life sucks," people have little hope or respect for themselves or others. Think street gangs.

> **Tribal Stage Two**, "My life sucks," believe their lives are awful, but others have happiness, excellence, and meaning that just *might* be attainable. Classic examples are hopeless workers in sterile cubicles, and depressed alcoholic wounded warriors like Jim.

> **Tribal Stage Three** is, "I'm great and you're not." We all know (or are) the egocentric high-achiever who's constantly busy, surrounded by "idiots," and overwhelmed by work/home demands and responsibilities. Tribal Three leaders don't delegate well, and structure communication patterns of other employees talking directly to him or her, rather than facilitating people talking with each other. Many business cultures orient around powerful Tribal Three individuals.

226

Tribal Stage Four is, "We're great, and you're not." These tribal groups are bound together by shared values and passionate purpose (Logan calls it "noble cause") and naturally work cooperatively to realize a shared vision. Tribal Four leaders have an instinct to connect others in service of the noble cause – constantly using their authority and social skills to hook people up into problem solving systems. I imagine the cast and crew of Saturday Night Live have spent many years on a Tribal Four level.

Tribal Stage Five is, "Life is great," groups work blissfully together to change the world. Steve Jobs had a mission to challenge and support his people in Apple (brimming with collective genius) to change the world. Tribal Four tribes can rise to Tribal Five when their noble cause is primarily for the benefit of mankind, and less about competing with others. One of Logan's favorite examples is the Apple engineer who was intoxicated with creating a home computer that was so easy to operate his grandmother could use it.

Tribal Four is as sophisticated as most businesses get, but Tribal Five still keeps showing up, reflecting evolution reaching through culture – groups self-organizing towards greater compassion and deeper consciousness. The more compassion and the deeper your consciousness, *the better it feels* to be changing the world, rather than just beating the competition.

Like most developmental stage models, you can't skip levels. Tribal One "Life sucks" has to up-level to Tribal Two "My life sucks" before he can get stable at Tribal Three, "I'm great." "I'm great" individuals can coordinate values/purpose with others into Tribal Four, "We're great." "We're great" groups can temporarily up-level to Tribal Five "Life is great" visionaries, but tend to regress back to Tribal Four let's-beat-the-competition after the project comes to fruition.

In general, tribes regress (for instance, "We're great" fractures into "I'm great and you're not") unless the community regularly reviews and refines core values while focusing on the current incarnation of noble cause.

Logan suggests that company core values be reexamined and refined every six months. (This is *so* like therapy. Ongoing self-reflection with growth-mindset goals of refining values and improving life accelerates progress during and after sessions – ask any therapist.)

The Tribal Leadership system was designed by Dave Logan, whose roots are in rhetoric – the study of persuasive dialogue. Logan is a professor of business at University of Southern California, and bases his evaluations and understanding purely on *language and behavior* – "true" validity standards. Language and behavior are dimensions that are especially useful for business because they are observable, don't require much psychological insight, and can be adjusted if someone is willing to examine their habits of language and behavior and exert some willpower to change them.

In other words, the Tribal Leadership system is minimally threatening to me-first egocentric and we-first communication-centric worldviews, and provides scaffolding to love-first worldcentric, serve-the-highest-good perspectives and practices.

Tribal Two Jim – lost in "my life sucks" – needs to up-level to Tribal Three "my life is great." To do this requires acknowledging his own gifts and skills, and speaking and acting from these strengths (*language and behavior*). We spend a lot of time on this, with me busting him each time he slips into "my life sucks" references, and encouraging and guiding him towards an "I'm great" identity.

Today, Jim starts talking about his job as a construction foreman. "I like framing. It's clean work because all you have to do is follow the blueprints and – wow! – a house starts taking shape. I just wish the morons on my crew didn't keep screwing things up."

Even though Jim is trashing his crew, the "I'm great" references reflect progress from "my life sucks." I do the classic Tribal Leadership maneuver of creating a triad – directing Jim to connect positively with someone else, "You told me a few weeks ago you usually like the guys on your crew. I'll bet if you spent a little time each morning going over the plans with them, getting them to talk to each other, and emphasizing how cool today's piece of the job is, there'd be fewer mistakes and more fun."

Jim looks thoughtful at this. He wants to talk about the crew being "morons," but this idea of sharing values and techniques appeals to him –

he is a dedicated worker, and can sense it would be productive. "I'll try it," he says, "But I don't expect too much."

I smile, "I don't know Jim. Usually when you put your mind to something, you're quite successful."

He smiles back, only half-sarcastically, "Yeah, I know… I'm great."

Procrastination – anxiously trying to hold back the future

Most of us work different jobs throughout a lifetime, and work habits travel with us from job to job. One bad habit that's particularly important to improve is procrastination.

Jason is a successful lawyer in his mid-forties, sitting in my office in a frozen state of procrastination.

In most of his life, Jason takes charge and stays fully resolved. His work gets done, his body gets exercised, and he shows up for his son's games and parent conferences.

What has him immobilized and unresolved is his inability to sell his boat and slip in the Santa Barbara harbor – something he *knows* he needs to do – but just can't bring himself to start. He got the boat primarily to entertain clients and learn how to sail, and it just isn't delivering. He hasn't used it for clients, his company needs the cash, and, as it turns out, he's not that keen on sailing these days.

When I ask, "Why not?" Jason says, "I just don't want to deal with it." Whenever the subject shows up, anxiety floods through him and Jason shuts down.

Some psychologists suggest the three sources of procrastination are avoiding something aversive, vague or weak intentions, and being easily distracted. Most agree the basic solution is challenging the self-deception inherent in all three, and getting on with taking care of business. I agree with these constructs, but think the deeper issue of procrastination involves our relationship with the future – a relationship that only self-aware humans (existing simultaneously in the past, present and future) can have.

In general, anxiety reflects fear of the future, with procrastination as a prime mechanism for keeping the future at bay – literally trying to *hold back* the future. This is one reason we're often reluctant to get specific about what we're anxious about – if we turn a general anxiety into a *specific fear* it becomes harder to avoid action to move forward.

Even when we identify a specific fear and what we need to do about it, some of us reflexively procrastinate – often with variants of "I don't want to deal with it right now," "I'll get to it later," or, "Maybe I can get someone else to do it."

Later in the session, Jason and I discuss this more deeply:

Jason: "I've been feeling uneasy this last week. It's been hard to concentrate."

Keith: "Has anything specific been on your mind?"

Jason: "I don't know. It's been hard to go down to the harbor."

Keith: "Really – you used to love hanging out at the harbor. What's been hard?"

Jason: "Well… I know I have to sell the boat and slip. I don't sail anymore. Tom [his son] never liked sailing to begin with, and I'm not taking clients out sailing like I thought I would. Money's tight and it's time to do it."

Keith: "So, you're procrastinating selling your boat?"

Jason looks out at my garden and lowers his voice: "I guess."

I can feel how Jason doesn't want to talk about this. His attention is wavering as he palpably resists examining a sell-the-boat future. As usual, there is something deeper below the surface:

Keith: "What does it mean to you to sell the boat and slip?"

Jason: Tears welling up – "Sandy [his wife who died eighteen months ago] and I had some of our best times on the boat. I suppose it's another way of saying 'goodbye.'"

Keith: I sit quietly for a minute, comfortably connected with this good man. It's important to honor grief. Big losses deserve grief – nervous systems usually mark the loss of someone who's gone with the "Denial, bargaining, depression, anger, acceptance" cycle that Elisabeth Kubler Ross made famous – and grief is our natural path to integrating the new world created by loss. "We've talked a lot about how hard it's been to accept Sandy's death."

Jason: Resisting the future – "Selling the boat seems like such a final step. Another part of our life that's gone." He suddenly brightens up. "Though, I have to say, talking about doing it sounds good. Maybe selling the boat will actually help."

Keith: "I've found that embracing the future is usually the best way to go, and that procrastinating actually amplifies dread."

230

Jason: "What? You mean like, 'A coward dies a thousand deaths, but a brave man only one?'"

Keith: Laughing a little – "That's a little harsh – but, yes, that's what I mean. Putting stuff off just increases anxiety. That's why procrastination – even though we do it to reduce tension in the short run – creates vastly more distress in the long run."

Jason: Suddenly resolved and more upbeat – "All right! I'll list it this week!"

Keith: "Great idea! Though, remember, there's a part of you still trying to talk yourself out of it. If you don't call today, you'll probably have to struggle a little harder to do it tomorrow, and so on. That's the secret of dealing with procrastination – indulging impulses to avoid important action can create phobic avoidance, while resolved action in the face of fear cultivates courage. Courage is doing what's right, even though we're scared or resistant."

This is a typical procrastination conversation. When you get to what's really happening – resisting the future by practicing a bad habit of avoidance – it becomes easier to figure out what the underlying issues are and resolve to do what needs to be done.

Also, like Jason feeling better about listing his boat, *deciding* to take action *is* assertive action, which reduces anxiety. It also illustrates procrastination as a potentially deadly habit – the more you practice it, the more deeply embedded the habit becomes. Research shows that the closer we get to having to do something scary, the more we try to talk ourselves out of it, so *allowing procrastination as an option* predisposes us to opt out of responsibilities as we approach action.

Back in the seventies, researchers found that deep relaxation and assertion dramatically reduced anxiety. This led to anxiety reduction approaches using deep relaxation and assertive action, which to some extent anticipated the Mindfulness Based Stress Reduction of Jon Kabat Zinn, and the Dialectical Behavior Therapy of Marsha Linehan. For years in the seventies and eighties, I taught assertion training groups where people learned how to face their fears, plan and practice effective action, and then go into the world and make things happen.

When Jason engaged in assertive action – the firm decision to list his boat – his distress plummeted. In subsequent sessions, the theme of not indulging procrastination became increasingly important – until finally

231

Jason began using *the impulse* to procrastinate as a cue to be especially sure to get something done. This is how we turn unhealthy habits like procrastination into healthy habits supporting growth and development.

It's useless to resist the future! It's especially bad at work, since procrastination costs money and irritates bosses and coworkers. We do much better embracing the future and doing what it takes to make a good future happen. If we notice procrastination and use it as a guide to self-reflection and assertive action, we're effectively turning one of our most dangerous capacities – avoiding the future through procrastination – into a strength, where the impulse to procrastinate leads to insight, creation, and success.

DIALED-IN WORK MATTERS

Every human possesses incredible powers. Each time you get behind the wheel of a car, walk down the street, fall in love, or go to work, you influence others profoundly. Most of us work, whether we're paid for it or not. We have responsibilities and tasks we've taken on, and dialed-in work naturally delivers superior results.

What if we all worked consistently dialed-in? Some professions, like Navy Seals and neurosurgery, involve cultures which demand dialed-in altitudes on key developmental lines like the warrior line, the technical line, the emotional self-regulation line, and the kinesthetic line. These professions are famous for delivering consistent quality and high standards.

Dialed-in work is contagious

One person committed to attunement and compassionate understanding as core personal standards up-levels a work environment. You've probably felt the impacts of dialed-in work from your best teachers, mentors, and valued team members.

You could be that person.

It reminds me of the last verse of Christopher Fry's *Waking in the Dark*, because work is "making," and the poem asks, "What are you making for?"

Thank God our time is now!
When wrong comes up to meet us everywhere
Never to leave, till we take the longest stride of soul men ever
took
Affairs are now soul sized
The enterprise is exploration into God
What are you making for?
It takes so many thousand years to wake,
Will you wake, for pity's sake?[2]

Dialed-in work has a sacred feel about it, and leads to progressive experiences of waking up to better perspectives. This leads us to the topic of our last Chapter, Dialed-in Spirituality. The deeper you get in any area – love, work, parenting, marriage, or art – the more of a sense of the sacred arises from that area.

Attunement, plus a sense of the sacred, plus a resolve to do the right thing right now almost insures dialed-in behavior!

Karma Yoga

Work involves action of some sort – service to people or a company – and there is an Eastern tradition of sacred service called Karma Yoga. Roger Walsh has written and taught about Karma Yoga for years. Karma Yoga is doing your best to make every act an expression of Spirit. You set your intent, perform the activity, observe the results with complete acceptance of all outcomes, and then dedicate your efforts to consciousness everywhere.

Karma Yoga comes from the famous Hindu text, the Bhagavad Gita, where the God Krishna is the Charioteer of the warrior Arjuna on a vast battlefield, and answers Arjuna's questions as they ride into combat. When Arjuna asks, "What is Karma Yoga?" Krishna replies, "Karma yoga is making every act an expression of God."

That's Dialed-in work.

Dialed-in work exercise

For two days, keep a record of Type One, Type Two, and Type Three employee behaviors in you and your coworkers. In addition:

Write down two episodes of relating with coworkers.

Write down two episodes of handling (either you handling someone else, or someone else handling you).

Notice when you're attuned and not attuned to yourself and others, and write down any patterns you observe.

Notice any activities that felt especially satisfying or meaningful to you at your job, and write about them.

Take all that you've written to a comfortable place, and read it with the intent of finding patterns, yums, and yucks – this will point you towards dialed-in work and satisfying service.

Chapter 12: Dialed-In Spirituality

Chop that wood, carry water.
What's the sound of one hand clapping?
Enlightenment, don't know what it is.
~from *Enlightenment* by Van Morrison~

Many times in the last forty years, someone has called about therapy, or walked into an initial session, and has asked, "Do you take spirituality into account in your work?"

The question always evokes such a flood of associations that, to this day, I pause for a moment to gather my thoughts before responding with some version of, "Yes, I think spirituality is central to everything."

That flash of confusion reflects the magnitude of spirituality – the sheer vastness. *We are all God all the time.* From pure emptiness arises tiny fields self-organizing towards greater complexity, ultimately reaching *through us* for unity of pure consciousness.

I look into your eyes, I feel Spirit communing with Spirit, God *as* you harmonizing with God *as* me in an inter-subjective dance. Nothing exists completely separate from the rest of the universe. There are permeable boundaries in multiple dimensions – time, space, and unqualifiable transtemporal, translocal, and transpersonal realities that I can sense, but only faintly understand.

Frankly, "Do you take spirituality into account in your work?" usually disorients me a bit.

I imagine fish would have the same problem if they had conscious awareness and you asked them if they took water into account in their work.

A dialed-in life naturally prefers harmony with spirit – with whatever is sacred – progressing towards more beautiful, good, and true.

Spiritual awakening and deepening is not a choice with growth, we are drafted by our souls as we wake up to new perspectives. It's like the wagon trains in the nineteenth century who had no choice in recognizing the Rockies, rising gradually into the sky for weeks as their wagons slowly migrated west across the great plains.

It's no coincidence that the more we mature on any developmental line, (like how we think, relate, play, sex, judge, or work) the more that line has spiritual luminance.

You have a unique spirituality

Often your spiritual orientation guides you towards the good response right now. Dialed-in spirituality utilizes attuned Integral understanding to keep reaching for that sweet spot, which for me evokes existential questions:

- What are enlightened states?

- What are the universal spiritual currents that move through all of us?

- Where's the scaffolding, the frameworks to lead us deeper?

- What characterizes your unique spirituality?

As we progress through this chapter, stay attuned. Look for stories and frameworks you find particularly wonderful or irritating.

"**Wonderful**" leads to your natural spiritual inclinations, which demand attention, and protest in frustration when blocked.

"**Irritating**" will reflect either some shadow material in you (such as biases, defensive states, previous traumas, or forbidden feelings/thoughts/practices), or just not agreeing or resonating with the perspectives.

"Wonderful" and "Irritating" can thus lead to deeper resonance and more maturity on moral, spiritual, self, and interpersonal lines of development.

Modern enlightenment as oneness with all states and stages

Ken Wilber sees modern enlightenment as a felt sense of unity with all states and stages existent in the world. Certainly, most contemplative traditions agree that spiritual development involves increasing care, decreasing identification with a separate sense of self, and increasing identification with both pure emptiness and everything that is arising. Given the multitude of transcendent experiences possible, I suspect there are a number of states that can loosely be grouped as enlightened states.

Enlightened states are indescribably delicious, and seekers who stably inhabit such states eventually yearn to share them – we become more generous and eager to give as we grow.

We can use transcendent states as guides and worthy goals, and endeavor to live them as completely as possible – we know intuitively that organizing our lives around what feels sacred is a good thing. If we experience enlightened states enough, they become more stable traits of consciousness, more easily accessible, and often associated with connecting experiences of faith, unity, and care.

A sense of the sacred is universal

Most of us have a sense of the sacred – feeling connected to some spiritual goodness. Spirituality ranks high in happiness surveys – apparently a central feature of satisfying lives.

"Spiritual, but not religious" is the fastest growing self-described spiritual orientation in the United States (currently about 25%). In one UCLA study, 75% of the students and 84% of the instructors described themselves as "Spiritual," and almost all of them kept it to themselves for fear of censure by other students or teachers. Some of us are ashamed of our natural spirituality, and some of us are so afraid of censure – even subtle censure – that we become reluctant to share our beliefs and experiences.

Dialed-in spirituality begins with the reality that all humans yearn towards connectedness with energetic forces, figures, and powers beyond themselves. Whether it's God, Spirit, the Void, the Tao, enlightenment, love, family, energy healing, meditation, yoga, or surfing (you have to be a surfer to get this one), most of us have areas of spiritual luminance we hold dear.

A sense of personal spiritual connectedness is associated with better health, less disease, better social relationships, and more ethical behavior.

One of my favorite areas of Integral studies is Integral Spirituality, where we can observe universal frameworks of spiritual experience, and then find our own emergent growth edges, often involving deep mutuality with like-minded others. Ken Wilber's book *Integral Spirituality* is a cornucopia of such frameworks.

Why bother with spiritual practices?

I find it fascinating that we are all born with an innate yearning for self-transcendence. I can understand other temperamental variables such as self-directedness, cooperativeness, novelty seeking, persistence, harm avoidance, and dependence, but why self-transcendence? If the Darwinian view of evolution being all about passing on genes and making the individual fitter to survive explains development, of what survival value is self-transcendence? If the instinct toward self-transcendence is not a spandrel – an inadvertent effect of some other mutation – are there other forces at work?

Rupert Sheldrake and Ken Wilber suggest that the "selfish gene" hypothesis of evolution – the idea popularized by Richard Dawkins that all evolution is about survival of the fittest – is an inadequate explanation of the evolutionary drive toward greater complexity and deeper consciousness.

Self-transcendence seems to involve a complex, but predictable path from before birth to after death, increasingly aided or blocked along the way by conscious choices. The direction of this drive is toward greater care and unity. The deeper – or higher, or more mature – we develop on practically every developmental line, the more of a felt sense of unity, care, and spirituality we tend to experience. Apparently, dialed-in spirituality is a human birthright and tendency.

In the following pages we'll look at different dimensions of spiritual experiences. Dialed-in spirituality involves you clarifying what best suits you.

Spirit in the first, second, and third person

There are central categories of relationship with Spirit – **nature mysticism** (God in the third person, as "it"), **deity mysticism** (God in the second person, as "you"), **formless mysticism** (pure emptiness), and **non-dual mysticism** (God in the first person – all emptiness and form simultaneously as "I").

Nature mysticism: "The clouds…"

When I was around eight or nine years old, I was lying on my back in the front yard of our family home in the suburbs of Los Angeles, looking at the clouds. As my attention was drawn into the huge, beautiful, shapes drifting across the sky, I felt a blissful sense of unity with nature. It was as if the clouds, sky, world, and I were all connected in the same wondrous dance. Everything seemed simple and beautiful, and I was completely transported. Now, I recognize this as nature mysticism, oneness with nature, Spirit in the third person as "it."

Suddenly, my father was jerking me up by the arm. I began attempting to explain, "The clouds…," but he had been calling me for dinner, and, assuming I had been deliberately ignoring him (rather than lost in cosmic unity!), he began hitting me as he marched me into the house.

My dad was a gentle man for his era, which made the episode all the more shocking. Ironically, his outrage probably helped me remember the experience. Zen literature is full of stories of a student having a moment of transcendence, running to his Master to explain, and the Zen Master whacking him soundly to mark his breakthrough.

It's common for us to project our filters onto someone else's outward expression of their experience, when where they're coming from can be much different than our interpretation, based on our own filters. Humans tend to project their perspectives onto others, and the dialed-in practice is to recognize our own tendencies to do this, and be aware that our perceptions of another's beliefs and behaviors usually need to be held lightly until we actually know why they behave the way they do – usually by asking. If my dad hadn't have been so mad, he might have been curious as to why I couldn't hear him calling, and thus lead us into an intimate conversation about spiritual experience.

Deity Mysticism: God in the second person

My Aunt Dorothy (who is a judge in the Ninth Federal Circuit Court, and senior elder in the Baha'i faith), told our family some details of my Aunt Nancy's death in 1965 that we'd never heard before.

Aunt Dorothy is the middle of three daughters. Her older sister, Elizabeth, is my mother. Her younger sister Nancy had three daughters, Julie, Janie, and Jill. When her children were still young, Nancy was diagnosed with brain cancer, and subsequently died on December 31, 1965. At our annual Thanksgiving gathering in 2013, Dorothy told us the following story:

"It was New Year's Day at our house, and Nancy's family was over. After dinner, Nancy said she felt tired and lay down on the couch and fell asleep. Later, I heard her wake up and I walked into the living room. Nancy said, 'Dorothy! I dreamed I died and went to Baha'u'llah [both Dorothy and Nancy's families were devout Baha'is]. I told him, "I can't die yet! My girls need me for two more years!"'

Aunt Dorothy said, 'You had a bad dream, Nancy. You ate too much turkey.'

Nancy was diagnosed with terminal brain cancer soon after, and the doctors gave her six months to live. Two years later to the day, December 31, 1965, she lay in a hospital bed, with two of her favorite Baha'i teachers sharing favorite prayers. That night she died."

"Dorothy!" I said, "Why didn't you tell us the story then?"

She said, "We didn't want to upset anyone."

This was an intimate experience of God in the second person, based in the spiritual community of the Baha'i Faith. We owe it to our families to share the stories, to inspire us and help us develop faith in Spirit – in this case, Spirit in the second person as "you." Nancy met Baha'u'llah in her dream, had a personal relationship with Him, and died feeling profoundly connected with her God and her Baha'i fellowship.

Belonging to a church tends to be good for your health

I was raised as an Episcopalian with mild prejudice against the Catholic Faith. When I broke from the Episcopal Church at 13, I was prejudiced against almost all western religions. I didn't realize it, but I was making the same mistake Voltaire made in the French Revolution, when he denounced religious oppression with his, "Remember the cruelties!" Voltaire's anger at church cruelties blinded him to the heart of the church – surrender to God in the second person, God as "you."

People active in churches live longer and are happier, and religions are evolving. I have a progressive Catholic client whose faith and commitment to God have influenced me greatly. Recently, he told me that at an eight day retreat, he was instructed by his spiritual advisor to meditate on a passage in Mathew describing Jesus the night before the crucifixion. She suggested he meditate on how Jesus obviously wished everyone would wake up to love. For the first time I can remember, a reference to the Bible made me hungry to find the passage. When I read it later, I felt a tingle of charged sacred awareness.

I laughed and told him, "This is missionary work! After all these years you have caused me to look to the Bible for a sacred truth from Christ, a messenger of God! He smiled a saintly smile. His story – his eight-day retreat, his pure-hearted spiritual advisor, the Bible passage he was given, and my vast respect for his goodness and integrity – had just given me a taste of *his* Catholic church, the spiritual community he loves and has dedicated his life to.

Formless mysticism: pure emptiness

During meditation, many report a sense of losing their separate identity in a boundless void of no "things," just pure emptiness. These are experiences of causal, or formless, mysticism – feeling oneness with a vast emptiness out of which the universe is constantly and miraculously being born.

I honestly can't remember my first experience of pure emptiness, and my most recent one is at this moment writing these words. Speaking about emptiness often evokes emptiness, and partly explains why all human societies come together for sacred ceremony – where they speak,

241

sing, dance, and touch each other into mutually amplified connections with the infinite.

Traffic Light

I used to be irritated stopping and waiting at red lights, so a number of years ago I started going into emptiness meditation every time I had to stop at an intersection. Now, I feel a vague sense of regret when the lights turn green.

Non-dual awareness: pure emptiness and pure fullness arising simultaneously.

When I was thirty years old and had been practicing martial arts and meditation for fifteen years, I was introduced to Myamoto Musashi's *A Book of Five Rings*. Mushashi wrote extensively about sourcing yourself in the void, and channeling it into dominating power in combat. Musashi said:

"What is called the spirit of the void is where there is nothing. It is not included in man's knowledge. Of course the void is nothingness. By knowing things that exist, you can know that which does not exist. That is the void."

As I incorporated his philosophy and techniques into my training, I began to have moments where there was the peculiar sense of inhabiting pure emptiness and absolute fullness simultaneously. As I later learned, these were non-dual experiences combining absolute cessation (emptiness) and complete presence in the world (fullness).

A young man once told me that he was planning on taking psychedelic mushrooms. I told him something I wish someone had told me in my late teens and twenties when I experimented with various psychedelic substances. "Look," I said, "When you feel a sense of unity with nature, or a sense of being part of an omnipresent, pervasive consciousness, or a sense that we are all joined in love and emptiness simultaneously, that's not just the drug. That's real. What the drug can sometimes do is

242

temporarily alter how you feel, see, taste, think, and sense in ways that make these things which are always present perceptible to you."

Feeling the absolute fullness of the universe simultaneously with the absolute emptiness out of which everything constantly arises is Spirit in the first person – as a boundless "I am."

How do I uncover my unique spiritual orientation?

Nature mysticism (Spirit in the third person – as "it"), deity mysticism (Spirit in the second person – as "you"), formless mysticism (Spirit as pure cessation – absolute nothingness), and non-dual mysticism (Spirit in the first person – as unified "I") are common paths that our instinct toward self-transcendence leads us to.

As you yearn for spiritual awaking and unity, a great way to grow is to experiment with them all, and incorporate what feels most natural and useful into your daily routines.

Spirituality from conception to death

Biologist Rupert Sheldrake, Ken Wilber, and others believe that there are countless, interpenetrating fields of energy associated with every physical being and form. They believe such fields associated with living organisms – sometimes called "morphic fields" – guide the development of each living thing. They suggest that such fields not only guide individual development, but are shaped as individuals, families, and species change and evolve. The "Hundredth monkey" story – where when enough macaque monkeys on one island started washing their sweet potatoes, monkeys on other islands mysteriously began routinely washing their sweet potatoes – is an example of the idea of energetic species tipping points that occur when enough individuals change. The Hundredth Monkey story turns out to almost certainly be an urban legend, but experiments have been conducted with rats where the effect has been demonstrated. These fields might exist for families, clans, and even nations. It is possible that *before conception,* multiple morphic fields are already guiding our development.

Within the scaffolding of such forces, genetically driven development takes place. Fetuses communicate with mother (and quite possible father and others) biochemically and energetically. During the third trimester – perhaps even sooner – babies are encoding implicit memories into their nervous systems. As we've discussed in previous chapters, these implicit memories are automatic, don't require conscious focus, and involve perceptual memory, emotional memory, body memory, constructs of repeated events, and behavioral priming. When they are recalled – cued by internal or environmental events – all the above aspects are evoked *with no sense of something being remembered.* It's possible that states of deep meditative equanimity are accessing implicit memories of oneness with the womb that were encoding during pregnancy, when the fetus *literally experienced oneness with everything.*

Two years after birth, we start talking. Since the brain circuitry for anticipating the future is the same as for remembering the past, language abilities and explicit memory in many ways initiate a child into a past, present, and future. Within this potentially terrifying realm of infinite perspectives, interior to the infinite array of relationships with self, others, and world in the past/present/future, self-aware consciousness awakens and grows.

Between age eighteen and thirty months, symbolic language takes off like a rocket. The left hemisphere, with its literal, linguistic, logical, linear bias, begins to dominate, and kids start pestering caregivers with, "Why..." questions. This increasing sense of self in the past, present, and future accelerates symbolic communication interiorly and with others, and deepens abilities to approve/disapprove of self and others. As we've talked about in Chapter 9, this is where much social learning and the foundations of defensive states are established.

Spiritually, toddlers and very small children have a magic orientation – they can believe people directly control the universe.

Older children have a more mythic orientation, where they find they can't control the world, but others – like parents, police, Gods, or superheroes – might.

As children grow into teens, they can continue to believe exclusively in traditional Gods, or include rational explanations and merit based systems that complement and expand the cosmologies and values of their grade school mythologies.

As we develop spiritually, we enter into energetic connections with others, nature, and Spirit – like my childhood experience with the clouds. Flashes of unity consciousness arise in prayer, yoga, shared practice, meditation, love, or other states.

Transcendental losses and gains through development

From a self-transcendence point of view, development involves progressive losses and gains.

Developmental losses?

- Loss of unity with the womb.

- Loss of unity with the physical universe after birth. In their first five or six months, children gradually discover through movement and sensation that their bodies are separate from the objects around them.

- Loss of faith in mythic figures able to perform supernatural feats.

- In adolescence, loss of absolute certainty, as the rational capacity to hold opposing concepts simultaneously shows shades of gray everywhere.

Developmental gains?

- The physical universe, as we discover it bit by bit.
- Relationship/intimacy with mother and others.

- A new vibrant growing body, changing almost weekly throughout the first year of life.

- New and increasing mental, physical, emotional, and social abilities.

- An expanding sense of the complexity and richness of self, others, and the world.

- Eventual capacities for felt unity with everything, and for a return of faith in God in the second person, as "you," but this time through depth of consciousness rather than neurobiological immaturity.

Complex systems like our brains and our relationships naturally self-organize toward greater complexity – development never ends. With the teenage advent of formal operational thought – the abilities to hold "What if?" perspectives, consider opposing viewpoints simultaneously, and establish deeper empathic resonance with others – comes capacities to re-own the losses we've necessarily had to endure through previous development.

Neurologically, this re-owning involves neural integration where – with practice – we can better harmonize our right and left brain hemispheres, synchronize our brainwaves and heart rhythms, create optimal self-regulatory balance between inner and outer experience, and be exquisitely attuned to what is happening in ourselves, others, and our environments. Such integration supports autonomous, coherent, autobiographical narratives continually refining in our right hemispheres, while we develop deepening left hemispheric capacities to reach for true, good, beautiful, and socially comfortable/appropriate perspectives and actions.

The frontal lobes develop with attunement and other mindfulness practices

The frontal lobes are prime organizing areas – especially the orbital frontal regions behind our eyes. Months of contemplative practices, including daily attunements, can change firing patterns in these and other brain areas. Years of such practices can increase both the reflexive activities and the *physical shapes* of these areas. Long-term meditators have thicker prefrontal cortexes (especially in the right hemisphere), more GABA based soothing neural connections to their amygdalas (a brain organ generating and regulating intense emotions), and abilities to optimize brain waves and heart rhythms.

Some contemplatives – like senior Tibetan lamas – can switch off time and space parts of their brains, releasing their minds into timelessness and infinity. Self-reflective awareness also tends to empower us to pause before acting, be aware of and improve habitual responses, and activate self-regulatory autonomic systems to lower blood pressure and increase immune function.

It also feels *really* good to be connected with the infinite.

Since we are social beings, much of our spirituality is social

We are social beings programmed to harmonize with others. I look in your eyes, and resonance circuits in both our brains "read" each other's states of mind, including intentionality. Left to their own devices, these resonance circuits harmonize. People (and all mammals) have mirror neurons, which are motor neurons that automatically copy what we see and hear in others. This resonance is great if both of us are feeling safe, interested, and friendly; it is problematic if we're pissed off, frightened, or lost in shame or sadness. When I seem unsafe – for instance if I'm in some distorted defensive state – it cues a defensive state in you, *unless* you can keep calm in the face of my distress, oriented in the face of my distortion, and compassionate in the face of my attacks.

Mindful awareness self-regulates stress – encouraging others to resonate with our more calm, compassionate, and oriented states. *Integral mindful awareness* – dialed-in – makes us generous, like the famous bodhisattva vow to not leave the wheel of karma until all have been liberated.

Social spirituality in groups is omnipresent in churches, temples, gatherings, and communities all around the globe. With relationships, much social spirituality reflects tantric practices we discussed in Chapter 7. When two or more people are mindfully generating, receiving, and resonating with intent and action to deepen pleasurable intimacy, they can harmonize all the way up to unity, while cherishing consciousness in every speck of creation. Such mutuality is a tantric spiritual practice of reciprocal waves of enlightened states.

Intending to serve the highest good reflects the Karma Yoga practices (as taught by Roger Walsh) that we discussed in Chapter 11, where the intent is to make every action an expression of Spirit.

Spiritual transformations arise from a seeking mind

If you pursue spiritual growth, your life will deliver opportunities, ordeals, challenges, and transformative experiences that guide and validate your seeking. One of mine was the Yoga of the Five Dragons.

The Five Dragons and consistent practice

At age thirty, I was completing two years of study with John Davidson, a Taoist priest. In his tradition, there was a yoga for senior students called The Five Dragons that the student could only learn when both teacher and student felt the time was right. After two years of study, John and I decided I was ready to receive "The Dragons."

The Five Dragons consists of learning a different Dragon (a series of yogic movement/energetic practices) each week for five weeks, while maintaining sexual abstinence, and – in my case – having to journey down to San Diego to participate in the fighting class that John and another instructor taught. I learned and practiced the movements, maintained sexual abstinence (with – I admit – a fair amount of whining and complaining), and I made it through the fighting class with no major injuries – no small feat, given how martial artists hate having their teachers bring in opponents from outside their schools.

At the end of all these processes, I asked John, "OK. I've learned the Dragons. Now what?" to which he replied, "Practice every day for years."

I must admit I was a little let down by his response. Wasn't there some sort of enlightenment, magical up-leveling, or transcendent insight that would change me forever? Was this my spiritual reward for all my study, training, and ordeals, the opportunity to engage in rigorous daily practice for more years? The answer, of course, was "Yes."

Since then, I've increasingly realized that effective spiritual practice requires patience and constancy, and spiritual practice *does* deliver extraordinary benefits. Charles Alexander and Ellen Langer researched daily Transcendental Meditation practitioners and found that regular meditation was associated with boosts of up to two levels on central developmental lines such as the self and values lines. Individuals not engaged in contemplative practice rarely grow a single level between age twenty-five and fifty-five.

Almost any contemplative approach, *practiced consistently over time,* is good for human bodies, spirits, and relationships. As we descend/ascend into the ocean of spiritual practices that have been generated by humans over the last six thousand plus years, it's helpful to remember that no matter how enjoyable, enlightening, or transformative a yoga, meditation, or other form of spiritual activity might be, consistent practice amplifies effects.

Ascending and descending spiritual practices

There are thousands of spiritual practices, and most of them lean towards either *ascending* or *descending.*

> **Ascending** practices reach for the many into one (searching for one taste, experience, or texture that includes everything), and ascending from the body into pure consciousness or pure emptiness. Ascending practices are often more solitary than communal, and more masculine than feminine. Examples are Zen meditation and Christian centering prayer.

> **Descending** practices move from the one into many – especially unity with nature, community, and sinking more deeply into the sensual bodily experiences of pure fullness. We are more often communal than solitary, playful as well as serious. Tantric practices, ecstatic dance, A. H. Almaas' Diamond Approach to spiritual transformation, and group yoga classes all rock with *us together.* These are more feminine approaches.

> **Pure Emptiness and Fullness**
>
> *Pure emptiness and pure fullness are different poles in a continuum of enlightened states. Ken Wilber once suggested in an interview that an optimal shorthand spiritual practice was noticing when you were not in touch with either pure emptiness or pure fullness, because noticing the disconnect would start to hook you back up to those states.*

Contemplative practice as ceremony

Evelyn Underhill (a 20th century writer of Christian mysticism), maintained that ceremony moves through stages – Ken Wilber calls them "state stages" to distinguish them from much more permanent shifts of trait stages. The state stages of ceremony are:

> **Awakening/initiation,** which is directing our attention to inherent yearning for transcendence and growth, and opening consciousness to both the process, and what the process will deliver.
>
> **Purification/pacification** involves self-reflective centering and inward focus, often utilizing technique and ritual.
>
> **Illumination** is the shift into expanded and ecstatic states of consciousness as we deepen our practice, or receive transmitted wisdom and compassion.
>
> **Dark night** is the emerging awareness of our blocks, our egoic senses of separation and attachment, and the suffering inherent in life.
> **Unity** is the final resolve of one taste, an experience or expression of pure consciousness, and/or an interior

atmosphere of identification with, and dedication to, all beings.

As we ceremonially plunge into the altered states of spiritual practices, we change the circuitry and eventually the shape of our brains.

Contemplative practice is like aerobic exercise. It's best practiced regularly, and yields phenomenal gains over time. Both relieve symptoms and suffering, and promote health and development.

An ascending practice at the Vedanta Temple on New Year's Eve

When my kids were young teens, each New Year's Eve Becky and I would take the family to the Vedanta Temple in Montecito – a beautiful community next to the city of Santa Barbara – and meditate at sunset. The temple is situated in a peaceful park of oak trees and chaparral in the foothills behind the city. We would come, get settled into chairs, and attend raptly as the monks first chanted and then sat in silent meditation.

I always found myself naturally meditating on "nameless." Each New Year's Eve I sat in the serene temple, surrendering to the present moment, allowing myself to drift into nameless spirit/consciousness/ love/all creation. Gradually, I'd become infused with bodily pleasure – so much so that it was actually distracting. Relaxing deeper into this pleasure, there always came a further shift into a sense of equanimity and balance.

A Zen practitioner, who built his own temple on an island in the archipelago directly off of Vancouver, once instructed one of my clients in Zen meditation. He told my client, "As you progress into your meditation you will feel rapture. Don't become distracted or confused. Sink deeper until you relax into equanimity."

It might seem remarkable to consider rapture a distraction from a deeper pleasure – from a more profoundly satisfying experience. Ascending practices *sense* the body – feeling *nothing* is dissociation – but identify with more than bodily experiences or needs. Long time meditators increasingly feel the unity of "one taste" with everything that is arising, has always been arising, and will always arise. Ken Wilber calls this identification "Self" – with a capital "S" – to discriminate it from our smaller, body and ego-identified "self."

251

Ascending practices attract the masculine in us who craves ordeal, self-discipline, and meaning at the edge of death. Our masculine resonates with the bliss of solitary meditation, communing alone with nature, one-on-one combat, extreme sports, or vision quests.

A descending practice of dancing and singing

In my early thirties, my friends and I would occasionally create a rock and roll band, rehearse a couple of sets, and then play a big party where people would come to drink, dance, and rock out. I was always struck by the incredible surges of pleasure and love resonating between the other members of the band, the audience, and myself. Singing and dancing together felt somehow sacred.

Curious, I studied tap-dancing for nine years and participated in more formal productions. Music, dance, song, performers, and audience always seemed to meld together in blissful celebration – communal ceremonies of descending spirituality, the one into many, sensual into the body.

Human cultures create ceremonies involving various combinations of singing, dancing, family, community, food, drink, touch, and euphoric substances. Anthropologists report ceremonies in some tribes where every man, woman, and child in the tribe is drunk simultaneously, but alcoholism is not a particular problem. Group ceremony serves our deep needs for self-transcendence in descending practices and attracts the feminine in us that yearns for pleasure, family, the body, and community.

Breakthroughs and dead ends

Back in the 60's and 70's, we didn't understand the differences between states and traits – especially transcendent states. Seekers, particularly those new to the path, tended to crave *one transformative experience* to wake them up to a stable larger consciousness.

In those days, most of us tried extended practices, different teachers, and psychedelic drugs. Martial arts was my primary area, but I branched into others, often with surprising results.

Does acid wake you up?

LSD and other psychedelics delivered amazing, often chaotic, altered states – gateways into other worlds – available for $5 a hit (I assume it costs more these days). Young and reckless, hardened by the Vietnam War and race riots in the streets of our cities, we children of the 60's blithely – sometimes recklessly – dropped acid and a wide array of other psychedelics. In retrospect, we were hoping for *that one transformative experience.*

The first time I took LSD, I was nineteen and had been meditating and practicing Shotokan Karate for over three years (in retrospect, I suspect this training prepared me for the drug that night). My high school friend, Steve (who enjoyed his new identity as a cool college stoner), said he had some great acid, and that four of us should take it Friday night at Disneyland.

I know now that the human brain doesn't become fully mature till around twenty-six, and that empathy, self-reflection, and response flexibility – the ability to pause and reflect before action – are among the last capacities to fully mature.

I'm not surprised I automatically took the challenge, "Sure, I'm in!"

LSD dosage varies from one to three hundred *micrograms* (millionths of a gram). Steve's acid was in tiny pills, but large doses, probably two or three hundred micrograms. Makers were still trying to figure out how much to take of a drug where one hundred micrograms radically altered consciousness for seven or more hours.

We swallowed our pills, bought tickets, and walked into the Magic Kingdom, looking with interest at the crowds and wondering what was so weird about all the young men we saw wandering around. I found out later that night that several gay organizations and Camp Pendleton Marine recruits had serendipitously chosen that night to have special Disneyland parties (not related I'm assuming), along with the usual hordes of high school and college students.

We walked into a Main Street Emporium, and I was instantly drawn to an old style electric endurance machine. You put in quarters, grasped two handles, and then slowly felt electric current build, monitored by a scale in the front panel, until the pain became too intense and you tore your hands away. I watched several people try their willpower, stepping

253

back as the current built towards the center of the scale. At that moment, I began to feel what was to become the familiar tingle of LSD taking over my consciousness, and I impulsively stepped up to the machine.

The handles were damp with the last person's sweat, and the current was mild at first, but some part of me relaxed and surrendered as the intensity built and the needle climbed. People started gathering round as my arms began vibrating and the current kept intensifying. I didn't feel pain as much as a flood of energetic sensation flooding through my body, building... building... becoming a universe of vibration obscuring all else, until the machine snapped off. I felt relief and loss as I turned to hear applause from the room, and realized that I had just come on to the acid. There was a sense of breaking through into another world – a feeling that persisted for the next five hours.

We left the Emporium to a night of typical acid adventures I won't go into.

A surprisingly enduring insight from that night was that I didn't seem to change much! I felt like the same guy two days later. The altered LSD states hadn't given me the stable bridge to the other world I craved. It appeared that more work lay ahead to transform altered states into stable traits, and, indeed, research such as Christopher Alexander's TM studies have born that out.

In the years since then, I've become convinced that drugs don't deliver stable unity with Spirit – at best they yield peeks into states of unity that can become more stable with contemplative practice and growth mindsets.

Seekers can expect to develop wise self-observation

As I write this, I'm almost sixty-four, and realized years ago that I'd lost most of my interest in attaining "enlightenment" as a goal. Simultaneously, I'm more committed to my practices, and I certainly feel daily states of profound unity. Such states often spontaneously arise looking at the sunrise, into a client's eyes, or laughing with Becky and my kids.

I still enter states of depression, anxiety, shame, anger at oppressive or uncaring institutions, obsessive worry or resentment, and egoic cravings, but I tend to observe them rather than be lost in them. As Ken Wilber suggests, over time spiritual practitioners feel more empathic suffering, but are more able to contain suffering.

Equanimity, deeper compassion, and wider perspectives are predictable outcomes of regular spiritual practice

I've found that teachers and friends with decades of practices under their belts say a lot of the same things. When someone is secure and growing, it seems that unity, compassion, and service to the world with like-minded others increasingly call them.

Buddhism

This all resonates with "The Three Jewels" of Buddhism – Buddha (the exemplar of freedom from attachments to suffering and the world), Dharma (the teachings of liberation), and Sangha (spiritual community).

So, "breakthroughs" tend to happen regularly when you take up a practice – including daily attunements – and breakthroughs point the way onward. Peak state experiences stretch you and let you know what deeper and more connected feels like – but states fade into our current worldview, sometimes faintly remembering a more expanded consciousness.

Gradually over time we transform – become more caring, wiser, less emotionally reactive, and more emotionally open – but by the time we get there, it doesn't feel like such a big deal.

You can sense this when hanging out with long term practitioners and teachers. They exude an aura of *personalness* – a human authenticity – that makes you feel relaxed and comfortable with them. If you know someone like this, ask them about "breakthroughs" – you'll hear some incredible stories.

Find combinations of practices that appeal to you, and let them permeate your life

Dialed-in spirituality includes practices and associations with groups that magnetize, along with living our principles in an ever changing world.

Ken Wilber suggests that we choose traditions and practices that appeal to us and "supplement" with teachings and ceremonies guided by "Body/mind/spirit in self/culture/nature."

Remember mindful awareness? *"Being aware with acceptance and caring intent, on purpose, with compassionate judgment, in the present moment."* All the practices and perspectives we've discussed in this chapter are directions to explore your natural spirituality. Ascending and descending, Spirit in the first-, second-, and third-person, yoga, dance, meditation, martial arts, prayer, and vision quests are all part of dialed-in spirituality, and your litmus tests are your own body, relationships, and love. When they thrive, you're dialed-in.

I'm in awe of human relationships and development. I'm in awe of each person's epic struggles and luminous potentials.

I think dialed-in spirituality is the foundation of Integral mindful living, and it makes everything better.

TRANSFORMATION OPPORTUNITIES

Skim through this chapter looking for ascending and descending practices that appeal to you. Find two that draw you to them, and create daily ceremonies incorporating them. Practice these ceremonies religiously – as if you have a sacred mission – for three months.

After three months, sit down with an intimate and ask if he or she has noticed any changes in you. Talk about your practices and experiences.

Either commit to continue, refine practices to be more beautiful, good, and true, or ask yourself, "Why am I not making this commitment?"

EPILOGUE

You and I share a rising wave of consciousness.

When ten percent of a population progresses into a more complex worldview, culture changes. We saw this in the industrial revolution, and the social convulsions of the 60's and 70's. The zeitgeist changed dramatically during these times in ways both predictable and unimaginable. For instance, during the industrial revolution we could have predicted a cornucopia of goods and a dramatic expansion of literacy with steam engines and printing presses, but not expected the banishment of slavery and the rise of democracy.

In 2014, the information revolution rewards cross-paradigmatic views – capacities to shift quickly in response to floods of new data driving the accelerating pace of modern life.

Integral worldviews harmonize

Felt appreciation for multiple points of view, and dramatically less fear of death, are signature characteristics of Integral worldviews.

Integral people can be Churched like Father Thomas Keating, or "Spiritual, but not religious."

Dialed-in worldviews recognize complementary partners, and enjoy natural authority in liberation hierarchies.

We want this for all people.

Integral worldviews could very well hit ten percent in the next decade, and there will be unexpected consequences we'll discover when we get there.

The Integral age is upon us.

We live in interesting times.

One way or another, dialed-in living will keep spreading through the world. People will discover some deeper perspective, share it with friends and family, and accelerate the evolutionary wave.

This book is dedicated to Integral consciousness

The salvations for the world's problems exist – we have the technology and wealth. What the world needs and evolution *demands* is expanding consciousness, which progresses one awakening at a time, always in relationship with the beautiful, good, and true.

Each of us is a unique part of this evolutionary wave. You matter! Your life matters!

Every dialed-in moment expands consciousness, so enjoy many dialed-in moments!

Integral mindful living doesn't just make everything better for you, it makes the world better for all of us.

BIBLIOGRAPHY

Anand, Margot. (1989). *The Art of Sexual Ecstasy.* New York Tarcher/ Putnam.

Barash, David. P. and Lipton, Judith Ever. (2009). *Strange Bedfellows: The surprising connection between sex, evolution and Monogamy.* New York: Bellevue Literary Press.

Barratt, Barnaby. (2005). *Sexual Health and Erotic Freedom.* Philadelphia: Xlibris.

Bateman, Anthony, and Fonagy, Peter. (2004). *Psychotherapy for Border- lind Personality Disorder: mentalization-based treatment.* Oxford: Oxford University Press.

Baumeister, R. F. and Leary M. R. (1995). *Desire For Interpersonal At- tachments as a fundamental human motivation.* Psychological Bulletin, 11. 7. 497-529.

Baumeister, R. F. *Willpower: Rediscovering the Greatest Human Strength.* New York: Penguin.

Beck, Don Edward, and Cowan, Christopher C. (1996). *Spiral Dynam- ics; mastering values, leadership, and change.* Malden, MA: Blackwell Publishing.

Bergner, Daniel. (2009). What Do Women Want? *The New York Times Magazine,* Jan 25, 2009.

Bodkin, J.A. (1995). Buprenorphine treatment of refractory depression. *Journal of Clinical Psychopharmacology.* 1995 Feb: 15(1):49-57.

Bowen, M. (1961). *Family Psychotherapy.* American Journal of Ortho- psychiatry. 31: 40-60.

Bowlby, J. (1988). *A secure base: Parent-child attachment and healthy hu- man development.* New York: Basic Books.

Brizendine, Louann. (2006). *The Female Brain.* New York: Morgan Road Books.

Buss, D. M. (1999). *Evolutionary Psychology: The New Science of Mind.* Boston, MA: Allyn and Bacon.

Cage, Arlan. (2008). *Modern Physics and the Science of Qi.* drcage@ southbaytotalhealth.com, www.southbaytotalhealth.com.

Campbell, Joseph. *The Hero With a Thousand Faces.* Princeton: Princeton University Press, 1949.

Carnes, Patric. (2002). *Out of the Shadows, Understanding Sexual Addiction. Center City,* Minn: Hazelden

Cassidy, J., & Shaver, P. (Eds.). (1999), *Handbook of attachment: Theory, research, and clinical applications.* New York: Guilford Press.

Chen, Ingfei. (2009). The Social Brain. *Smithsonian,* June, 2009.

Cloniger, Robert C. (2004). *Feeling Good, the Science of Well-Being.* Oxford University Press.

Combs, Allan. Krippner, Stanly. (2003). Process, Structure, and form: An Evolutionary Transpersonal Psychology of Consciousness. *The International Journal of Transpersonal Studies,* 2003, V. 22.

Coyle, Daniel. (2009). *The Talent Code.* New York. Bantam.

Cozolino, Louis J. (2002). *The Neuroscience of Psychotherapy.* New York: W.W. Norton & Co.

Darwin, Charles. (1872). *The Expression of Emotions in Man and Animals.* London: John Murray.

De Becker, Gavin. (1997). *The Gift of Fear, and other survival signals that protect us from violence.* New York: Dell Publishing.

Debroski, T. M., MacDougal J. M., (1985). *Components of Type A, hostility, and anger-in: relationship to angiographic findings.* Psychosomatic Medicine. Volume 47, Issue 3.

de Chardin, Teilhard. (1955). *Le Phenomene Humain (The Phenomenon of Man)*. Bernard Wall translation. New York: Harper and Row, 1975.

Deida, David. (2004). *Enlightened Sex*. Boulder, Colorado: Sounds True (audio recording).

—. (1995). *Intimate Communion*. Deerfield Beach: Health Communications, Inc.

—. (1997). *The Way of the Superior Man*. Austin: Plexus.

—. (2006). *David Deida, live, volumes 1, 2, 3.*

Dement, William C. and Vaughan, Christopher. (1999). *The Promise of Sleep*. New York: Dell.

Diagnostic and Statistical Manual of Mental Disorders 4th edition: Washington D.C. American Psychiatric Association.

Dixit, Jay. (2010). Heartbreak and home runs: the power of first experiences. *Psychology Today:* Jan/Feb 2010.

Duhigg, Charles. (2012). *The Power of Habit*. New York: Random House.

Eliot, Lise (2009). *Pink Brain, Blue Brain*. New York: Houghton Miflin Harcourt Publishing Company.

Elton, Catherine. (2010). Learning to Lust. *Psychology Today:* May/June, 2010.

Fisher, Helen. (2004). *Why We Love: the Nature and Chemistry of Romantic Love*. New York: Henry Holt.

—. (2009). *Why Him? Why Her? Finding real love by understanding your personality type*. New York: Henry Holt.

Fosha, Diana. (2008). *Transformation: Recognition of Self by Self, and effective action*. In K. J. Schnieder (ed.), *Existential-Integrative Psychotherapy: Guideposts to the core of Practice*. New York: Routledge.

Frankl, Viktor. (2004). *Man's Search for Meaning. An Introduction to Logo-therapy.* Boston: Beacon and Random House, first published 1946.

Freud, Sigmund. (1961) *Civilization and its Discontents.* New York: Notion.

Freud, Sigmund. (1949). *An Outline of Psycho-Analysis.* New York: W.W. Norton and Company.

Gardner, Howard. (1983). *Frames of Mind.* New York: Basic Books.

Gigy, L. & Kelly, J. B. (1993). Reasons for Divorce: – Perspectives of Divorcing Men and Women. *Journal of divorce & Remarriage, 18(1).*

Gilligan, Carol. (1993). *In a Different Voice: Psychological Theory and Women's Development.* Cambridge, Mass.: Harvard University Press.

Gottman, John, M., Silver, Nan. (1999). *The Seven Principles for Making Marriage Work.* New York: Three Rivers Press.

—. (2005). Presented at a conference, *The Anatomy of Intimacy.* Foundation for the Contemporary Family, UC Irvine, November 5 and 6.

—. (2007). Meta-Communication, *Presented at the conference,"The Healing Power of Emotion."* By the Lifespan Learning Institute, www.lifespan-learn.org.

—. (2001). *The Relationship Cure, a 5 Step Guide for Building Better Connections with Family, Friends, and Lovers.* New York: Crown Publishing.

Gawande, Atul. (2009). Hellhole: The United States holds tens of thousands of inmates in long-term solitary confinement. Is this torture? *New Yorker Magazine.* March 30.

Hanes, Stephanie. (2010). In an Affair's Wake. *Christian Science Monitor,* February 14.

Hanes, Stephanie. (2012). Time for Play. *Christian Science Monitor,* January 23, 2012.

Hawkins, Jeff. (2000). *On Intelligence.* New York: Henry Holt and Company..

262

Hebb, Donald. (1949). *The organization of behavior: A neuropsychological theory.* New York: Wiley.

Hill, Catey. (2013)...Spouses Won't Tell You. *The Wall Street Journal,* August 25, 2013.

Hutson, Matthew. (2006). *The heat of the moment: what will you do when in the mood?* Psychology Today, September 1, 2006.

Johnson, Susan. (2005). Presented at a conference, *The Anatomy of Intimacy.* Foundation for the Contemporary Family, UC Irvine, November 5 and 6.

Jung, Carl G. (1961) *Memories, Dreams, and Reflections.* New York: Random House.

—, (1959). *The Archetypes and the Collective Unconscious.* Princeton: Princeton University Press.

—, (1959). *The Basic Writings of C. G. Jung,* ed. Violet Staub De Laszlo, New York: The Modern Library.

Kahneman, Daniel. (1999). *Well-Being: Foundations of Hedonic Psychology.* Portland, Oregon: Book News, Inc.

Kegan, Robert. (1982) *The Evolving Self: Problems and Process in Human Development.* Cambridge, Mass: Harvard University Press.

Kernberg, Otto. (1975). *Borderline Conditions and Pathological Narcissism.* Northvale, New Jersey: Jason Aronson Inc.

Kettlewell, Julianna. (2004). "Fidelity gene" found in voles. *BBC Online News,* June 16.

Kinsey, Alfred Charles. (1948). *Sexual Behavior in the Human Male.* Indiana University Press.

—. (1953). *Sexual Behavior in the Human Female.* Indiana University Press.

Kohn, Alfie. (1993). *Punished by Rewards: The Trouble with Gold Stars, Incentive Plans, A's, Praise, and Other Bribes.* New York: Houghton Mifflin Company.

Kolbert, Elizabeth, (2011). Sleeping with the Enemy. *The New Yorker,* August 15 & 22, 2011.

Langer, Ellen J. (1997). *The Power of Mindful Learning.* Cambridge, MA: Da Capo Press.

Lehmiller, J. J. (2009). Secret romantic relationships: Consequences for personal and relational well-being. *Personality and Social Psychology Bulletin,* 35, 1452-1466.

Lemonick, Michael D. (2004). *The Chemistry of Desire.* New York: Time Magazine, Jan. 19, 2004.

Levine, Judith. (2002). *Harmful to Minors.* Minneapolis: University of Mineapolis Press.

Liedloff, Jean. (1975). *The Continuum Concept.* Reading Mass: Addison-Wesley Publishing Company, Inc.

Lipton, Bruce. *The Biology of Belief.* (2005). www.hayhouse.com: Hay House.

MacTaggart, Lynne. (2007). *The Intention Experiment: Using Your Thoughts to Change Your Life and the World.* New York: Free Press.

MacTaggart, Lynne. (2012). *The Bond.* New York: Free Press.

Maltz, Wendy. (2009). *Private Thoughts.* New York: Magna Publishing.

Mareno, Hara Estroff. (2010). The Expectation Trap. *Psychology Today:* March/April 2010.

Masterson, James F. (1981). *The Narcissistic and Borderline Disorders, an integrated developmental approach.* New York: Brunner/Mazel.

McGonigal, Kelly. (2012). *The Willpower Instinct.* New York: Penguin Books.

Mushashi, Miyamoto. (1974). *A Book of Five Rings.* Woodstock, New York: The Overlook Press.

Nichols, Michael. (2007). *The Essentials of Family Therapy.* New York: Pearson.

O'neil, George and Nena, (1972). *Open Marriage.* New York: M. Evans and Company, Inc.

Paris, Wendy. (2010). Still doing it. *Psychology Today:* May/June 2010

Pearce, Joseph Chilton. (2002). *The Biology of Transcendence: A Blueprint of the Human Spirit.* Rochester, Vermont: Park Street Press.

Perel, Esther. (2006). *Mating in Captivity.* New York: Harpers.

Pink, Daniel. (2007). How to make your own luck. *Fast Company,* December, 2007.

Porges, S. W. (2006). Presented at a conference, *The Embodied Mind: Integration of the Body, Brain, and Mind in Clinical Practice.* UCLA, March 4 and 5.

Porter, Bruce. (1998). Is Solitary Confinement Driving Charley Chase Crazy? *New York Times Magazene,* November 8.

Prabhavananda, swami, and Isherwood, Christopher. (1944). *The Song of God: Bhagavad-Gita.* New York: The New American Library.

Radin, Dean. (2006). *Entangled Minds: Extrasensory Experiences in a Quantum Reality.* New York: Paraview Pocket Books.

—. *(2007).* Theater of the Mind Interview with Dean Radin. *Podcast by Kelley Howell.*

Resnick, Michael D. et al. (1997). Protecting Adolescents From Harm: Findings From the National Longitudinal Study on Adolescent Health. *Journal of the American Medical Association,* 1997; 278 (10): 823-832.

Schnarch, David. (1997). *Passionate Marriage, Keeping Love and Intimacy Alive in Committed Relationships.* New York: Henry Holt and Company.

Schiller, Daniela. (2009). Preventing the return of fear in humans using reconsolidation update mechanisms. *Nature, 12-9-09.*

Schore, Allan. (2006). Presented at a conference, *The Embodied Mind: Integration of the Body, Brain, and Mind in Clinical Practice.* UCLA, March 5.

Schore, Allan. (2003). *Affect Regulation and the Repair of the Self.* New York: W.W. Norton and Company.

Sharot, Tali, (2012). The Optimism Bias. *Time Magazine,* March 26, 2012.

Siegel, Daniel J. (1999). *The Developing Mind.* New York: The Guilford Press.

Siegel, Daniel J. and Hartzell, Mary. (2003). *Parenting from the Inside Out.* New York: Penguin.

Siegel, Daniel J. (2005). *The Mindsight Lectures: cultivating insight and empathy in our internal and interpersonal lives.* Mind Your Brain, Inc.

Slater, Lauren. (2006). Love. *National Geographic,* February.

Salmon, C. and Symons, D. (2003) *Warrior Lovers.* Yale University Press.

Talbott, Shawn. (2007). *The Cortisol Connection.* Berkeley, CA: Hunter-House.

Taylor, Shelley E. (2002). *The Tending Instinct: How Nurturing is Essential to Who We Are and How We Live.* New York: Henry Holt and Co.

Twinge, Jean, M. and Campbell, W. Keith. (2009). *The Narcissim Epidemic: Living in the Age of Entitlement.* New York: Free Press.

van der Kolk, Bessel. (2005). Presented at a conference, *The Anatomy of Intimacy.* Foundation for the Contemporary Family. UC Irvine, Nov. 5 and 6.

Vanity Fair Interview, Jan 2012, *Lady Gaga Opens Up About Bad Romance and Marriage Proposals.*

Wade, Nicholas. (2010). New adventures in recent evolution. *New York Times News Service.* July 25, 2010.

Wahoo, Jade. (2005). Personal communication, at a men's retreat on the green river in Arizona.

Wedekind, C. et al. (1995). "MHC-dependent preferences in humans." *Proceedings of the Royal Society of London* 260: 245-49.

Wilber, Ken. (2000). Sex, Ecology, Spirituality, the spirit of evolution. (revised from 1995). Boston: Shambhala Publications.

— . (2000). *Integral Psychology.* Boston and London: Shambala.

— . (2000). *A Brief History of Everything.* Boston: Shambala.

— . (2003). *Kosmic Consciousness.* Boulder: Sounds True (audio recording).

— . (2006). *Integral Spirituality.* Boston: Shambala.

— . (2004). *The Simple Feeling of Being.* Boston: Shambala.

—. (2013). *Address in The Integral Living Room.* Boulder, Nov. 1, 2013.

Wiseman, Richard. (2003). *The Luck Factor: Changing Your Luck, Changing Your Life: The Four Essential Principles.* Miramax.

Witt, Keith. (2006). *The Attuned Family: How to be a Great Parent to Your Kids and a Great Lover to Your Spouse.* Santa Barbara Graduate Institute Publishing/iUniverse.

Witt. Keith. (2006). *The Gift of Shame: Why we need shame and how to use it to love and grow.* Santa Barbara Graduate Institute Publishing/iUniverse.

Witt, Keith. (2006). *Sessions, All Therapy is About Relationships integrating toward unity.* Santa Barbara Graduate Institute Publishing/iUniverse.

Witt, Keith. (2008). *Waking Up; Integrally Informed Individual and Conjoint Psychotherapy.* Santa Barbara Graduate Institute Publishing/iUniverse.

Wormser, Gary. (2010). Voice indicator of male strength. *Santa Barbara Newspress,* July 25, 2010.

Wright, S. C., & Aron, A. (2009). The Extended Contact Effect. In J. M. Levine & M. A. Hogg (eds.), <u>Encyclopedia of group processes and inter-group relations</u>, Thousand Oaks, CA: Sage Publications.

Zimmerman, Eilene, (2012). Modern Romance. *Christian Science Monitor, February 13, 2112.*

Zuk, Marlene. (2010). Is the man you call Dad really your father? *L.A. Times, June 30, 2010.*

CPSIA information can be obtained at www.ICGtesting.com
Printed in the USA
BVOW03s0122180915

418236BV00008B/216/P